$v = \sqrt{600} = \sqrt{6(100)} =$

THE GOLD STANDARD
OAT PHY & GS-1

Optometry Admission Test Physics [OAT PHY]
and GS Full-length Practice Test [GS-1]

Book IV of IV

$ET = Ek + Ep = 1/2mv2 + mgh$

Gold Standard Contributors
• 4-Book GS OAT/DAT Set •

Brett Ferdinand BSc MD-CM
Karen Barbia BS Arch
Brigitte Bigras BSc MSc DMD
Ibrahima Diouf BSc MSc PhD
Amir Durmic BSc Eng
Adam Segal BSc MSc
Da Xiao BSc DMD
Naomi Epstein BEng
Lisa Ferdinand BA MA
Jeanne Tan Te
Kristin Finkenzeller BSc MD
Heaven Hodges BSc
Sean Pierre BSc MD
James Simenc BS (Math), BA Eng
Jeffrey Cheng BSc
Timothy Ruger MSc PhD
Petra Vernich BA
Alvin Vicente BS Arch

Gold Standard Illustrators
• 4-Book GS OAT/DAT Set •

Daphne McCormack
Nanjing Design
· Ren Yi, Huang Bin
· Sun Chan, Li Xin
Fabiana Magnosi
Harvie Gallatiera
Rebbe Jurilla BSc MBA

RuveneCo

The Gold Standard OAT was built for the OAT.

The OAT is one exam. There is no difference between the OAT taken in Canada and the OAT taken in the US.

The Gold Standard DAT 4-book set is identical to OAT prep except DAT PAT, which is replaced by OAT Physics in this book. To supplement your Gold Standard Physics review and OAT practice test in this book, consider completing your OAT prep with Gold Standard DAT books in Biology, General and Organic Chemistry, QR & RC, and our website oatbooks.com.

Be sure to register at www.oatbooks.com by clicking on GS OAT Owners and following the directions for Gold Standard OAT Owners. Please Note: benefits are for 1 year from the date of online registration, for the original book owner only and are not transferable; unauthorized access and use outside the Terms of Use posted on oatbooks.com may result in account deletion; if you are not the original owner, you can purchase your virtual access card separately at oatbooks.com.

Visit The Gold Standard's Education Center at www.gold-standard.com.

ISBN 978-1-927338-19-3

Address all inquiries, comments, or suggestions to the publisher. For Terms of Use go to: www.oatbooks.com

RuveneCo Inc
Gold Standard Multimedia Education
559-334 Cornelia St
Plattsburgh, NY 12901
E-mail: learn@gold-standard.com
Online at www.gold-standard.com

Table of Contents

EXAM SUMMARY

The Optometry Admission Test (OAT) consists of 220 multiple-choice questions distributed across quite a diversity of question types in four tests. The OAT is a computer-based test (CBT). This exam requires approximately five hours to complete - including the optional tutorial, break, and post-test survey. The following are the four subtests of the Optometry Admission Test:

1. Survey of the Natural Sciences (NS) – 100 questions; 90 min.
    - General Biology (BIO): 40 questions
    - General Chemistry (CHM): 30 questions
    - Organic Chemistry (ORG): 30 questions
2. Reading Comprehension (RC) – 40 questions; 3 reading passages; 50 min.
3. Physics (PHY) - 40 questions; 50 min.
4. Quantitative Reasoning (QR) – 40 questions; 45 min.
    - Mathematics Problems: 30 questions
    - Applied Mathematics/Word Problems: 10 questions

You will get six scores from: (1) BIO (2) CHM (3) ORG (4) PHY (5) QR (6) RC.

You will get two additional scores which are summaries:
(7) Academic Average (AA) = BIO + CHM + ORG + PHY + QR + RC
(8) Total Science (TS) = BIO + CHM + ORG + PHY

Common Formula for Acceptance:

GPA + OAT score + Interview = Optometry School Admissions*

*Note: In general, Optometry School Admissions Committees will only examine the OAT score if the GPA is high enough; they will only admit or interview if the GPA + OAT score is high enough. Some programs also use autobiographical materials and/or references in the admissions process. Different optometry schools may emphasize different aspects of your OAT score, for example: PHY, BIO, TS, AA. The average score for any section is approximately 300; the average AA for admissions is usually 290-350 depending on the optometry school.

PREFACE

The OAT is challenging, get organized.

oatbooks.com/oat-study-schedule

1. How to study:

1. Study the Gold Standard (GS) OAT/DAT books and videos to learn
2. Do GS Chapter review practice questions
3. Consolidate: create and review your personal summaries (= Gold Notes) daily

2. Once you have completed your studies:

1. Full-length practice test
2. Review mistakes, all solutions
3. Consolidate: review all your Gold Notes and create more
4. Repeat until you get beyond the score you need for your targeted optometry school

3. Full-length practice tests:

1. ASCO practice exam
2. Gold Standard OAT exams
3. TopScore Pro exams
4. Other sources if needed

4. How much time do you need?

On average, 3-6 hours per day for 3-6 months

WARNING: Study more or study more efficiently. You choose. The Gold Standard has condensed the content that you require to excel at the OAT.

To make the content easier to retain, you can also find aspects of the Gold Standard program in other formats such as:

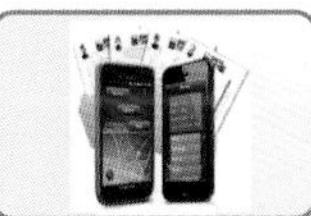

Is there something in the Gold Standard that you did not understand? Don't get frustrated, get online.

oatbooks.com/forum oatbooks.com/QRchanges-2015

Good luck with your studies!

Gold Standard Team

GOLD STANDARD
MULTIMEDIA EDUCATION

OATbooks.com

OPTOMETRY SCHOOL ADMISSIONS

PART I

IMPROVING ACADEMIC STANDING

1.1 Lectures

Before you set foot in a classroom you should consider the value of being there. Even if you were taking a course like 'Basket Weaving 101', one way to help you do well in the course is to consider the value of the course to **you**. The course should have an *intrinsic* value (i.e. 'I enjoy weaving baskets'). The course will also have an *extrinsic* value (i.e. 'If I do not get good grades, I will not be accepted...'). Motivation, a positive attitude, and an interest in learning give you an edge before the class even begins.

Unless there is a student 'note-taking club' for your courses, your attendance record and the quality of your notes should both be as excellent as possible. Be sure to choose a seat in the classroom that ensures you will be able to hear the professor adequately and see whatever she may write. Whenever possible, do not sit close to friends!

Instead of chattering before the lecture begins, spend the idle moments quickly reviewing the previous lecture in that subject so you would have an idea of what to expect. Try to take good notes and pay close attention. The preceding may sound like a difficult combination (especially with professors who speak and write quickly); however, with practice you can learn to do it well.

And finally, do not let the quality of teaching affect your interest in the subject nor your grades! Do not waste your time during or before lectures complaining about how the professor speaks too quickly, does not explain concepts adequately, etc. When the time comes, you can mention such issues on the appropriate evaluation forms! In the meantime, consider this: despite the good or poor quality of teaching, there is always a certain number of students who still perform well. You must strive to count yourself among those students.

1.2 Taking Notes

Unless your professor says otherwise, if you take excellent notes and learn them inside out, you will *ace* his course. Your notes should always be up-to-date, complete, and separate from other subjects.

To be safe, you should try to type or write everything! You can fill in any gaps by comparing your notes with those of your friends. You can create your own shorthand symbols or use standard ones. The following represents some useful symbols:

|·|	*between*
=	*the same as*
≠	*not the same as*
∴	*therefore*
Δ	*difference, change in*
cf.	*compare*
c̄ or w	*with*
c̄out or w/o	*without*
esp.	*especially*
∵	*because*
i.e.	*that is*
e.g.	*for example*

Many students rewrite their notes at home. Should you decide to rewrite your notes, your time will be used efficiently if you are paying close attention to the information you are rewriting. In fact, a more useful technique is the following: during class, write your notes only on the right side of your binder. Later, rewrite the information from class in a complete but condensed form on the left side of the binder (*this condensed form should include mnemonics, which we will discuss later*).

Some students find it valuable to use different colored pens. Juggling pens in class may distract you from the content of the lecture. Different colored pens would be more useful in the context of rewriting one's notes.

Of course, typing can be more efficient but time should still be set aside to actively condense and organize notes after class. If the professor has supplied handouts, ideally you would condense those notes as well to include only the most important information or content that you find challenging to remember.

1.3 The Principles of Studying Efficiently

If you study efficiently, you will have enough time for extracurricular activities, movies, etc. The bottom line is that your time must be used efficiently and effectively.

During the average school day, time can be found during breaks, between classes, and after school to quickly review notes in a library or any other quiet place you can find on campus. Simply by using the available time in your school day, you can keep up to date with recent information.

You should design an individual study schedule to meet your particular needs. However, as a rule, a certain amount of time every evening should be set aside for more in-depth studying. Weekends can be allotted for special projects and reviewing notes from the beginning.

On the surface, the idea of regularly reviewing notes from the beginning may sound like an insurmountable task that would take forever! The reality is just the opposite. After all, if you continually study the information, by the time midterms approach you would have seen the first lecture so many times that it would take only moments to review it. On the other hand, had you not been reviewing regularly, it would be like reading that lecture for the first time!

You should study wherever you feel most comfortable and effective (i.e., library, at home, etc.). Should you prefer studying at home, be sure to create an environment, which is conducive to the task at hand.

Studying should be an active process to memorize, synthesize, and understand a given set of material. Memorization and comprehension are best achieved by the **elaboration** of course material, **attention, repetition,** and practicing **retrieval** of the information. All these principles are carried out in the following techniques.

1.4 Studying from Notes and Texts

Successful studying from either class notes or textbooks can be accomplished in three simple steps:

- **Preview the material:** Read all the relevant headings, titles, and sub-titles to give you a general idea of what you are about to learn. You should never embark on a trip without knowing where you are going!

- **Read while questioning:** Passive studying is when you sit in front of a book and just read. This can lead to boredom, lack of concentration, or even worse - difficulty remembering what you just read! Active studying involves reading while actively questioning yourself. For example, how does this fit in with the 'big picture'? How does this relate to what we learned last week? What cues about these words or lists will make it easy for me to memorize them? What type of question would my professor ask me? If I was asked a question on this material, how would I answer?

- **Recite and consider:** Put the notes or text away while you attempt to recall the main facts. Once you are able to recite the important information, consider how it relates to the entire subject.

N.B. If you ever sit down to study and you are not quite sure with which subject to begin, always start with either the most difficult subject or the subject you like least (usually they are one and the same!).

1.5 Study Aids

The most effective study aids include practice exams, mnemonics and audio MP3s.

Practice exams (*exams from previous semesters*) are often available from the library, upper level students, online or directly from the professor. They can be used like maps, which guide you through your semester. They give you a good indication as to what information you should emphasize when you study; what question types and exam format you can expect; and what your level of progress is.

Practice exams should be set aside to do in the weeks and days before 'the real thing.' You should time yourself and do the exam in an environment free from distractions. This provides an ideal way to uncover unexpected weak points.

Mnemonics are an effective way of memorizing lists of information. Usually a word, phrase, or sentence is constructed to symbolize a greater amount of information (i.e. LEO is A GERC = Lose Electrons is Oxidation is Anode, Gain Electrons is Reduction at Cathode). An effective study aid to active studying is the creation of your own mnemonics.

Audio MP3s can be used as effective tools to repeat information and to use your time efficiently. Information from the left side of your notes (*see 1.2 Taking Notes*) or your summarized typed notes including mnemonics, can be dictated and recorded. Often, an entire semester of work can be summarized in one 90-minute recording.

Now you can listen to the recording on an MP3 player or an iPod while waiting in line at the bank, or in a bus or with a car stereo on the way to school, work, etc. You can also listen to recorded information when you go to sleep and listen to another one first thing in the morning. You are probably familiar with the situation of having heard a song early in the morning and then having difficulty, for the rest of the day, getting it out of your mind! Well, imagine if the first thing you heard in the morning was: "Hair is a modified keratinized structure produced by the cylindrical down growth of epithelium..."! Thus MP3s become an effective study aid since they are an extra source of repetition.

Some students like to **record lectures**. Though it may be helpful to fill in missing notes, it is not an efficient way to repeat information.

Some students like to use **study cards** (flashcards) on which they may write either a summary of information they must memorize or relevant questions to consider. Then the cards are used throughout the day to quickly flash information to promote thought on a course material. Smartphone apps, like the ones designed by Gold Standard, can make flashcards more interactive.

1.5.1 Falling Behind

Imagine yourself as a marathon runner who has run 25.5 km of a 26 km race. The finishing line is now in view. However, you have fallen behind some of the other runners. The most difficult aspect of the race is still ahead.

In such a scenario, some interesting questions can be asked: Is now the time to drop out of the race because 0.5 km suddenly seems like a long distance? Is now the time to reevaluate whether or not you should have competed? Or is now the time to remain faithful to your goals and to give 100%?

Imagine one morning in mid-semester, you wake up realizing you have fallen behind in your studies. What do you do? Where do you start? Is it too late?

You should see the situation as one of life's challenges. Now is the worst time for doubts, rather, it is the time for action. A clear line of action should be formulated such that it could be followed.

For example, you might begin by gathering all pertinent study materials like a complete set of study notes, relevant text(s), sample exams, etc. As a rule, to get back into the thick of things, notes and sample exams take precedence. Studying at this point should take a three pronged approach: i) a regular, consistent review of the information from your notes from the beginning of the section for which you are responsible (i.e., *starting with the first class*); ii) a regular, consistent review of course material as you are learning it from the lectures (*this is the most efficient way to study*); iii) regular testing using questions given in class or those contained in sample exams. Using such questions will clarify the extent of your progress.

It is also of value, as time allows, to engage in extracurricular activities, which, you find helpful in reducing stress (e.g., sports, piano, creative writing).

THE OPTOMETRY SCHOOL INTERVIEW

2.1 Introduction

The application process to most optometry schools includes interviews. Only a select number of students from the applicant pool will be given an offer to be interviewed. The optometry school interview is, as a rule, something that you achieve. In other words, after your school grades, OAT scores and/or references, and autobiographical materials have been reviewed, you are offered the ultimate opportunity to put your best foot forward: a personal interview.

Depending on the optometry school, you may be interviewed by one, two or several interviewers (i.e., panel or committee interview). You may be the only interviewee or there may be others (i.e., a group interview). There may be one or more interviews lasting from 20 minutes to two hours. Some optometry schools are introducing the multiple mini-interview (MMI) which includes many short assessments in a timed circuit. Despite the variations among the technical aspects of the interview, in terms of substance, most optometry schools have similar objectives. These objectives can be arbitrarily categorized into three general assessments: (i) your personality traits, (ii) social skills, and (iii) knowledge of optometry as a profession.

Personality traits such as maturity, integrity, compassion, originality, curiosity, self-directed learning, intellectual capacity, confidence (not arrogance!), and motivation are all components of the ideal applicant. These traits will be exposed by the process of the interview, your mannerisms, and the substance of what you choose to discuss when given an ambiguous question. For instance, bringing up specific examples of academic achievement related to school and related to self-directed learning would score well in the categories of intellectual capacity and curiosity, respectively. Nevertheless, highlighting significant insights about support to and interaction with patients in say, a recent involvement in community service might set you apart from equally qualified candidates as more emotionally matured and compassionate.

Motivation is a personality trait, which may make the difference between a high and a low or moderate score in an interview. A student must clearly demonstrate that he or she has the energy and eagerness to survive (typically) four long years of optometry school! If you are naturally shy or soft-spoken, you will have to give special attention to this category. In other instances, a student must display the desire to learn and the zest to think critically in a problem-based learning framework.

Social skills such as leadership, ease of communication, ability to relate to others and work effectively in groups, volunteer work, cultural and social interests, all constitute skills that are often viewed as critical for future optometrists. It is not sufficient to say in an interview: "I have good social skills"! You must display such skills via your interaction with the interviewer(s) and by discussing specific examples of situations that clearly portray your social skills.

Knowledge of optometry includes at least a general understanding of what the field of optometry involves, the curriculum you are applying to, and knowledge of common optometry issues like vision care and the aging population, the development of new lens materials and treatments, the expanding scope of lasers, improved diagnostic instrumentation, the development of new medications to treat eye disease, special needs services, the health care system, and ethical decision-making issues involving patient autonomy, confidentiality, and practice values. It is striking to see the number of students who apply to optometry schools each year whose knowledge of optometry is limited to headlines and popular TV shows! It is not logical for someone to dedicate their lives to a profession they know little about.

Doing volunteer work in a hospital or a community clinic is a good start. Alternatively, job shadowing at a private optometry office or a relative who is in the profession can help expose you to the daily goings-on. The key is to get a good grasp of the profession in diverse settings – from the public health care delivery system to private practice to, if possible, optometry specialties (i.e. neuro-optometry, pediatric or geriatric eye care, etc.). Here are some more suggestions: (i) keep up-to-date with the details of optometry-related controversies in the news. You should also be able to develop and support opinions of your own; (ii) skim through an optometry journal at least once; (iii) read any articles about the eye or vision in a popular science magazine (i.e., Scientific American, Discover, Popular Science, etc.); (iv) keep abreast of changes in optometry school curricula in general and specific to the programs to which you have applied. You can access such information online or at most university libraries and by writing individual optometry schools for information on their programs; (v) get involved in a laboratory research project.

2.2 Preparing for the Interview

If you devote an adequate amount of time for interview preparation, the actual interview will be less tense for you and you will be able to control most of the content of the interview.

Reading from the various sources mentioned in the preceding sections would be helpful. Also, read over your curriculum vitae and/or any autobiographical materials you may have prepared. Note highlights in your life or specific examples that reflect the aforementioned personality traits, social skills or your knowledge of optometry. Zero in on qualities or stories that are important, memorable, interesting, amusing, informative or "all of the above"! Once in the interview room, you will be given the opportunity to elaborate on the qualities you believe are important about yourself. Be ready to respond to an interviewer should they ask you: "What do you want to know about us?" In many cases, students tend to concentrate on preparing their most brilliant answers to various interview questions that they tend to overlook another means for the admission committee to gauge an applicant's sincere interest in the course and the university itself – by letting the applicant himself or herself ask and/or clarify essential information about the school and how the program could ultimately help advance a successful career in optometry.

Once you have received the invitation, do not lose time to get to know the optometry college with which you will be having the interview. Go online or call and inquire about the structure of the interview (e.g., one-on-one, group, MMI, etc.). Ask them if they can tell you who will interview you. Many schools have no qualms volunteering such information. Now you can determine the person's expertise by either asking or looking through staff members of the different faculties or optometry specialties at that university or college. A primary eye care provider, an academician, and a specialist in pre/post-operative laser surgery care, all may have different areas of interest and will likely orient their interviews differently. Thus you may want to read from a source, which will give you a general understanding of their area of interest.

Choose appropriate clothes for the interview. Every year some students dress for a optometry school interview as if they were going out to dance! Optometry is still considered a conservative profession; you should dress and groom yourself likewise. First impressions are very important. Your objective is to make it as easy as possible for your interviewer(s) to imagine you as an optometrist.

Do practice interviews with people you respect but who can also maintain their objectivity. Let them read this entire chapter on optometry school interviews. They must understand that you are to be evaluated *only* on the basis of the interview. On that basis alone, they should be able to imagine you as an ideal candidate for a future optometrist.

2.3 Strategies for Answering Questions

Always remember that the interviewer controls the *direction* of the interview by his questions; you control the *content* of the interview through your answers. In other words, once given the opportunity, you should speak about the topics that are important to you; conversely, you should avoid volunteering information that renders you uncomfortable. You can enhance the atmosphere in which the answers are delivered by being polite, sincere, tactful, well-organized, outwardly oriented and maintaining eye contact. Motivation, intellectual interest, and a positive attitude must all be evident.

As a rule, there are no right or wrong answers. However, the way in which you justify your opinions, the topics you choose to discuss, your mannerisms and your composure all play important roles. It is normal to be nervous. It would be to your advantage to channel your nervous energy into a positive quality, like enthusiasm.

Do not spew forth answers! Take your time - it is not a contest to see how fast you can answer. Answering with haste can lead to disastrous consequences as what happened to this student in an actual interview:

Q: *Have you ever doubted your interest in optometry as a career?*
A: *No! Well . . . ah . . . I guess so. Ah . . . I guess everyone doubts something at some point or the other . . .*

Retractions like that are a bad signal, but it illustrates an important point: there are usually no right or wrong answers in an interview; however, there are right or wrong ways of answering. Through this example we can conclude the following: listen carefully to the question, try to relax, and think before you answer!

Do not sit on the fence! If you avoid giving your opinions on controversial topics, it will be interpreted as indecision, which is a negative trait for a prospective optometrist. You have a right to your opinions. However, you must be prepared to defend your point of view in an objective, rational, and informative fashion. It is also important to show that, despite your opinion, you understand both sides of the argument. If you have an extreme or unconventional perspective and if you believe your perspective will not interfere with your practice of optometry, you must let your interviewer know that.

Imagine a student who is uncomfortable with the idea of cosmetic optometry as a legitimate medical practice (i.e. removing small 'lumps and bumps' strictly for the purpose of esthetics). If asked about her opinion on cosmetic optometry, she should clearly state her opinion objectively, show she understands the opposing viewpoints, and then use data to reinforce her position. If she feels that her opinion would not interfere with her objectivity when practicing optometry, she might volunteer: "If I were in a position where my perspective might interfere with an objective management of a patient, I would refer that patient to another optometrist."

Carefully note the reactions of the interviewer in response to your answers. Whether the interviewer is sitting on the edge of her seat wide-eyed or slumping in her chair while yawning, you should take such cues to help you determine when to continue, change the subject, or when to stop talking. Also, note the more subtle cues. For example, gauge which topic makes the interviewer frown, give eye contact, take notes, etc.

Lighten up the interview with a well-timed story. A conservative joke, a good analogy, or anecdote may help you relax and make the interviewer sustain his interest. If it is done correctly, it can turn a routine interview into a memorable and friendly interaction.

It should be noted that because the system is not standardized, a small number of interviewers may ask overly personal questions (i.e., about relationships, religion, etc.) or even questions that carry sexist tones (e.g., *What would you do if you got pregnant while attending optometry school?*). Some questions may be frankly illegal. If you do not want to answer a question, simply maintain your composure, express your position diplomatically, and address the interviewer's real concern (i.e., *Does this person have the potential to be a good optometrist?*). For example, you might say in a non-confrontational tone of voice: "I would rather not answer such a question. However, I can assure you that whatever my answer may have been, it would in no way affect either my prospective studies in optometry or any prerequisite objectivity I should have to be a good optometrist."

2.4 Sample Questions

There are an infinite number of questions and many different categories of questions. Different optometry schools will emphasize different categories of questions. Arbitrarily, ten categories of questions can be defined: ambiguous, medically related, academic, social, stress-type, problem situations, personality-oriented, based on autobiographical material, miscellaneous, and ending questions. We will examine each category in terms of sample questions and general comments.

Ambiguous Questions:

* * *Tell me about yourself.*

How do you want me to remember you?

What are your goals?

There are hundreds if not thousands of applicants, why should we choose you?

Convince me that you would make a good optometrist.

Why do you want to study optometry?

COMMENTS: These questions present nightmares for the unprepared student who walks into the interview room and is immediately asked: "Tell me about yourself." Where do you start? If you are prepared as previously discussed, you will be able to take control of the interview by highlighting your qualities or objectives in an informative and interesting manner.

Optometry/Health Care Questions:

What are the pros and cons to our health care system?

If you had the power, what changes would you make to our health care system?

How are optometrists responsible for educating the general public about vision care/health?

Do optometrists make too much money?

Describe your experiences with the optometrists you shadowed.

Would you prefer a private practice or a group practice setting, and why?

If you were pre-med, why didn't you pursue medical school to become an ophthalmologist?

What are the differences between clinicians and technicians?

What influenced you to get into optometry?

What are the main differences between an optometrist, an optician and an opthalmologist, and why did you choose optometry?

COMMENTS: The health care system, your motivation and knowledge of optometry, patient confidentiality, patient autonomy, health insurance, and other ethical issues are very popular topics in this era of technological advances, skyrocketing health care costs, and ethical uncertainty. A well-informed opinion can set you apart from most of the other interviewees.

Questions Related to Academics:

Why did you choose your present course of studies?

What is your favorite subject in your present course of studies? Why?

Would you consider a career in your present course of studies?

Can you convince me that you can cope with the workload in optometry school?

How do you study/prepare for exams?

Do you engage in self-directed learning?

What is Problem-Based Learning or PBL?

How do you feel about the online delivery format in optometry education?

COMMENTS: Optometry schools like to see applicants who are well-disciplined, committed to optometry as a career, and who exhibit self-directed learning (i.e., such a level of desire for knowledge that the student may seek to study information independent of any organized infrastructure). Beware of any glitches in your academic record. You may be asked to give reasons for any grades they may deem substandard. On the other hand, you should volunteer any information regarding academic achievement (i.e., prizes, awards, scholarships, particularly high grades in one subject or the other). At some point, you may also be asked to discuss aspects that you mentioned in your personal statement, essay or autobiographical materials.

Questions Related to Social Skills or Interests:

Give evidence that you relate well with others.

Give an example of a leadership role you have assumed.

Have you done any volunteer work?

Have you engaged in any sports?

What are the prospects for a lasting peace in Afghanistan? Libya? The Sudan? The Middle-East?

COMMENTS: Questions concerning social skills should be simple for the prepared student. If you are asked a question that you cannot answer, say so. If you pretend to know something about a topic in which you are completely uninformed, you will make a bad situation worse.

Stress-Type Questions:

How do you handle stress?

What was the most stressful event in your life? How did you handle it?

The night before your final exam, your father has a heart-attack and is admitted to a hospital, what do you do?

COMMENTS: The ideal optometrist has positive coping methods to deal with the inevitable stressors of a optometry practice. Stress-type questions are a legitimate means of determining if you possess the raw material necessary to cope with optometry school and optometry as a career. Some decide to introduce stress <u>into</u> the interview and see how you handle it. For example, they may decide to ask you a confrontational question or try to back you into a corner (e.g., You do not know anything about optometry, do you?). Alternatively, the interviewer might use silence to introduce stress into the interview. If you have completely and confidently answered a question and silence falls in the room, <u>do not</u> retract previous statements, mutter, or fidget. Simply wait for the next question. If the silence becomes unbearable, you may consider asking an intelligent question (e.g., a specific question regarding their curriculum).

Questions on Problem Situations:

You are about to administer local anesthesia to a sixteen-year-old patient. She suddenly expresses apprehension about the procedure and confesses that she is pregnant. She begs you to keep the information in utmost confidentiality. Would you still inform the girl's parents?

How would you deal with a group member who does not submit his assigned tasks for a small group project?

You have a very nervous patient who is about to undergo a procedure. What would you do to ease the anxiety?

Your patient is at the top of his career. How do you tell him that he has eye cancer?

COMMENTS: As for the other questions, listen carefully and take your time to consider the best possible response. Keep in mind that the ideal optometrist is not only knowledgeable, but is also compassionate, empathetic, and is objective enough to understand both sides of a dilemma. Be sure such qualities are clearly demonstrated.

Personality-Oriented Questions:

If you could change one thing about yourself, what would it be?

How would your friends describe you?

What do you do with your spare time?

What is the most important event that has occurred to you in the last five years?

If you had three magical wishes, what would they be?

What are your best attributes?

COMMENTS: Of course, most questions will assess your personality to one degree or the other. However, these questions are quite direct in their approach. Forewarned is forearmed!

Questions Based on Autobiographical Materials:

COMMENTS: Any autobiographical material you may have provided to the optometry school is fair game for questioning. You may be asked to discuss or elaborate on any point the interviewer may feel is interesting or questionable.

Miscellaneous Questions:

Should the federal government reinstate the death penalty? Explain.

What do you expect to be doing 10 years from now?

How would you attract optometrists to rural areas?

Why do you want to attend our optometry school?

What other optometry schools have you applied to?

Have you been to other interviews?

COMMENTS: You will do fine in this grab-bag category as long as you stick to the strategies previously iterated.

Ending Questions:

What would you do if you were not accepted to optometry school?

How do you think you did in this interview?

Do you have any questions?

COMMENTS: The only thing more important than a good first impression is a good finish in order to leave a positive lasting impression. They are looking for students who are so committed to optometry that they will not only re-apply to optometry school if not accepted, but they would also strive to improve on those aspects of their application that prevented them from being accepted in the first attempt. All these questions should be answered with a quiet confidence. If you are given an opportunity to ask questions, though you should not flaunt your knowledge, you should establish that you are well-informed. For example: "I have read that you have changed your curriculum to a more patient-oriented and self-directed learning approach. I was wondering how the optometry students are getting along with these new changes." Be sure, however, not to ask a question unless you are genuinely interested in the answer.

2.4.1 Interview Feedback: Questions, Answers and Feedback

Specific interview questions can be found online for free at studentdoctor.net. Dr. Ferdinand reproduced and captured the intense experience of a medical school interview on video which, of course, is very similar to the content, process and interaction of an optometry school interview. "The Gold Standard Medical School Interview: Questions, Tips and Answers + MMI" DVD was filmed live in HD on campus in front of a group of students. A volunteer is interviewed in front of the class and the entire interview is conducted as if it were the real thing. After the interview, an analysis of each question and the mindset behind it is discussed in an open forum format. If you are not sure that you have the interviewing skills to be accepted to optometry school, then it is a must-see video.

$$\mathcal{A} + \mathcal{B} = ?$$

OATbooks.com

UNDERSTANDING THE OAT

PART II

THE STRUCTURE OF THE OAT

1.1 Introduction

The Optometry Admission Test (OAT) is required by all optometry schools in the United States, its territories, as well as the University of Waterloo, Canada, for applicants seeking entry into the O.D. program (Doctor of Optometry). The test is standardized by the Association of Schools and Colleges of Optometry (ASCO) through its Department of Testing Services and is available throughout the year by testing appointments in Prometric Test Centers around the US, Guam, Puerto Rico, the US Virgin Islands, and Canada.

In most instances, the weight given to OAT scores in the admissions process varies from school to school. However, results in the different sections of the test tend to be used in a way similar to your university GPA (i.e. your academic standing). Some schools consider the Academic Average and Total Science scores as significant criteria in their selection of candidates. Some combine the Academic Average and Total Science scores, and a few others give as much emphasis to the Reading Comprehension score. Consult programs directly about their evaluation guidelines.

1.1.1 When to Take the OAT

Taking the OAT requires registering with ASCO and meeting their eligibility requirements. Usually, applicants have successfully completed at least one year of undergraduate studies, including the prerequisite courses in physics, biology, general chemistry, and organic chemistry at the time of application. Note that the majority of applicants complete two or more years of college before taking the OAT.

Upon approval of your application, the Department of Testing Services (DTS) will notify you, through email or letter, of the procedure in securing a testing appointment with the Prometric Contact Center. As a registered examinee, you will have the next six months from your application and payment to confirm a testing date.

Prospective students commonly arrange for their OAT roughly a year before their intended matriculation into optometry school. However, varying circumstances may call for careful planning when choosing the appropriate time for you to take this exam. The following are common factors to consider:

1. The Admissions Cycle

Most optometry schools begin reviewing applications around June, the majority of successful candidates start receiving acceptance letters as early as the 1st of December. Getting over the OAT hurdle well ahead of the submission deadlines will put you in a more favorable position in several ways: you will have ample time to procure any supplemental materials that the schools might request; you will have a less stressful time preparing for your interview; and, you would have a better chance of belonging to the initial bulk of the entering classes.

Many schools observe a rolling admissions process - they continue to accept applications until all vacant spots are filled. Applicants with remarkable credentials who wait until the last minute may miss admission into their schools of preference if the number of early applicants who satisfactorily meet the entry requirements quickly closes the enrollment seats.

2. Course Requirements

Optometry colleges usually impose certain curricular prerequisites as part of their entry requirements. Some applicants opt to take their OAT a year before completing any required coursework. They can then focus on improving their GPAs in the remaining semesters. Others take the opposite route. You should weigh which schedule would work best for you. In any case, be sure to check the individual schools regarding their rules and criteria for OAT scores – some might consider scores received three years before the date of your application, while others may only look at scores from two years ago.

3. Contingent Results

If you are not satisfied with your OAT score, ASCO permits you to retake the exam 90 days later. As a precaution, you should provide some allowance for such an event.

1.1.2 Retaking the OAT

To reiterate, an applicant who is unsatisfied with his or her OAT scores must wait 90 days before retesting. If approved, students are permitted to retake the OAT once per twelve-month period. Results of the four most recent OATs taken, as well as the total number of attempts, are reported on the official score reports. Admissions committees may consider either the best, or the most recent marks. There is currently no limit as to the number of times to take the OAT.

For the most up-to-date guidelines on registration, scheduling and pertinent information about the OAT, consider consulting your undergraduate advisor and accessing the following:

ASCO's general OAT information
https://www.ada.org/oat/index.html

OAT™ Program Guide
https://www.ada.org/oat/oat_examinee_guide.pdf

Prometric Centers
https://www.prometric.com/en-us/clients/oat/Pages/landing.aspx

1.2 The Format of The OAT

Part of doing well in a standardized test includes being familiar with the format of the actual exam, what it covers, and what skills and level of knowledge are being assessed. Accurate information of this sort helps identify your study needs and as a result, allows you to judge which prep materials and courses would help to address your weak areas.

The Optometry Admission Test measures your general academic aptitude, and understanding of scientific information. Memory, comprehension, and problem solving are essential cognitive skills needed for this exam.

The OAT is a timed computer-based test divided into four sections. All questions are in multiple choice format with four or five options per question. You are to work on only one section at a time. A timer is visible on the upper right hand corner of the computer screen. If you are unsure of your answer on a specific item, you may click the "Mark" button. You can then review your marked and/or incomplete responses if you have enough time left. Otherwise, a message that says "The time limit for this test has expired" will appear and you will have to move on to the next segment of the test.

REMEMBER

Once you exit a test section, you cannot go back to it.

The test center administrator provides two laminated note boards and two low-odor, fine-tip permanent markers. The laminated sheets are 8.5" x 11" in size with one side in the form of graph paper and the other side just a blank page. Should you require additional pieces, you only need to raise your hand so that the test center administrator will replace them with new ones. No scratch paper is permitted within the testing area during the exam.

The following table shows the sequence of the different OAT test sections:

Optional Tutorial	
Time	15 minutes
Survey of Natural Sciences	
Time	90 minutes
Number of Questions	100
Reading Comprehension Test	
Time	50 minutes
Number of Questions	40
Optional Break	
Time	15 minutes
Physics	
Time	50 minutes
Number of Questions	40
Quantitative Reasoning Test	
Time	45 minutes
Number of Questions	40
Optional Post-Test Survey	
Time	15 minutes
Total Time	**4 hours 40 minutes**

The Natural Sciences on the OAT collectively include biology, general and organic chemistry at introductory university levels. The subject material is apportioned as follows:

Biology	40 items
General Chemistry	30 items
Organic Chemistry	30 items

Some pages contain an Exhibit button that allows you to open a new window showing the periodic table.

The RC Test presents three short, science-based articles to read followed by questions. There are 40 multiple choice style questions. For each article, you will first be displayed the article without any questions to read through it. Then when you are ready to go through the questions, a pop-up box appears underneath each question to allow you to refer back to the article.

You can choose whether or not to take the 15-minute break. If you choose to take it, the timer will continue to monitor the minutes remaining on the upper right hand corner of the computer screen. Once 15 minutes has elapsed, the test will resume automatically. If you decide to continue without any break, you can click the "End" button and you will be immediately directed to the Physics test.

OAT Physics includes the following topics at the introductory university level: units and vectors, statics and dynamics (i.e. objects not moving vs. moving), linear and rotational kinematics, energy and momentum, simple harmonic motion and waves, fluid statics (i.e. fluids not in motion), thermal energy and thermodynamics, electrostatics/DC circuits and magnetism, optics, and modern physics. Unlike Quantitative Reasoning, there is no access to a calculator during the Physics test.

The Quantitative Reasoning Test (QR) is the last exam section of the OAT. It covers Number Operations, Algebra, Geometry, Trigonometry, Probability and Statistics, and Applied Mathematics problems. In this particular section only, a basic four-function calculator appears on the computer screen. It is expected that this section will undergo significant changes in 2015.

Overall, you will have a total of 3 hours and 55 minutes, without the three optional portions of the test, or 4 hours and 40 minutes if you go through each segment.

1.3 English as a Second Language (ESL)

Many ESL students will need to pay extra attention to the Reading Comprehension Test of the OAT. Although specific advice for all students will be presented in the sections that follow, extra tips are discussed for ESL students in Section 3.2.3 of the Reading Comprehension part of this book series.

Having said that, OAT scores are subjected to a statistical analysis to check that each question is fair, valid and reliable. Test questions in development are scrutinized in order to minimize gender, ethnic or religious bias, and to affirm that the test is culturally fair.

Depending on your English skills, you may or may not benefit from an English reading summer course. Certainly, you have the option of deciding whether or not you would want to take such a course for credit.

1.4 How the OAT is Scored

ASCO reports eight standard scores. The first six scores are from the individual tests themselves, i.e. biology, general chemistry, organic chemistry, physics, reading comprehension, and quantitative reasoning. The multiple choice questions are first scored right or wrong resulting in a raw score. Note that wrong answers are worth the same as unanswered questions so ALWAYS ANSWER ALL THE QUESTIONS even if you are not sure of certain answers. The raw score is then converted to a scaled score ranging from 200 (lowest) to 400 (highest). A test section that is skipped will be scored 200. This is neither a percentage nor a percentile. The test is not based on a curve. Essentially, OAT performance is measured using an ability-referenced system. Based on standard scores, an individual examinee's abilities (i.e. knowledge and problem solving skills) are directly compared to that of the other OAT examinees'. It is not possible to accurately replicate this scoring system at home.

The remaining two scores are Total Science and Academic Average. The Total Science score is the standard score for the 140 questions in the Survey of Natural Sciences (100 questions) + Physics (40 questions) – NOT THE AVERAGE OF THE STANDARD SCORES of the Science subtests. This is derived from the sum of your raw scores each in biology, general chemistry, organic chemistry and physics. The total score is then converted to a standard score for Total Science. In contrast, a score in the Academic Average is the rounded average of the standard scores from physics (PHY), reading comprehension (RC), quantitative reasoning (QR), biology (BIO), general chemistry (CHM), and organic chemistry (ORG) tests. Here is an example of an Academic Average calculation:

QR – 280
RC – 290
BIO – 350
CHM – 320
ORG – 330
PHY – 340

TOTAL: 1910 ÷ 6 = 318.33; rounded up to the nearest 10 points, the Academic Average for these scores would be reported as 320.

Standards for interviews or admissions may vary for the individual scores, Total Science and the Academic Average. For example, one particular optometry school may establish a cutoff (minimum) of 300 for all sections. In other cases, admissions committees assess candidates against a mean of OAT scores in a particular batch of applicants; therefore, the range can vary from year to year. We have placed a table in the following pages to guide you but you should contact individual programs for specific score requirements.

The OAT may include a small number of questions, called pretest questions, which will not be scored. These questions are trial questions which may be used in the future. If you see a question that you think is off the wall, unanswerable or inappropriate for your level of knowledge, it could well be one of these questions, so never panic! And of course, answer every question because guessing may provide a 25% chance of being correct while not answering provides a 0% chance of being correct!

1.4.1 Average, Good, and High OAT Scores

Because the OAT employs an ability-referenced measurement, there are no established cutoff scores, or Pass and Fail marks. Rather, the standard score indicates your test performance relative to all the students who did the same test on the same day. This means that the national average of 300 on the scored sections is not always a guarantee for acceptance in an optometry program. In most instances, what is considered "average" depends on the entering batch of a particular academic year. This could range from as low as 290 to as high as 350 for the Academic Average and 280 to 360 for Total Science. Likewise, a "good" score may be good enough for admittance to one optometry school but below the cutoff of another. The best way to find out is to consult the websites of the optometry institutions to which you intend to apply.

Your main aim is to achieve the scores that will put you on a competitive footing among all the other applicants. Statistics of enrollees entering optometry school in 2012 are reported in Table 1.1 and 1.2 on the following page.

1.4.2 When are the Scores Released?

Right after completing the OAT, an unofficial score report is immediately generated at the Prometric Test Center. This report will then be audited for accuracy and verified by the Department of Testing Services. Official scores are forwarded within three to four weeks to the optometry schools, which are indicated in the OAT application of the examinee.

Requests of additional copies and/or recipients mean additional fees and transmittal time. For more details about this process, please check the ASCO website.

State	Institution	# first-year slots	Average GPA	AA Average	TS Average	# Out-of-State	# Foreign Country
Alabama	University of Alabama at Birmingham	40-45	3.65	321	318	23	1
Arizona	Midwestern University, Arizona College of Optometry	54	3.26	318	313	41	7
California	Southern California College of Optometry	100	3.44	332	330	32	2
California	University of California, Berkeley	68	3.46	354	359	15	3
California	Western University of Health Sciences	86	3.18	316	314	21	2
Florida	Nova Southeastern University	103	3.33	320	318	44	14
Illinois	Illinois College of Optometry	165	3.38	324	318	80	32
Indiana	Indiana University	76	3.53	321	316	36	0
Massachusetts	Massachusetts College of Pharmacy and Health Sciences	64	3.17	298	290	52	6
Massachusetts	New England College of Optometry	115	3.41	327	325	58	28
Michigan	Michigan College of Optometry	38	3.57	324	320	5	0
Missouri	Univ. of Missouri at St. Louis	46	3.51	316	307	30	0
New York	State University of New York	88	3.53	342	347	36	3
Oklahoma	Northeastern State University	28	3.62	315	306	14	0
Ohio	The Ohio State University	62	3.54	325	322	25	0
Oregon	Pacific University	91	3.55	320	320	58	23
Pennsylvania	Pennsylvania College of Optometry at Salus University	159	3.38	310	300	89	13
Puerto Rico	Inter American University	60	3.08	293	280	45	6
Tennessee	Southern College of Optometry	130	3.54	324	321	109	0
Texas	Rosenberg School of Optometry	67	3.23	308	301	44	2
Texas	University of Houston	104	3.48	326	323	20	3

Table 1.1: Profile of the 2012 Optometry Entering Class adapted from the Association of Schools and Colleges of Optometry (ASCO; www.opted.org). Note that Berkeley considers the BIO, CHM and PHY GPA, not the overall GPA.

Country	Institution	# first-year slots	Average Grades	Range	AA Average
Canada	University of Waterloo	90	86%	79-95%	370

Table 1.2: Profile of the 2012 Optometry Entering Class at the University of Waterloo which is one of two schools of optometry currently in Canada. The other institution, Université de Montréal, is French and does not require the OAT.

THE RECIPE FOR OAT SUCCESS

2.1 The Important Ingredients

- Time, Motivation
- Read from varied sources/Check SDN and optometrystudents.com websites for advice (read essential sources; familiarize with the actual test content and the skills demanded)
- A review of the basic OAT sciences

OAT-Specific Information

- The Gold Standard OAT/DAT Books
- optional: The Gold Standard Natural Sciences DVDs, smartphone apps/ flashcards, MP3s or online programs (OATbooks.com)
- optional: speed reading/comprehension course if necessary

OAT-Specific Problems

- Gold Standard (GS) chapter review problems online
- Gold Standard OAT tests (full lengths GS-1 and GS-2; + GS free mini test)
- Official OAT Sample Test Items (free download in PDF format from https://www.ada.org/oat/index.html)
- TopScore Pro: 3 full length practice OATs

2.2 The Proper Mix

1) Study regularly and start early. Creating a study schedule is often effective. Adhering to it is even more productive. Even the best study plans will unlikely yield the scores that you want if you do not follow your own preparation regimen. A lot of material needs to be covered and you will need sufficient time to review. Starting early will highlight your weak areas and give you ample time to remedy them. This will also reduce your stress level in the weeks leading up to the exam and may make your studying easier. Make sure that you get a good grasp of what each section of the test is designed to assess.

   Depending on your English skills and the quality of your science background, a good rule of thumb is: 3-6 hours/day of study for 3-6 months.

2) Keep focused and enjoy the material you are learning. Forget all past negative learning experiences, so you can

open your mind to the information with a positive attitude. Given an open mind and some time to consider what you are learning, you will find most of the information tremendously interesting. Motivation can be derived from a sincere interest in learning and by keeping in mind your long-term goals.

3) Preparation for the Sciences: The Gold Standard (GS) OAT/DAT books are the most comprehensive review guides for the OAT ever to be sold in bookstores. Thus the most directed and efficient study plan is to begin by reviewing and understanding the science sections in the GS. While doing your science survey, you should take notes specifically on topics that are marked Memorize or Understand on the first page of each chapter. Your notes - we call them Gold Notes (!!) - should be very concise (no longer than one page per chapter). Every week, you should study from your Gold Notes at least once.

   As you are incorporating the information from the science review, do the practice problems in the books and/or those included in the free chapter review questions online at OATbooks.com. This is the best way to more clearly define the depth of your understanding and to get you accustomed to the questions you can expect on the OAT.

   You may be wondering: What does the DAT have to do with the OAT and how does that work to your advantage? Well, first you should know that the Dental Admission Test (DAT) is constructed and trademarked by the American Dental Association (ADA), which also constructs the OAT questions for ASCO. The DAT tests the identical content as the OAT, from the same test makers, except that DAT PAT is replaced with OAT Physics.

   This means that you can get another free test! Besides the OAT test in this book (GS-1), and the GS free mini test online, and the free official OAT test, ada.org has a free practice DAT test with Natural Sciences, RC and QR questions of the same caliber required for the OAT (of course, just ignore the DAT PAT section). Also, beware that DAT standard scores are less forgiving than OAT standard scores (approximately 4 times more students apply to dental school so the competition is more stiff). So use the standard score tables from your ASCO OAT free practice test.

   Of course, it is because the skills and knowledge for DAT and OAT Natural Sciences, RC and QR are identical, you can use Gold Standard (GS) DAT Biology, Chemistry, RC and QR books for a comprehensive preparation for the OAT.

4) Preparation for Reading Comprehension: Begin by reading the advice and techniques given in GS RC. Time yourself and practice, practice, practice with various resources for this section as needed (in the book, online at OATbooks.com, TopScore, and of course, the ASCO and ADA materi-

als). You should be sure to understand each and every mistake you make so as to ensure there will be improvement.

5) Preparation for Quantitative Reasoning: Similar to your preparation for the section on the Sciences, take note of the scope and demands of the test, which are listed on the first page of GS QR. Your aim is to determine your deficiencies and work on the foundations that will help address these.

6) Do practice exams. Ideally, you would finish your science review in The Gold Standard texts and/or the science review DVDs at least a couple of months prior to the exam date. Then each week you can do a practice exam under simulated test conditions and thoroughly review each exam after completion. Scores in practice exams should improve over time. Success depends on what you do between the first and the last exam. You can start with OAT Sample Test Items then continue with the GS and TopScore practice exams. You should do practice exams as you would the actual test: in one sitting within the expected time limits. Doing practice exams serves two important purposes in your preparation. First, it will increase your confidence and allow you to see what is expected of you. It will make you realize the constraints imposed by time limits in completing the entire test. Second, it will allow you to identify the areas in which you may be lacking.

Some students can answer all OAT questions quite well if they only had more time. Thus you must time yourself during practice and monitor your time during the test. On average, you will have a little less than a minute per question for Natural Sciences, just over 15 minutes per passage and its accompanying questions for the RC, and just over 1 minute per question for Physics and QR. In other words, every 30 minutes, you should check to be sure that you have completed an approximate number of questions for that section; for example, 34 questions or more in the first 30 minutes for Science, 70 or more in the next, and so on. If not, then you always guess on "time consuming questions" in order to catch up and, if you have time at the end, you return to properly evaluate the questions you skipped. Set aside at least the equivalent of a full day to review the explanations for EVERY test question. Do NOT dismiss any wrong answer as a "stupid mistake." You made that error for a reason, so you must work that out in your mind to reduce the risk that it occurs again. You can reduce your risk by test-proofing answers (i.e. spending 5-10 seconds being critical of your response) and by considering the following questions:

1. Why did you get the question wrong (or correct)?
2. What question-type or passage-type gives you repeated difficulty?

3. What is your mindset when looking at a particular diagram?
4. Did you monitor your time during the test?
5. Are most of your errors at the beginning or the end of the test?
6. Did you eliminate answer choices when you could?
7. For the Reading Comprehension Test, did you effectively scan for the detail questions? Did you comprehend the fundamental concepts presented in each passage?
8. Was your main problem a lack of content review or a lack of practice?
9. In which specific science or QR content areas do you need improvement?
10. Have you designed a study schedule to address your weaknesses?

8) Remember that the OAT will primarily measure your basic knowledge and understanding of concepts. Evidently, a lot of material in the GS books must simply be memorized; for example, some very basic science equations (i.e. weight W = mg, Ohm's Law, Newton's Second Law, etc.), rules of logarithms, trigonometric functions, the phases in mitosis and meiosis, naming organic compounds and many, many basic science facts. Nonetheless, for the most part, your objective should be to try to understand, rather than memorize, the biology, chemistry, physics, and math material you review. This may appear vague now, but as you immerse yourself in the review chapters and practice material, you will more clearly understand what is expected of you.

9) Relax once in a while! While the OAT requires a lot of preparation, you should not forsake all your other activities. Try to keep exercising, maintain a social life and do things you enjoy. If you balance work with things that relax you, you will study more effectively overall.

2.3 It's OAT Time!

1) On the night before the exam, try to get a good night sleep. The OAT can be physically draining and it is in your best interest to be well rested when you do the exam.

2) Avoid last minute cramming. On the morning of the exam, do not begin studying ad hoc. You will not learn anything effectively, and noticing something you do not know or will not remember might reduce your confidence and lower your score unnecessarily. Just get up, eat a good breakfast, consult your Gold Notes (the top level information that you personally compiled) and go do the exam.

3) Eat breakfast! You need the food energy to get through the exam.

4) If you are taking an afternoon schedule, eat a light lunch. Avoid greasy food that will make you drowsy. You do not want to feel sleepy while taking the test. A chocolate bar or other sweet highly caloric food could, however, be very useful during the break when you may be tired for the last section. The 'sugar low' will hit you only after you have completed the exam when you do not have to be awake!

5) Make sure you answer all the questions! You do not get penalized for incorrect answers, so always choose something even if you have to guess. If you run out of time, pick a letter and use it to answer all the remaining questions. ASCO performs statistical analyses on every test so no one letter will give you an unfair advantage. Just choose your "lucky" letter and move on!

6) Pace yourself. Do not get bogged down trying to answer a difficult question. If the question is very difficult, mark it, guess, move on to the next question and return later if you have enough time remaining.

7) Remember that some of the questions may be thrown out as inappropriate, used solely to calibrate the test or trial questions. If you find that you cannot answer some of the questions, do not despair. It is possible they could be questions used for these purposes.

8) Do not let others psyche you out! Some people might be leaving an earlier exam saying, 'It went great. What a joke!' Ignore them. Often these types may just be trying to boost their own confidence or to make themselves look good in front of their friends. Just focus on what you have to do and tune out the other examinees.

9) Relax during the short break. You need the time to recuperate and rest.

10) Before reading the RC passage, some students find it more efficient to quickly read the questions first. In this way, as soon as you read something in the passage which brings to mind a question you have read, you can answer immediately. Otherwise, if you read the text first and then the questions, you may end up wasting time searching through the text for answers.

11) Read the text and questions carefully! Often students leave out a word or two while reading, which can completely change the sense of the problem. Pay special attention to words in italics, CAPS, bolded, or underlined. You will certainly find the word "EXCEPT" in CAPS in a question on the real OAT!

12) You must be both diligent and careful with the way you choose the correct answer because you will not be given

extra time to make corrections when time expires.

13) If you run out of time, just do the questions. In other words, only read the part of the passage which your question specifically requires in order for you to get the correct answer.

14) Expel any relevant equation onto your note board! Even if the question is of a theoretical nature, sometimes equations contain the answers and they are much more objective than the reasoning of a nervous pre-optometry student!

15) Consider your choice of clothing on test day. Be ready for too much heat or an overzealous air conditioning unit.

16) Some problems involve algebraic manipulation of equations and/or numerical calculations. Be sure that you know what all the variables in the equation stand for and that you are using the equation in the appropriate circumstance. In physics, chemistry, and QR, the use of dimensional analysis will help you keep track of units and solve some problems where you might have forgotten the relevant equations. Dimensional analysis relies on the manipulation of units. For example, if you are asked for the energy involved in maintaining a 60 watt bulb lit for two minutes you can pull out the appropriate equations or: i) recognize that your objective (unknown = energy) is in joules; ii) recall that a watt is a joule per second; iii) convert minutes into seconds. {note that minutes and seconds cancel leaving joules as an answer}

$$60\ \frac{\text{joules}}{\text{second}} \times 2\ \text{minutes} \times 60\ \frac{\text{seconds}}{\text{minutes}}$$

$$= 7200\ \text{joules or } 7.2\ \text{kilojoules}$$

17) The final step in problem solving is to ask yourself: is my answer reasonable? For example, if you would have done the preceding problem and your answer was 7200 kilojoules, intuitively this should strike you as an exorbitant amount of energy for an everyday light bulb to remain lit for two minutes! It would then be of value to recheck your calculations. This is where your intuition serves as a guide. But to be frank, 'intuition' in the context of the OAT is really learned through the experience of a comprehensive review and completing many practice problems and tests.

18) Whenever doing calculations, the following will increase your speed: (i) manipulate variables but plug in values only when necessary; (ii) avoid decimals, use fractions wherever possible; (iii) square roots or cube roots can be converted to the power (exponent) of 1/2 or 1/3, respectively; (iv) before calculating, check to see if the possible answers are sufficiently far apart such

that your values can be approximated (i.e. 19.2 ≈ 20, 185 ≈ 200). In fact, the OAT will provide gravity $g = 9.8\ m/s^2$ at the beginning of the Physics test as $g = 10\ m/s^2$.

We, at The Gold Standard, will do our best - on paper and online - to guide you through the content and strategies you can use to be successful. Let's continue . . .

OATbooks.com

PHYSICS

TRANSLATIONAL MOTION
Chapter 1

Memorize

'rigonometric functions: definitions
'ythagorean theorem
)efine: displacement, velocity,
cceleration
:quations: acceleration, kinematics

Understand

* Scalar vs. vector
* Add, subtract, resolve vectors
* Determine common values of functions
* Conversion of the angle to other units
* Displacement, velocity, acceleration (avg. and instant.) including graphs

Importance

5 to 7 out of the 40 PHY

OAT questions are based on content in this chapter (in our estimation).

*Note that between 55% and 85% of the questions in OAT Physics are based on content from 6 chapters: 1, 2, 3, 6, 7 and 11.

OATbooks.com

Introduction 

Transitional motion is the movement of an object (or particle) through space without turning (rotation). Displacement, velocity and acceleration are key vectors — specified by magnitude and direction — often used to describe transitional motion. Being able to manipulate and resolve vectors is critical for problem solving in OAT physics. Please note that this chapter overlaps with our DAT QR book's Appendix.

Additional Resources

Free Online Q&A + Forum

Video: Online or DVD

Flashcards

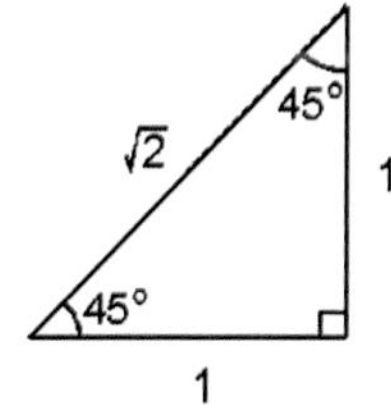

Special Guest

1.1 Scalars and Vectors

Scalars, such as speed, have magnitude only and are specified by a number with a unit (55 miles/hour). Scalars obey the rules of ordinary algebra. *Vectors*, like velocity, have both magnitude **and** direction (100 km/hour, west). Vectors are represented by arrows where: i) the length of the arrow indicates the magnitude of the vector, and ii) the arrowhead indicates the direction of the vector. Vectors obey the special rules of vector algebra. Thus vectors can be moved in space but their orientation must be kept the same.

Addition of Vectors: Two vectors **a** and **b** can be added geometrically by drawing them to a common scale and placing them head to tail. The vector connecting the tail of **a** to the head of **b** is the sum or resultant vector **r**.

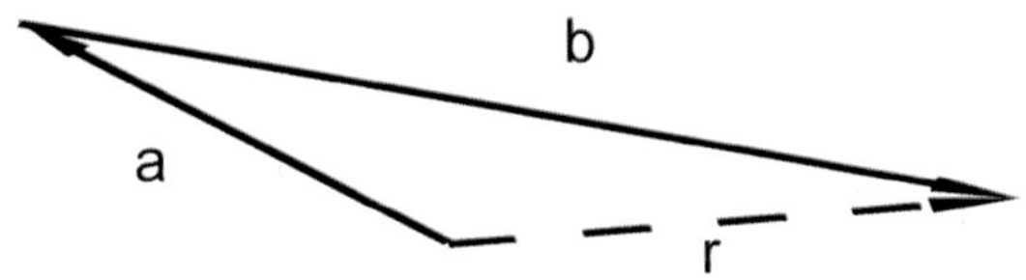

Figure III.B.1.1: The vector sum a + b = r.

Subtraction of Vectors: To subtract the vector **b** from **a**, reverse the direction of **b** then add to **a**.

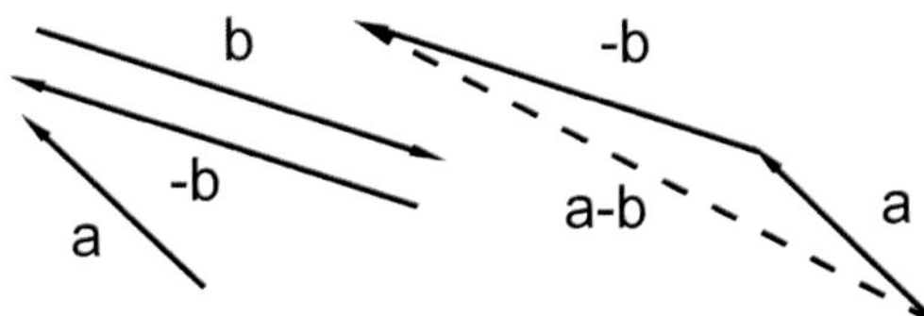

Figure III.B.1.2: The vector difference a - b = a + (-b).

Resolution of Vectors: Perpendicular projections of a vector can be made on a coordinate axis. Thus the vector **a** can be *resolved* into its x-component (a_x) and its y-component (a_y).

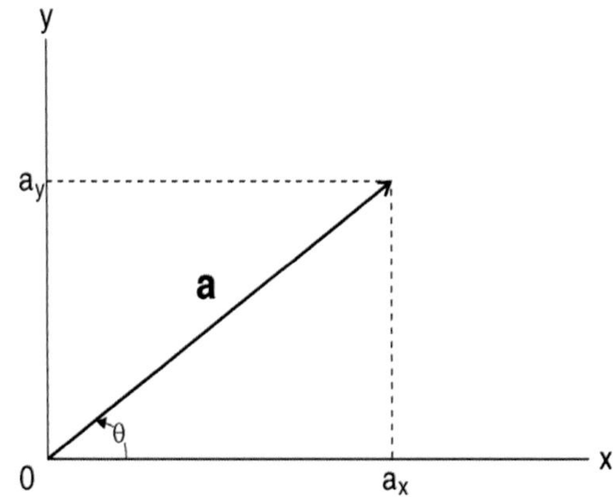

Figure III.B.1.3: The resolution of a vector into its scalar components in a coordinate system.

Analytically, the resolution of vector **a** is as follows:

$$a_x = \mathbf{a} \cos\theta \quad \text{and} \quad a_y = \mathbf{a} \sin\theta$$

Conversely, given the components, we can reconstruct vector **a**:

$$\mathbf{a} = \sqrt{a_x^2 + a_y^2} \quad \text{and} \quad \tan\theta = a_y / a_x$$

Another concept which is sometimes useful is the unit vector. It is a vector of one unit given the special symbols **i**, **j**, and **k** which represent a unit vector in the *x-*, *y-* and *z*-directions, respectively.

Examples of Scalar Quantities
distance, speed, time, temperature, mass, area, volume, energy, entropy, electric charge

Examples of Vector Quantities
displacement, velocity, acceleration, force, momentum, gravitational field, electrical field

1.1.1 Trigonometric Functions

The power in trigonometric functions lies in their ability to relate an angle to the ratio of scalar components or *sides* of a triangle. These functions may be defined as follows:

$$\sin\theta = opp/hyp = y/r$$

$$\cos\theta = adj/hyp = x/r$$

[*opp* = *the length of the side opposite* angle θ, *adj* = the length of the side *adjacent* to angle θ, *hyp* = the length of the *hypotenuse*]

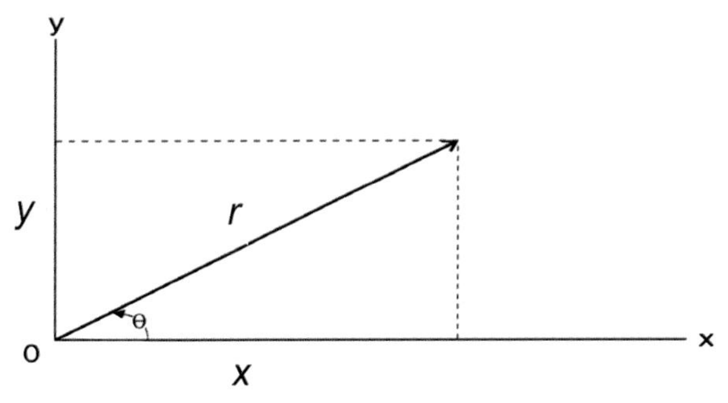

Thus sine ($r\sin\theta$) gives the *y*-component and cosine ($r\cos\theta$) gives the x-component of vector r. The tangent function ($\tan\theta$) and two important trigonometric identities relate sine and cosine:

$$\tan\theta = \sin\theta/\cos\theta = opp/adj = y/x$$

$$\sin^2\theta + \cos^2\theta = 1$$

and

$$\sin 2\theta = 2\sin\theta\cos\theta$$

Other functions of less importance for OAT test physics include: cotangent ($\cot\theta = x/y$), secant ($\sec\theta = r/x$) and cosecant ($\csc\theta = r/y$).

The Pythagorean Theorem relates the sides of the right angle triangle according to the following:

$$r^2 = x^2 + y^2.$$

1.1.2 Common Values of Trigonometric Functions

There are special angles which produce standard values of the trigonometric functions. These values should be memorized. Several of the values are derived from the following triangles:

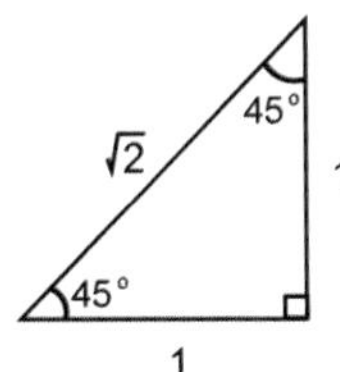

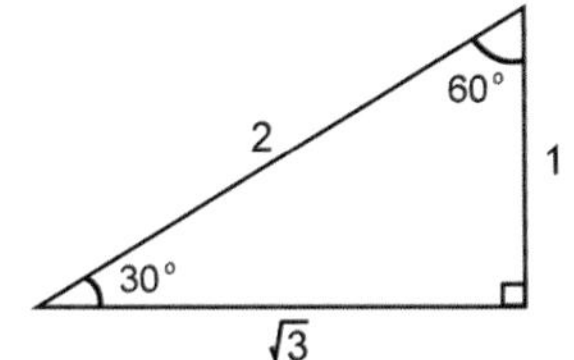

θ	$\sin\theta$	$\cos\theta$	$\tan\theta$
0°	0	1	0
30°	1/2	$\sqrt{3}/2$	$1/\sqrt{3}$
45°	$1/\sqrt{2}$	$1/\sqrt{2}$	1
60°	$\sqrt{3}/2$	1/2	$\sqrt{3}$
90°	1	0	∞
180°	0	-1	0

Table III.B.1.1:
Common values of trigonometric functions. The angle θ may be given in radians (R) where $2\pi^R$ = 360°= 1 revolution. Recall $\sqrt{3} \approx 1.7$, $\sqrt{2} \approx 1.4$.

Note that 1° = 60 arcminutes, 1 arcminute = 60 arcseconds.

Each trigonometric function (i.e. sine) contains an inverse function (i.e. $\sin^{-1}$), where if sin θ = x, θ = $\sin^{-1}$ x. Thus cos 60° = 1/2, and 60° = $\cos^{-1}$ (1/2). Some texts denote the inverse function with "arc" as a prefix. Thus arcsec (2) = $\sec^{-1}$ (2).

1.2 Distance and Displacement

Distance is the amount of separation between two points in space. It has a magnitude but no direction. It is a scalar quantity and is always positive. Another concept which is sometimes useful is the unit vector.

Displacement of an object between two points is the difference between the final position and the initial position of the object in a given referential system. Thus, a displacement has an origin, a direction and a magnitude. It is a vector.

The sign of the coordinates of the vector displacement depends on the system under study and the chosen referential system. The sign will be positive (+) if the system is moving towards the positive axis of the referential system and negative (-) if not.

The International System of Units (SI), the standard for the OAT and science in general, uses the meter for length.

Speed is the rate of change of distance with respect to time. It is a scalar quantity, it has a magnitude but no direction, like distance, and it is always positive.

Velocity is the rate of change of displacement with respect to time. It is a vector, and like the displacement, it has a direction and a magnitude. Its value depends on the position of the object. The sign of the coordinates of the vector velocity is the same as that of the displacement.

The instantaneous velocity of a system at a given time is the slope of the graph of the displacement of that system vs. time at that time.The magnitude of the velocity decreases if the vector velocity and the vector acceleration have opposite directions.

The units of speed and velocity are expressed in length divided by time such as *feet/sec., meters/sec. (m/s)* and *miles/hour.*

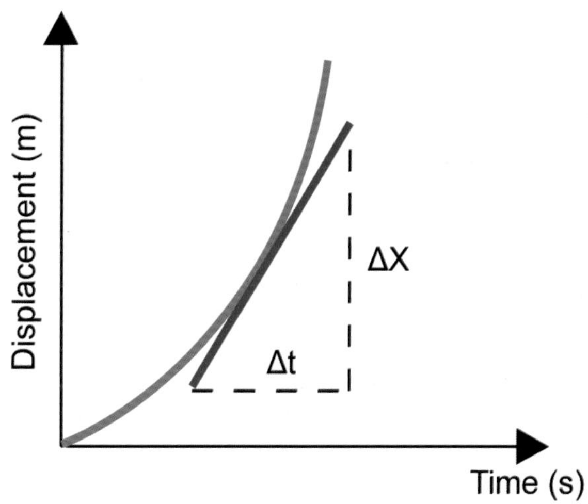

Figure III.B.1.4: Displacement vs. time. Please note that the capital letter X denotes displacement as opposed to referring to the x-axis (small letter x) which is time.

Dimensional Analysis: remember from High School math that a slope is "rise over run" meaning it is the change in the y-axis divided by the change in the x-axis (see GS QR book). This means when we pay attention to the units, we get, for example, m/s which is velocity.

1.4 Acceleration

Acceleration (a) is the rate of change of the velocity (v) with respect to time (t):

$$a = v/t$$

Like the velocity, it is a vector and it has a direction and a magnitude.

The sign of the vector acceleration depends on the net force applied to the system and the chosen referential system. The units of acceleration are expressed as velocity divided by time such as *meters/sec²*. The term for negative acceleration is deceleration.

1.4.1 Average and Instantaneous Acceleration

The average acceleration av between two instants t and t′ = t + Δt, measures the result of the increase in the speed divided by the time difference,

$$a_v = \frac{v' - v}{\Delta t}$$

The instantaneous acceleration can be determined either by calculating the **slope** (*see* QR for the math) of a velocity vs. time graph at any time, or by taking the limit when Δt approaches zero of the preceding expression.

$$a_v = \lim_{\Delta t \to 0} \frac{v' - v}{\Delta t}$$

Math involving "limits" does not exist on the OAT test. So let's discuss what this definition is describing in informal terms. The limit is the value of the change in velocity over the change in time as the time approaches 0. It's like saying that the change in velocity is happening in an instant. This allows us to talk about the acceleration in that incredibly fast moment: the instantaneous acceleration which can be determined graphically.

Consider the following events illustrated in the graph (Fig. III.B.1.4): your car starts at rest (0 velocity and time = 0); you steadily accelerate out of the parking lot (the change in velocity increases over time = acceleration); you are driving down the street at constant velocity (change in velocity = 0 and thus acceleration is 0 divided by the change in time which means: a = 0); you see a cat dart across the street safely which made you slow down temporarily (change in velocity is negative thus negative acceleration which, by definition, is deceleration); you now enter the on-ramp for the highway so your velocity is now increasing at a faster and faster rate (increasing acceleration). You can examine the instantaneous acceleration at any one point (or instant) during the period that your acceleration is increasing.

To determine the displacement (*not* distance), take the area under the graph or curve. To calculate area: a rectangle is base (b) times height (h); a triangle is ½b × h; and for a curve, they can use graph paper and expect you would count the boxes under the curve to estimate the area.

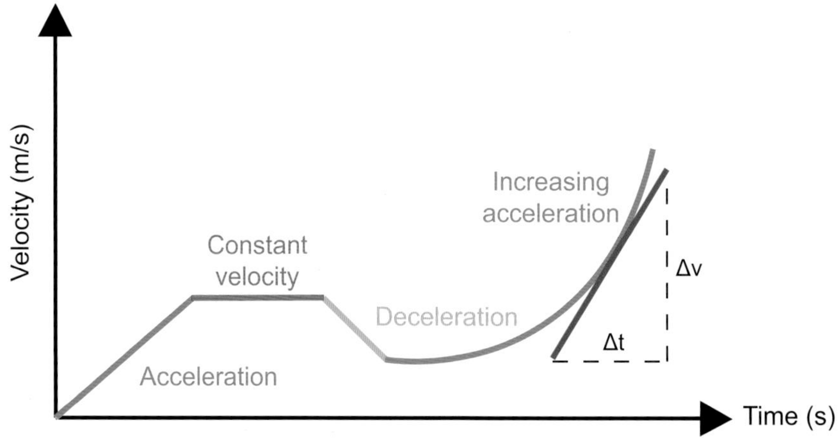

Figure III.B.1.4: Velocity vs. time. Note that at constant velocity, the slope and thus the acceleration are both equal to zero.

1.5 Uniformly Accelerated Motion

The magnitude and direction of the acceleration of a system are solely determined by the exterior forces acting upon the system. If the magnitude of these forces is constant, the magnitude of the acceleration will be constant and the resulting motion is a *uniformly accelerated motion*. The initial displacement, the velocity and the accelera-tion at any given time contribute to the over-all displacement of the system:

$x = x_0$ – displacement due to the initial displacement x_0.

$x = v_0 t$ – displacement due to the initial velocity v_0 at time t.

$x = ½at^2$ – displacement due the acceleration at time t.

The total displacement of the uniformly-accelerated motion is given by the following formula:

$$x = x_0 + v_0 t + ½at^2$$

The translational motion is the motion of the center of gravity of a system through space, illustrated by the above equation.

1.6 Equations of Kinematics

Kinematics is the study of objects in motion with respect to space and time. There are three related equations which must be memorized. The first is above (PHY 1.5), the others are:

$$v = v_0 + at \quad \text{and}$$
$$v^2 = v_0^2 + 2ax$$

where v is the final velocity; we will put these equations to use in PHY 2.6.

Chapter review questions are available online for free. Doing practice questions will help clarify concepts and ensure that you study in a targeted way. We also have a Physics equation list that you can print to help your review.

First, register at oatbooks.com, then login and click on OAT Textbook Owners in the right column. Your online access continues for one full year from your online registration.

FORCE, MOTION, AND GRAVITATION
Chapter 2

Memorize	Understand	Importance
efine with units: weight, mass ewton's laws, Law of Gravitation quation for uniformly accelerated motion	* Mass, weight, center of gravity * Newton's laws * Law of Gravitation, free fall motion * Projectile motion equations and calculations	**5 to 7 out of the 40 PHY** OAT questions are based on content in this chapter (in our estimation). *Note that between 55% and 85% of the questions in OAT Physics are based on content from 6 chapters: 1, 2, 3, 6, 7 and 11.

Introduction

Force is a vector (often a push or pull) that can cause a mass to change velocity thus motion. Forces can be due to gravity, magnetism or anything that causes a mass to accelerate. Nuclear forces (strong) are far greater than electrostatic forces (opposite charges attract), which in turn are far greater than gravitational forces (one of the weakest forces in nature).

Additional Resources

Free Online Q&A + Forum

Video: Online or DVD

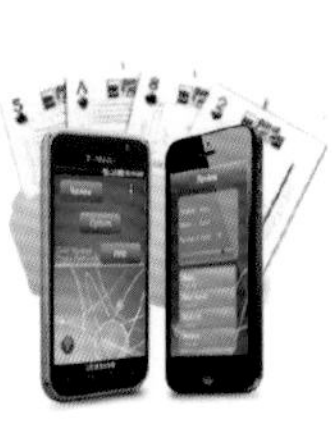

Flashcards

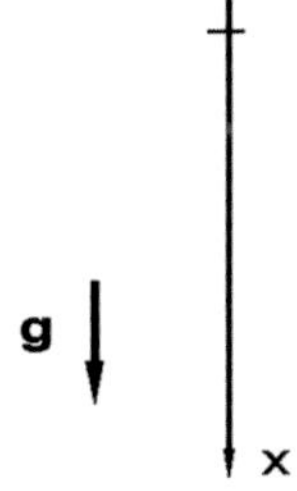

Special Guest

2.1 Mass, Center of Mass, Weight

The mass (m) of an object is its measure of inertia. It is the measure of the capacity of that object to remain motionless or to move with a constant velocity if the sum of the forces acting upon it is zero. This definition of inertia is derived from Newton's First Law.

The *center of mass* of an object is a point whose motion can be described like the motion of a particle through space. The center of mass of an object always has the simplest motion of all the points of that object.

The center of gravity (COG) is also the center of mass seen as the center of application of all the gravitational forces acting on the object. For example, for a uniform plank hanging horizontally, the COG is at half the length of the plank.

The COG can be determined experimentally by suspending an object by a string at different points and noting that the direction of the string passes through the COG. The intersection of the projected lines in the different suspensions is the COG.

An object is in *stable equilibrium* if the COG is as low as possible and any change in orientation will lead to an elevation of the COG. An object is in *unstable equilibrium* if the COG is high relative to the support point or surface and any change in orientation will lead to a lowering of the COG.

The *weight* is a force (i.e. newtons, pounds). It is a vector unlike the *mass* which is a scalar (i.e. kilograms, slugs). The weight is proportional to the mass. It is the product of the mass by the vector gravitational acceleration *g*.

$$W = m \times g$$

2.2 Newton's Second Law

Newton's Second Law, also called the fundamental dynamic relation, states that the sum of all the exterior forces acting upon the center of mass of a system is equal to the product of the mass of the system by the acceleration of its center of mass.

Therefore, if there is a net force, the object must accelerate. It is a vectorial equality which asserts that <u>a net force against an object *must* result in acceleration:</u>

$$\Sigma F = m \times a$$

It is important to note that for a system in complex motion, Newton's Second Law can only determine the acceleration of the center of mass. It does not give any indication about the motion of the other parts of the system.

Whereas, for a system in translational motion, Newton's Second Law gives the acceleration of the system.

In your daily life, you would already have the sense that objects with a greater mass (m) require a greater force (F) to get it to move with increasing speed (a). If you maintain a net force on an object, it will not only move, it must accelerate. We will be exploring more consequences of Newton's Second Law both in this and later chapters.

2.3 Newton's Third Law

For every action there is an equal and opposite reaction. If one object exerts a force, *F*, on a second object, the second object exerts a force, *F'* , on the first object. *F* and *F'* have opposite direction but the same magnitude.

One conclusion would be that forces are found in pairs. Consider the time you sit in a chair. Your body exerts a force downward (mg) and that chair needs to exert an equal force upward (the normal force N) or the chair will collapse. There is symmetry. Acting forces encounter other forces in the opposite direction. Consider shooting a cannonball. When the explosion fires the cannonball through the air, the cannon is pushed backward. The force pushing the ball out is equal to the force pushing the cannon back, but the effect on the cannon is less noticeable because it has a much larger mass and it may be restrained. Similarly, a gun experiences a "kick" backwards when a bullet is fired forward.

2.4 The Law of Gravitation

The Law of Gravitation states that there is a force of attraction existing between any two bodies of masses m_1 and m_2. The force is proportional to the product of the masses and inversely proportional to the square of the distance between them.

$$F = K_G(m_1 m_2 / r^2)$$

r is the distance between the bodies; K_G is the universal constant of gravitation, and its value depends on the units being used.

2.5 Free Fall Motion

The free fall motion of an object is the upward or downward vertical motion of that object with reference to the earth.

The motion is always uniformly accelerated with the acceleration g: vertical, directed towards the center of the earth and the magnitude is considered constant during the free fall motion.

Also, during the free fall motion, the air resistance is considered negligible. The equation of the motion can easily be derived from Newton's Second Law.

$$\Sigma F = ma$$

Where ΣF represents all the forces acting on the object, m is the mass of the object and a is the acceleration of the center of mass of the object. Hence, a can be replaced by g since $a = g$ by definition. In the free fall motion, the only force acting on the object is the gravitational force, which gives the following equality:

$$K_G m_{object} \frac{M_{earth}}{r^2_{earth}} = m_{object}\, g$$

dividing both sides by m_{object} we get :

$$g = K_G \frac{M_{earth}}{r^2_{earth}}$$

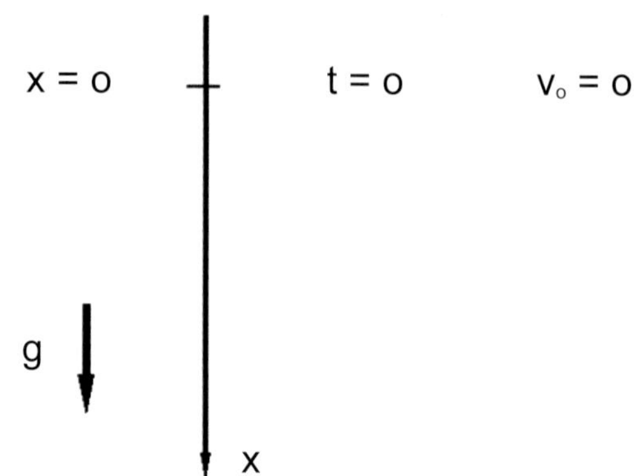

Figure III.B.2.1: Free fall motion.

The values of g are: 32 ft/s^2 (Imperial units), 980 cm/s^2 (CGS units), or 9.8 m/s^2 (**SI** units). The equation for uniformly accelerated motion is applicable by replacing a by g:

$$x = x_0 + v_0 t + 1/2gt^2$$

$$v = gt$$

$$a = g$$

Before doing any calculation, the reference point and a positive direction must be chosen. In the free fall of an actual object, the value of g is modified by the buoyancy of air and resistance of air. This results in a *drag force* which depends on the location on earth, shape and size of the object, and the velocity of the object (as free fall velocity increases, the drag force increases). When the drag force reaches the force of gravity, the object reaches a final velocity called the terminal velocity and continues to fall at that velocity.

The projectile motion is the motion of any object fired or launched at some angle α from the horizontal. The motion defines a parabola (*see Figure III.B.2.2*) in the plane *O-x-y* that contains the initial (*original*) vector velocity v_o.

The motion can be decomposed into two distinct motions: a vertical component, affected by *g*, and a horizontal component, independent of *g*.

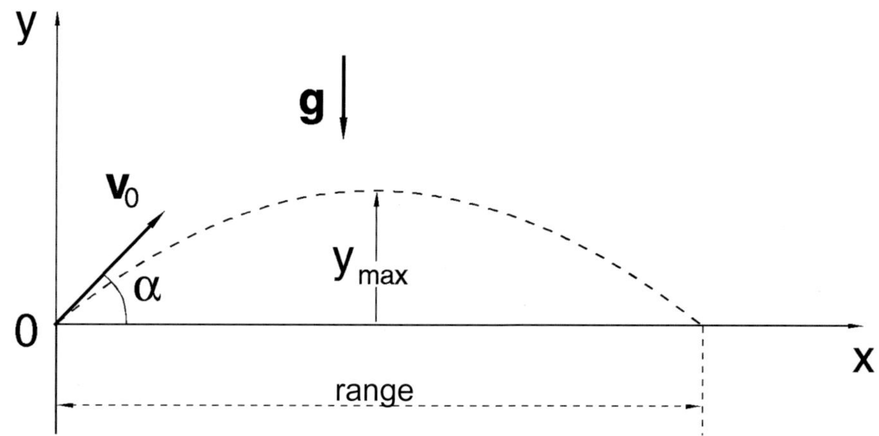

Figure III.B.2.2: Projectile motion.

Vertical component (free fall)

- initial speed : $V_{oy} = V_o \sin \alpha$
- displacement at time t: $y = V_{oy}t + 1/2gt^2$
- speed at any time t: $V_y = V_{oy} + gt$

Horizontal component (linear with constant speed)

- initial speed : $V_{ox} = V_o \cos \alpha$
- displacement at any time t: $x = V_{ox}t$
- speed at any time t: $V_x = V_{ox}$ (speed is constant)

Initial velocity

- magnitude: $|V_o| = \sqrt{V^2_{ox} + V^2_{oy}}$
- direction: *alpha*: $\tan \alpha = V_{oy}/V_{ox}$
- important points to consider:

1) Neglecting air resistance, there is no acceleration in the horizontal direction: V_x is constant.

2) V_y is zero at Y_{max}, then $V_y = 0 = V_{oy} + gt_{up}$ or $-V_{oy} = gt_{up}$ can be solved for t.

3) Also, by eliminating the variables y and t in the equations, we can get the following equality :

$$x = \frac{V_o^2 \sin 2\alpha}{g}$$

The horizontal distance from the origin to where the object strikes the ground (= *the range*) is maximum for a given V_o when $\sin 2\alpha = 1$, hence for $2\alpha = (\pi/2)^R \Rightarrow \alpha = (\pi/4)^R$ or α = 45 degrees.

2.6.1 Projectile Motion Problem (Imperial units)

In the Super Bowl, a player kicks the ball at an angle of 30° from the horizontal with an initial speed of 75 ft/s. Assume that the ball moves in a vertical plane and that air resistance is negligible.

(a) *Find the time at which the ball reaches the highest point of its trajectory.*

{*key: height* refers to the y-component; we can define *gravity* as a negative vector since it is directed downwards}

V_y is zero at Y_{max} (= *the highest point*), thus:

$$V_y = 0,\quad V_o = 75 \text{ ft/s},\quad \alpha = 30°,\quad g = -32 \text{ ft/s}^2$$

$$V_y = V_o \sin\alpha + g t_{up}$$

Isolate t_{up}:

$$t_{up} = \frac{V_y - V_o \sin\alpha}{g} = \frac{-75(\sin 30°)}{-32}$$

$$= 1.2 \text{ seconds}$$

(b) *How high does the ball go?*

$$Y_{max} = V_o (\sin\alpha)\, t_{up} + 1/2 g t_{up}^2$$

$Y_{max} = 75(\sin 30°)1.2 + 1/2(-32)(1.2)^2 =$ 22 feet

(c) *How long is the ball in the air and what is its range?*

{*key: time* is the same for *x*- and *y*-components, *range* = *x*-component}

Once the ball strikes the ground its vertical displacement $y = 0$, thus:

$$y = 0 = V_o (\sin\alpha)\, t + 1/2 g t^2$$

Divide through by t then isolate:

$$t = 2V_o(\sin\alpha)/g = 2.4 \text{ seconds.}$$

Since $t = 2t_{up}$, we can conclude that the time required for the ball to go up to Y_{max} is the same as the time required to come back down: 1.2 seconds in either direction.

The range $x = V_o(\cos\alpha)t$

$$x = 75(\cos 30°)2.4 \approx 150 \text{ feet}$$

or

$$x \approx 150 \text{ ft } (1 \text{ yd}/ 3 \text{ ft}) = 50 \text{ yards}$$

{Had the player kicked the ball at 45° from the horizontal he would have maximized his range. He should be benched for not having done his physics!}

(d) *What is the velocity of the ball as it strikes the ground?*

{*key: velocity* is the resultant vector of V_x and V_y - the final velocities in the *x* and *y* directions}

$$V_x = V_o \cos \alpha = 75(\cos 30^\circ) = 65 \text{ ft/s}$$

$$V_y = V_o \sin \alpha + gt$$

$$= 75(\sin 30^\circ) + (-32)(2.4) = -39 \text{ ft/s}$$

$$V = \sqrt{V_x^2 + V_y^2} = \sqrt{(65)^2 + (-39)^2}$$

$$= \sqrt{(13 \times 5)^2 + (13 \times -3)^2}$$

$$V = 13\sqrt{(5)^2 + (-3)^2} = 13\sqrt{34}$$

To estimate $\sqrt{34}$ we must first recognize that the answer must be at least 5 ($5^2 = 25$) but closer to 6 ($6^2 = 36$). Try squaring 5.7, 5.8, 5.9. Squaring 5.8 is the closest estimate (= *33.6*), thus

$$V = 13(5.8) = 75 \text{ ft/s.}$$

Please note:

- With no air resistance and a symmetric problem (the ball is launched and returns to the same vertical point), the initial and final speeds are the same (75 ft/s).
- Usually the OAT will use SI units in exam problems, but many problems are solved using dimensional analysis, with or without SI units.
- Please be sure you can do all the preceding calculations efficiently.
- There is no use of a calculator in OAT physics so please do not use one when doing practice problems.

Go online to OATbooks.com for free chapter review Q&A and forum.

PARTICLE DYNAMICS
Chapter 3

Memorize

* Centripetal force and acceleration
* Circumference and area of a circle

Understand

* Equations: f_{max}, μ_s
* Static vs. kinetic friction
* Resolving vectors, calculate for incline plane
* Uniform circular motion
* Solve pulley system, free body diagram

Importance

3 to 5 out of the 40 PHY

OAT questions are based on content in this chapter (in our estimation).

*Note that between 55% and 85% of the questions in OAT Physics are based on content from 6 chapters: 1, 2, 3, 6, 7 and 11.

Introduction

Particle dynamics is concerned with the physics of motion. Among other topics, particle dynamics includes Newton's laws, frictional forces, and problems dealing with incline planes, uniform circular motion and pulley systems.

Additional Resources

Free Online Q&A + Forum

Video: Online or DVD

Flashcards

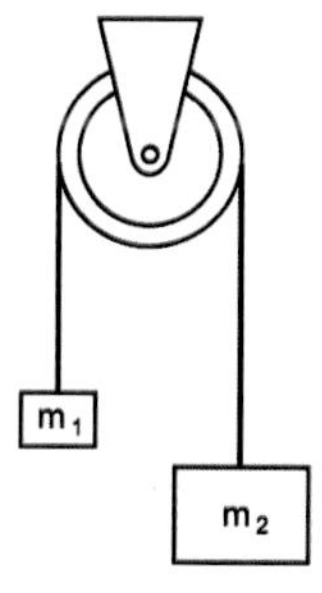

Special Guest

3.1 Overview

For the OAT test, particle dynamics is concerned with the physics of motion. Among other topics, particle dynamics includes Newton's laws, frictional forces, and problems dealing with incline planes, uniform circular motion and pulley systems.

3.2 Frictional Forces

Frictional forces are nonconservative (mechanical energy is not conserved) and are caused by molecular adhesion between tangential surfaces but are independent of the area of contact of the surfaces. Frictional forces always oppose the motion. The maximal frictional force has the following expression: $f_{max} = \mu N$, where μ is the coefficient of friction and N is the normal force to the surface on which the object rests, it is the reaction of that surface against the weight of the object. Thus N always acts perpendicular to the surface.

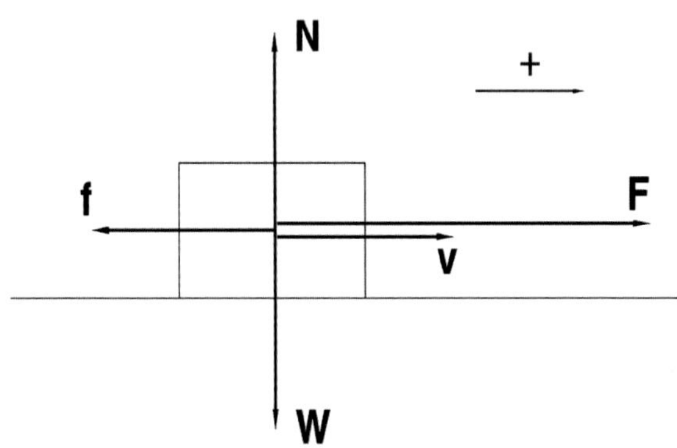

Figure III.B.3.1: Frictional force f and force normal N.

Static friction is when the object is not moving, and it must be overcome for motion to begin. The coefficient of static friction μ_s is given as :

$$\mu_s = \tan \alpha$$

where α is the angle at which the object first begins to move on an inclined plane as the angle is increased from 0 degrees to α degrees (*see Figure III.B.3.2*). There is also a coefficient of kinetic friction, μ_k, which exists when surfaces are in motion; $\mu_k < \mu_s$ always.

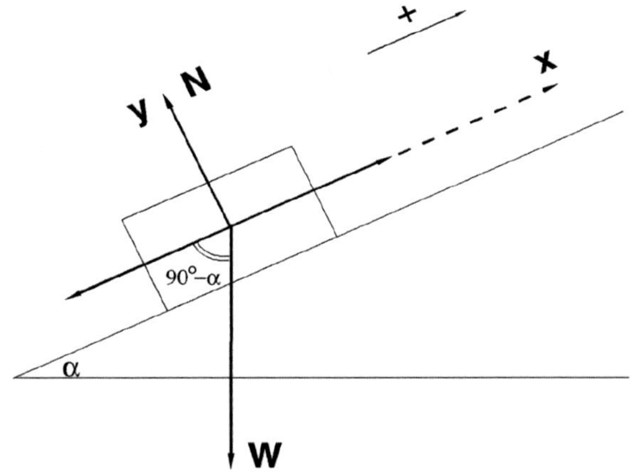

Figure III.B.3.2: Analysis of motion on an incline.

The weight (W) due to gravity (g) may be sufficient to cause motion if friction is overcome. The reference axes are usually chosen as shown such that one (the x) is along the surface of the incline.

Note that W is directed downward and N is directed upward but *perpendicular* to the surface of the incline (i.e. in the positive *y* direction).

3.2.1 Incline Plane Problem with Friction (SI units)

A 50 kilogram block is on an incline of 45°. The coefficient of sliding (= *kinetic*) friction between the block and the plane is 0.10.

Determine the acceleration of the block. {*key: motion* is along the plane, so only the *x*-components of the force is relevant to the acceleration}

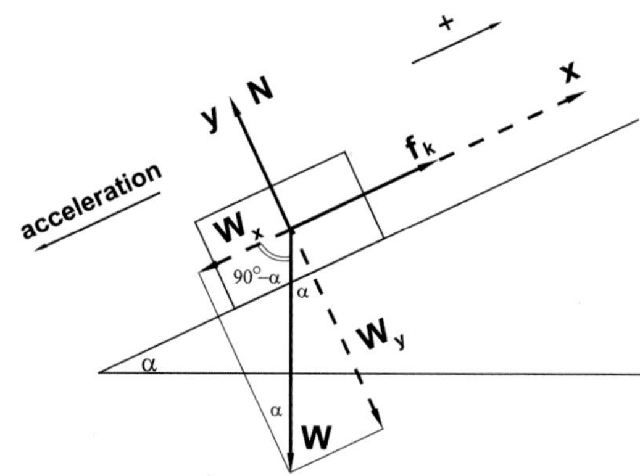

Figure III.B.3.3: Resolving the weight W into its x-component (W sinα) and its y-component (W cosα).

Begin with Newton's Second Law:

$$F = m \times a$$

thus

$$F_x = f_k - W\sin\alpha = \mu_k N - W\sin\alpha = m \times a$$

The force normal (*N*) can be determined by summing the forces in the y direction where the acceleration is zero:

$$F_y = N - W\cos\alpha = m \times a = 0$$

Therefore,

$$N = W\cos\alpha$$

Solving for a and combining our first and last equations we get (*recall:* $W = mg$):

$$a = (\mu_k W\cos\alpha - W\sin\alpha)/m$$
$$= mg(\mu_k\cos\alpha - \sin\alpha)/m = g(\mu_k\cos\alpha - \sin\alpha)$$

Substituting the values:

$$a = 9.8\ m/s^2(0.10\cos45° - \sin45°) = -6.2\ m/s^2$$

• Thus the block accelerates at 6.2 m/s^2 *down* the plane. Also note that the *mass* of the block is irrelevant.

3.3 Uniform Circular Motion

In Chapter 1 we saw that acceleration is due to a change in velocity (PHY 1.4). For a particle moving in a circle at constant speed (= *uniform circular motion*), the velocity vector changes continuously in direction but the magnitude remains the same.

The velocity is always tangent to the circle and since it is always changing (i.e. *direction*) it creates an acceleration directed radially inward called the *centripetal* acceleration (a_c). The magnitude of the acceleration a_c is given by v^2/r where r is the radius of the circle.

Every accelerated particle must have a force acting on it according to Newton's Second Law. Thus we can calculate the *centripetal* force,

$$F_c = ma_c = mv^2/r.$$

The centripetal force can be produced in many ways: a taut string which is holding a ball at the end that is spinning in a circle; a radially directed frictional force like when a car drives around a curve on an unbanked road; a contact force exerted by another body like driving around a curve on a banked road or like the wall of an amusement park rotor.

Any particle moving in a circle with *non-uniform* speed will experience both centripetal and tangential forces and accelerations. {Reminder: the circumference of a circle is $2\pi r$ and the area is πr^2}

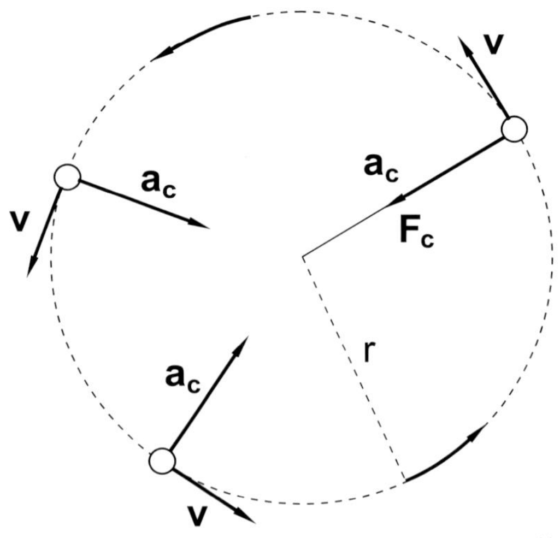

Figure III.B.3.4: Uniform Circular Motion.

In PHY 4.5, Rotational Motion, we will establish how to calculate the tangential acceleration (i.e. the acceleration in the direction of **v** in the diagram above), which, just as mentioned, only becomes an issue with non-uniform speed.

Consider two unequal masses connected by a string which passes over a frictionless, massless pulley (*see* Figure III.B.3.5). Let us determine the following parameters: i) the tension T in the string which is a force and ii) the acceleration of the masses given that m_2 is greater than m_1.

Always begin by drawing vector or *free-body* diagrams of a problem. The position of each mass will lie at the origin O of their respective axes. Now we assign positivity or negativity to the directions of motion. We can arbitrarily define the upward direction as positive. Thus if the acceleration of m_1 is a then the acceleration of m_2 must be $-a$.

Using Newton's Second Law we can derive the equation of motion for m_1:

$$F = T - m_1 g = m_1 a$$

and for m_2:

$$F = T - m_2 g = - m_2 a$$

Subtracting one equation from the other eliminates T then we can solve for a:

$$a = \frac{m_2 - m_1}{m_2 + m_1} g$$

Solve for a using the equations of motion, equate the formulas, then we can solve for T:

$$T = \frac{2 m_1 m_2}{m_1 + m_2} g$$

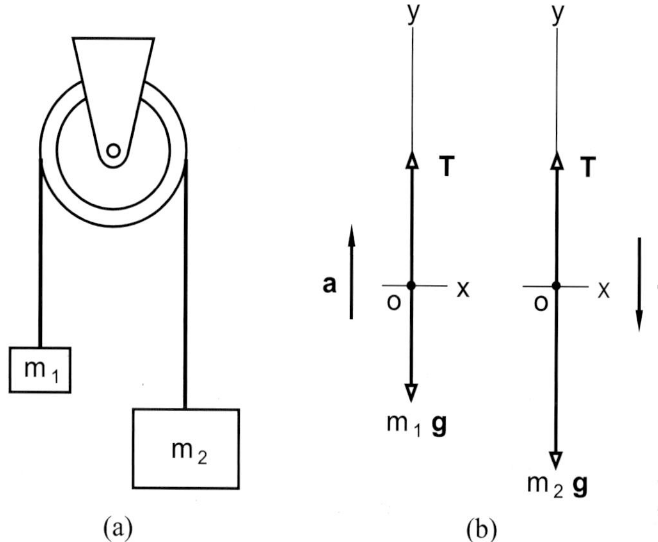

Figure III.B.3.5: A Pulley System.
(a) Two unequal masses suspended by a string from a pulley (= Atwood's machine). (b) Free-body diagrams for m_1 and m_2.

Let us solve the problem using Imperial units where m_2 is 3.0 slugs ($W_2 = m_2 g = 96$ pounds - lb) and m_1 is 1.0 slug ($W_1 = m_1 g = 32$ lb):

$$a = \frac{3.0 - 1.0}{3.0 + 1.0} g = g/2 = 16 \ ft/s^2$$

and

$$T = \frac{2\,(1.0)\,(3.0)}{1.0 + 3.0} (32) = 48 \text{ lb.}$$

• Note that T is always between the weight of mass m_1 and that of m_2. The reason is that T must exceed $m_1 g$ to give m_1 an upward acceleration, and $m_2 g$ must exceed T to give m_2 a downward acceleration.

EQUILIBRIUM
Chapter 4

Memorize	Understand	Importance
* Definitions and equations to solve torque problems * Newton's First Law, inertia * Equations for momentum, impulse * Equations for rotational motion	* Solve torque, collision problems * Choosing an appropriate pivot point * Create vector diagrams * Elastic vs. inelastic vs. conservation of E. * Solve momentum problem, significant figures * Rotational motion	**2 to 4 out of the 40 PHY** OAT questions are based on content in this chapter (in our estimation). *Note that between 55% and 85% of the questions in OAT Physics are based on content from 6 chapters: 1, 2, 3, 6, 7 and 11.

Introduction 

Equilibrium exists when a mass is at rest or moves with constant velocity. Translational (straight line) and rotational (turning) equilibria can be resolved using linear forces, torque forces, Newton's first law and inertia. Momentum is a vector that can be used to solve problems involving elastic (bouncy) or inelastic (sticky) collisions.

Additional Resources

Free Online Q&A + Forum

Video: Online or DVD

Flashcards

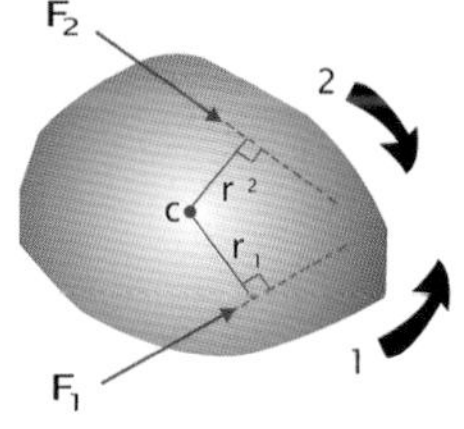

Special Guest

4.1 Translational, Rotational and Complex Motion

When a force acts upon an object, the object will undergo translational, rotational or complex (translational and rotational) motion.

Rotational motion of an object about an axis is the rotation of that object around that axis caused by perpendicular forces to that axis. The effective force causing rotation about an axis is the torque (L).

The torque is like a *turning force*. Consider a hinged door. If you were to apply a force F at the pivot point (*the hinge*), the door would not turn (L=0). If you apply the *same* force further and further from the pivot point, the turning force multiplies and the acceleration of the door increases. Thus the torque can be defined as the force applied multiplied by the perpendicular distance from the pivot point (= *lever or moment arm* = r).

$$L = \text{(force)} \times \text{(lever arm)}$$

Thus according to Figure III.B.4.1:

$$L_1 = F_1 \times r_1 = \text{counterclockwise torque (1)} = \text{positive}$$

and

$$L_2 = F_2 \times r_2 = \text{clockwise torque (2)} = \text{negative.}$$

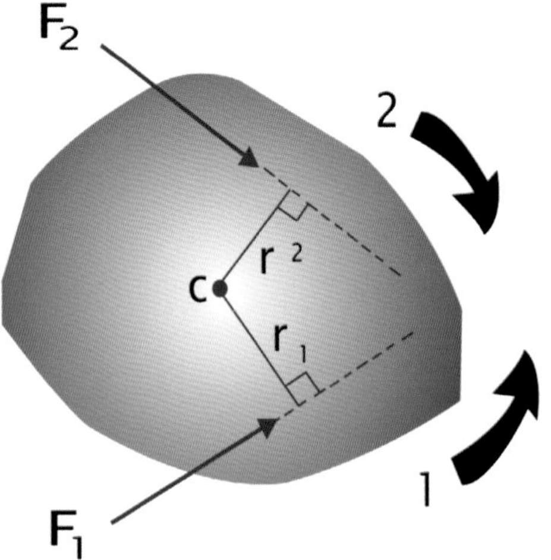

Figure III.B.4.1: Rotational Motion.

Positivity and negativity are arbitrary designations of the two opposite directions of motion. To determine the direction of rotation caused by the torque, imagine the direction the object would rotate if the force is pushing its moment arm at right angles. The net torques acting upon an object is obtained by summing the counterclockwise (+) and the clockwise (-) torques. An object is at equilibrium when the net forces and the net torques acting upon the object is zero. Thus, the object is either motionless or moving at a constant velocity due to its internal inertia.

<u>The conditions of equilibrium are</u>:

For translational equilibrium:

$$\Sigma F_x = 0 \text{ and } \Sigma F_y = 0$$

For rotational equilibrium:

$$\Sigma L = 0$$

If the torques sum to zero about one point in an object, they will sum to zero about any point in the object. If the point chosen as reference *(= pivot point or fulcrum)* includes the line of action of one of the forces, that force need not be included in calculating torques.

4.1.1 Torque Problem (SI units)

A 70 kg person sits 50 cm from the edge of a non-uniform plank which weighs 100 N and is 2.0 m long (*see Figure III.B.4.2*). The weight supported by point *B* is 250 N. Find the center of gravity (COG) of the plank.

{key: draw a vector diagram then choose an unknown value as the pivot point i.e. point A; see section 2.1 for a definition of COG}

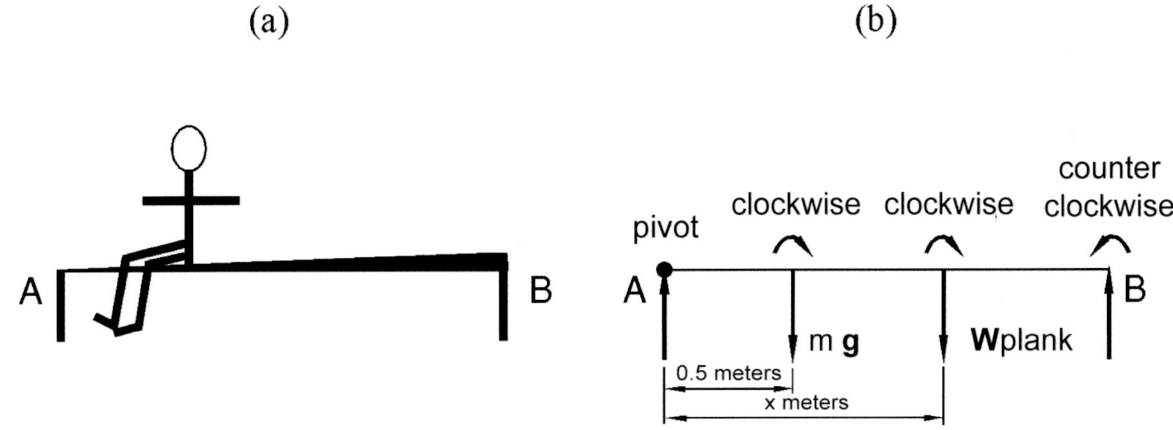

Figure III.B.4.2: Torque Problem.
(a) A person sitting on a non-uniform bench which is composed of a plank with two supports A and B. (b) Vector diagram with point A as the reference point. The torque force at point A is zero since its distance from itself is zero.

The counterclockwise torque (CCW) is given by the force at point *B* multiplied by its distance from the reference point *A*:

$$CCW = F_B r_B = 250(2.0) = 500 \text{ Nm}$$

The clockwise torques (CW) are given by the force exerted by the person (= the weight *mg*) multiplied by the distance from the pivot point (*r* = 50 cm = 0.5 m) *and* the force exerted by the plank (= the weight) multiplied by the distance from the pivot point where the weight of the plank acts (= COG):

$$CW = mgr + W(COG)$$
$$= 70(10)0.5 + 100(COG)$$
$$= 350 + 100(COG)$$

Gravity was estimated as 10 m/s^2. Now we have:

$$\Sigma L = CCW - CW = 500 - 350 - 100(COG) = 0$$

Isolate *COG*

$$COG = 150/100 = 1.5 \text{ m from point } A.$$

• Note that had the plank been uniform its COG would be at its center which is 1.0 m from either end.

• Had the problem requested the weight supported at point *A*, it would be easy to determine since $\Sigma F_y = 0$. If we define upward forces as positive, we get:

$$\Sigma F_y = F_A + F_B - mg - W_{plank} = 0$$

Isolate F_A

$$F_A = 70(10) + 100 - 250 = 550 \text{ N}.$$

4.2 Newton's First Law

Newton's First Law states that objects in motion or at rest tend to remain as such unless acted upon by an outside force. That is, objects have inertia (resistance to motion). For translational motion, the mass (*m*) is a measure of inertia.

For rotational motion, a quantity derived from the mass called the moment of inertia (*I*) is the measure of inertia. In general $I = \Sigma mr^2$ where r is the distance from the axis of rotation. However, the exact formulation depends on the structure of the object.

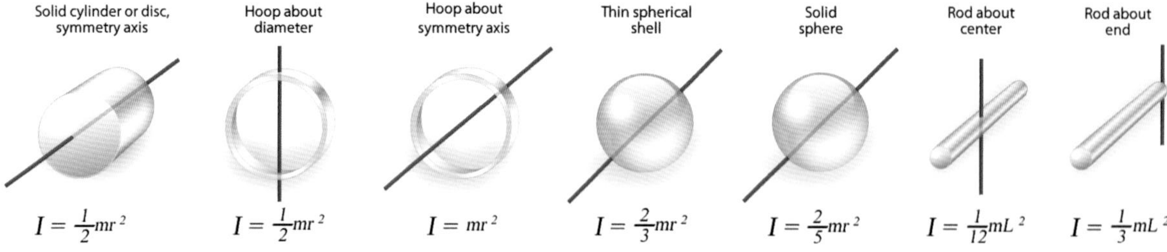

4.3 Momentum

The momentum (*M*) is a vector quantity. The momentum of an object is the product of its mass and its velocity.

$$M = m\,v$$

Linear momentum is a measure of the tendency of an object to maintain motion in a straight line. The greater the momentum (*M*), the greater the tendency of the object to remain moving along a straight line in the same direction. The momentum (M) is also a measure of the force needed to stop or change the direction of the object.

The impulse *I* is a measure of the change of the momentum of an object. It is the product of the force applied by the time during which the force was applied to change the momentum.

$$I = F\,\Delta t = \Delta M$$

where *F* is the acting force and Δt is the elapsed time during which the force was acting. *The* momentum is also conserved just like energy. The total linear momentum of a system is constant when the resultant external force acting on the system is zero.

4.4 Collisions

During motion, objects can collide. There are two kinds of collisions: *elastic* and *inelastic*. During an elastic collision (objects rebound off each other), there is a conservation of momentum and conservation of kinetic energy. Whereas, during an inelastic collision (objects stick together), there is conservation of momentum but not conservation of kinetic energy. Kinetic energy is lost as heat or sound, so total energy is conserved.

Examples of elastic collisions include 2 rubber balls colliding, particle collisions in ideal gases, and the slingshot type gravitational interactions between satellites and planets popularized in science fiction movies. Examples of inelastic collisions include 2 cars colliding at high speed becoming stuck together and a ballistic pendulum which can be a huge chunk of wood used to measure the speed of a moving object (i.e. bullet) which becomes completely embedded in the wood. If, however, the bullet were to emerge from the wood block, then it would be an elastic collision since the objects did not stick together.

Imagine two spheres with masses m_1 and m_2 and the velocity components before the collision v_{1i} and v_{2i} and after the collision v_{1f} and v_{2f}. If the momentum and the velocity are in the same directions, and we define that direction as positive, from the conservation of momentum we obtain:

$$m_1v_{1i} + m_2v_{2i} = m_1v_{1f} + m_2v_{2f}\,.$$

If the directions are not the same then each momentum must be resolved into x- and y-components as necessary.

• In the explosion of an object at rest, the total momentum of all the fragments must sum to zero because of the conservation of momentum and because the original momentum was zero.

• If one object collides with a second identical object that is at rest, there is a total transfer of kinetic energy, that is the first object comes to rest and the second object moves off with the momentum of the first one.

4.4.1 Collision Problem (CGS units)

A bullet of mass 10 g and a speed of 5.0 × 10^4 cm/s strikes a 700 g wooden block at rest on a very smooth surface. The bullet emerges with its speed reduced to 3.5 × 10^4 cm/s.

Find the resulting speed of the block. {*CGS uses centimeters, grams, and seconds as units; the CGS unit of force is a dyne*}

Let m_1 = the mass of the bullet (10 g), v_{1i} = the speed of the bullet before the collision (5.0 × 10^4 cm/s), m_2 = the mass of the wooden block (700 g), v_{2i} = the speed of the block before the collision (0 cm/s), v_{1f} = the speed of the bullet after the collision (3.5 × 10^4 cm/s), and v_{2f} = the speed of the block after the collision (*unknown*), now we have:

$$m_1v_{1i} + m_2v_{2i} = m_1v_{1f} + m_2v_{2f}$$

Solving for v_{2f}

$$v_{2f} = (m_1v_{1i} - m_1v_{1f})/m^2$$
$$= (5.0 \times 10^5 - 3.5 \times 10^5)/(700)$$
$$= 2.1 \times 10^2 \text{ cm/s.}$$

• Note: the least precise figures that we are given in the problem contain at least two digits or significant figures. Thus our answer can not be more precise than two significant figures. The exponent 10^x is not considered when counting significant figures unless you are *told* that the measurement was more precise than is evident {For more on significant figures *see* PHY 8.5.1 and CHM 12.4}.

• Note: you should be comfortable solving physics problems in Imperial, SI or CGS units.

The OAT usually has about 2 questions covering rotational motion which includes angular kinematics. We have already discussed 2 important aspects of "turning" or rotational motion - torque forces and the moment of inertia - and now we will look at angular velocity, acceleration and momentum of rigid bodies (i.e masses that hold a rigid shape). Many of the equations for the mechanics of rotating objects are very similar to the linear motion equations we have seen. The equivalent terms are listed in the table below.

Linear motion	Rotational motion
Force	Torque
Mass	Moment of inertia
Distance traveled (displacement)	Angle rotated (angular displacement)
Velocity	Angular velocity
Acceleration	Angular acceleration
Momentum	Angular momentum

The angular displacement is the angle through which a point or line has been rotated about an axis. The SI units are radians (see PHY 1.1.2 or GS QR). For example, if the wheel on your bicycle makes one full turn then the angular displacement θ is 2π radians (= 360°).

The average angular velocity (ω, Greek letter omega), measured in radians per second (sometimes: degrees/s), is the change of angle with respect to time. The average angular acceleration (α, Greek letter alpha) also has a form similar to the linear quantity and is measured in radians/second/second or rad/s² (sometimes degrees/s²).

$$\omega = \Delta\theta/\Delta t \quad \text{and} \quad \alpha = \Delta\omega/\Delta t$$

The following are the angular kinematics equations (i.e. for rotational motion) at constant angular acceleration. Notice the similarity with the kinematics equations of linear motion (PHY 1.5, 1.6, 2.6).

$$\omega = \omega_0 + \alpha t$$
$$\theta = \theta_0 + \omega_0 t + \tfrac{1}{2}\alpha t^2$$
$$\omega^2 = \omega_0^{\ 2} + 2\alpha(\theta - \theta_0)$$

Is there a direct connection between linear quantities and rotational quantities? Yes, and it is very simple. Let's return to your bicycle's wheel! Consider that your bicycle wheel is rolling without slipping in a straight line. The forward displacement of the wheel would be equal to the linear displacement of a point fixed on the tire. Yes, this gives another equation, but you will find that all the "connections" between translational and rotational quantities only require that you multiply by the radius r (technically, r represents the distance from the center of rotation, like your wheel's axle which is the axis about which the wheel turns, to the point on the object or wheel in question). So the forward displacement $d = r\theta$.

The average forward speed of the wheel is $v = d/t = (r\theta)/t = r\omega$. The direction of the velocity is tangent to the path of the point of rotation (see PHY 3.3).

The average forward or transverse ($_T$) acceleration of the wheel is $a_T = r(\Delta\omega)/t = r\alpha$. This component of the acceleration is tangential to the point of rotation and represents the changing speed of the object. The direction is the same as the velocity vector.

The radial component of the linear acceleration (PHY 3.3) is $a_r = v^2/r = \omega^2 r$.

Angular momentum is rotational momentum and it is conserved in the same way that linear momentum is conserved (PHY 4.3). For a rigid body, the angular momentum (L) is the product of the moment of inertia (PHY 4.2) and the angular velocity: $L = I\omega$. For a point of mass, angular momentum can be expressed as the product of linear momentum and the radius (r): $L = mvr$. The SI units for L is kilograms-meters^2 per second, or more commonly, joule-seconds.

The law of conservation of angular momentum states that the angular momentum of a system of objects is conserved if there is no external net torque (τ, Greek letter tau) acting on the system. So instead of "mv is constant" (PHY 4.3), we are left with the moment of inertia times angular velocity ($I\omega$) is constant. Remember that the moment of inertia is directly proportional to the radius (PHY 4.2). So when a figure skater is turning in a circle, when she pulls her arms towards her body, she reduces her radius thus her angular velocity increases (she spins faster) since $I\omega$ is constant.

The following table compares the equations for linear and rotational motion.

	Linear motion	***Rotational motion***
Newton's 2nd law (PHY 2.2)	$F = ma$	$\tau = I\alpha$
Momentum (PHY 4.3)	$M = mv$	$L = I\omega$
Work (PHY 5.2)	$W = F\Delta x$	$W = \tau\Delta\theta$
Kinetic energy (PHY 5.3)	$E_k = \frac{1}{2}mv^2$	$E_k = \frac{1}{2}I\omega^2$
Power (PHY 5.7)	$P = Fv$	$P = \tau\omega$

WORK AND ENERGY
Chapter 5

Memorize

efine, equation, units: work
 quations and units: potential energy
 quations and units: kinetic energy, power

Understand

* Path independence of work done in a g field
* Work-Energy Theorem
* Conservation of E.; conservative forces
* Solving Conservation of E. problems

Importance

2 to 4 out of the 40 PHY

OAT questions are based on content in this chapter (in our estimation).

*Note that between 55% and 85% of the questions in OAT Physics are based on content from 6 chapters: 1, 2, 3, 6, 7 and 11.

Introduction

Work and energy are used to describe how bodies or masses interact with the environment or other bodies or masses. Conservation of energy, work and power describe the forms of energy and the changes between these forms.

Additional Resources

Free Online Q&A + Forum

Video: Online or DVD

Flashcards

Special Guest

5.1 Work

The work of a force F on an object is the product of the force by the distance travelled by the object where the force is in the direction of the displacement.

• *Units*: both work and energy are measured in joules where 1 *joule (J)* = 1 *N* × 1 *m*. {Imperial units: the *foot-pound*, CGS units: the *dyne-centimeter* or *erg*}

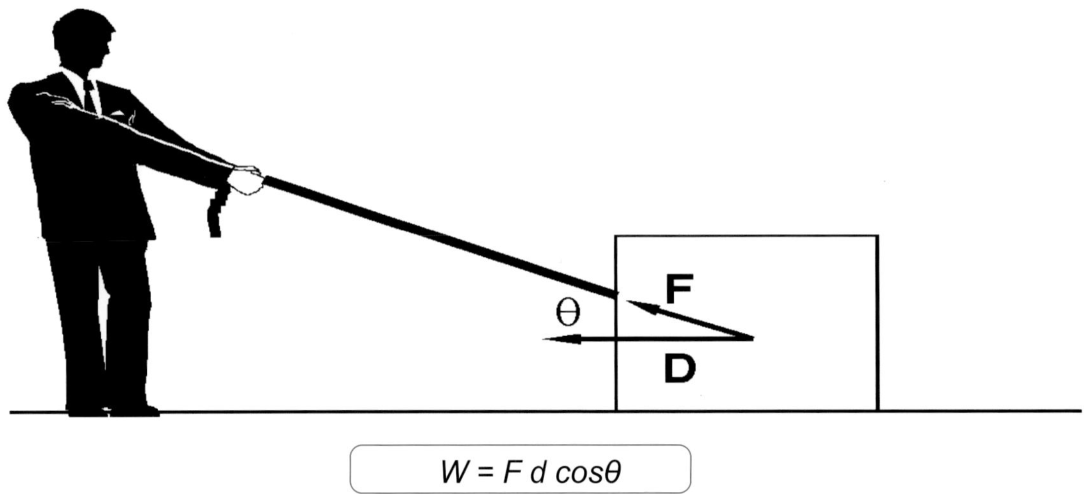

$$W = F\, d\, \cos\theta$$

Figure III.B.5.1: Work. The displacement depends on the final and initial positions of the object. The angle θ is necessary to determine the component of a constant force F in the same direction of the displacement. Note that if F acts perpendicular to the displacement then the work $W = F\, d\, \cos(90^\circ) = 0$.

5.2 Energy

We usually speak of mechanical, electrical, chemical, potential, kinetic, atomic and nuclear energy, to name a few. In fact, these different kinds of energy are different forms or manifestations of the same energy. Energy is a scalar. It is defined as a physical quantity capable of producing work.

5.3 Kinetic Energy

1) *Definition of kinetic energy*

Kinetic energy (E_k) is the energy of motion which can produce work. It is proportional to the mass of the object and its velocity:

$$E_k = 1/2\ mv^2.$$

2) *The Work-Energy Theorem*

A net force is the sum of interior and exterior forces acting upon the system. The variation of the kinetic energy of a system is equal to the work of the net force applied to the system:

$$W \text{ (of the resultant force)} = \Delta E_k\ .$$

Consequently, if the speed of a particle is constant, $\Delta E_k = 0$, then the work done by the resultant force must be zero. For example, in uniform circular motion the speed of the particle remains constant thus the centripetal force does no work on the particle. A force at right angles to the direction of motion merely changes the direction of the velocity but not its magnitude.

5.4 Potential Energy

Potential energy (E_p) is referred to as potential because it is accumulated by the system that contained it. It varies with the configuration of the system, i.e., when distances between particles of the system vary, the interactions between these particles vary. The variation of the potential energy is equal to the work performed by the interior forces caused by the interaction between the particles of the system. The following are examples of potential energy:

a) potential energy (= electric potential = E_p) derived from the Coulomb force (r is the distance between point charges q_1 and q_2, PHY 9.1.4):

$$E_p = k\ q_1 q_2/r$$

b) potential energy derived from the universal attraction force (r is the distance between the COG of masses m_1 and m_2):

$$E_p = G\ m_1 m_2/r$$

c) potential energy derived from the gravitational force (h is the height):

$$E_p = mgh$$

d) potential energy derived from the elastic force (i.e. a compressed spring):

$$E_p = kx^2/2\ .$$

{k = the spring constant, x = displacement, cf. PHY 7.2.1}

5.5 Conservation of Energy

a) *Definition*

The mechanical energy (E_T) of a system is equal to the sum of its kinetic energy and its potential energy:

$$E_T = E_k + E_p.$$

b) *Theorem of mechanical energy*

The variation of the mechanical energy of a system is equal to the work of exterior forces acting on the system.

c) *Consequence*

An isolated system, i.e., which is not being acted upon by any exterior force, keeps a constant mechanical energy. The kinetic energy and the potential energy may vary separately but their sum remains constant. This makes conservation of energy a very simple way to solve many different types of physics problems.

5.5.1 Conservation of Energy Problem (SI units)

A 6.8×10^3 kg frictionless roller coaster car starts at rest 30 meters above ground level. Determine the speed of the car at (a) 20 m above ground level; (b) at ground level.

$$E_T = E_k + E_p = 1/2mv^2 + mgh$$

Initially v = 0 since the car starts at rest, h = 30 m, and the constant g ≈ 10 m/s², thus

$$E_T = 0 + m(10)(30) = 300m \text{ joules.}$$

Situation (a) where h = 20 m:

$$E_T = 300m = 1/2mv^2 + mgh$$

m cancels, multiply through by 2, solve for *v*:

$$v = \sqrt{2(300) - 2(10)20} = \sqrt{2(100)}$$

$$= \sqrt{2}(10) = 14 \text{ m/s}$$

Situation (b) at ground level $h = 0$:

$$E_T = 300m = 1/2mv^2 + 0$$

m cancels, multiply through by 2, solve for *v*:

$$v = \sqrt{600} = \sqrt{6(100)} = 10\sqrt{6} = 24 \text{ m/s}$$

- Note: the mass of the roller coaster is irrelevant!

- Note: you must be able to quickly estimate square roots (PHY 1.1.2, 2.6.1).

5.6 Conservative Forces

The three definitions of a conservative force are: i) after a round trip the kinetic energy of a particle on which a force acts must return to its initial value; ii) after a round trip the work done on a particle by a force must be zero; iii) the work done by the force on a particle depends on the initial and final positions of the particle and not on the path taken.

Examples: Friction disobeys all three of the preceding criteria thus it is a non-conservative force. The force $F_s = -kx$ (Hooke's Law, PHY 7.2.1) of an ideal spring on a frictionless surface is a conservative force. Gravity is a conservative force. If you throw a ball vertically upward, it will return with the same kinetic energy it had when it left your hand (*neglect air resistance*).

5.7 Power

The power P applied during the work W performed by a force F is equal to the work divided by the time necessary to do the work. In other words, power is the rate of doing work:

$$P = \Delta W/\Delta t.$$

- The SI unit for power is the *watt* (W) which equals one *joule per second* (J/s).

- Power can also be expressed as the product of a force on an object and the object's velocity: $P = Fv$.

Go online to OATbooks.com for free chapter review Q&A and forum.

GOLD NOTES

FLUID STATICS AND THERMODYNAMICS
Chapter 6

Memorize

* Equation: density
* Density of water
* Equations for pressure, pressure change

Understand

* Buoyancy force, SG and height immersed
* Basics of thermodynamics
* Archimedes' principle, surface tension
* Vapor press, atm. press.
* Boiling point changes with altitude

Importance

3 to 5 out of the 40 PHY

OAT questions are based on content in this chapter (in our estimation).

*Note that between 55% and 85% of the questions in OAT Physics are based on content from 6 chapters: 1, 2, 3, 6, 7 and 11.

Introduction 

A fluid is a substance that flows (*deforms*) under shear stress. This includes all gases and liquids. It is important to focus on the properties of fluids without movement (= *statics* like hydrostatic pressure, Archimedes' principle, etc.) since fluid dynamics (= continuity, Bernouilli's equation, etc.) is not on the official topic list for the OAT test. The section in this chapter on Surface Tension overlaps CHM 3.5 but here we introduce some new equations. We will not however, repeat GS DAT General Chemistry Thermodynamics content but we will present non-overlapping content in PHY 6.2 and we will make sure that you have access to that information in case you do not own that book.

Additional Resources

Free Online Q&A + Forum

Video: Online or DVD

Flashcards

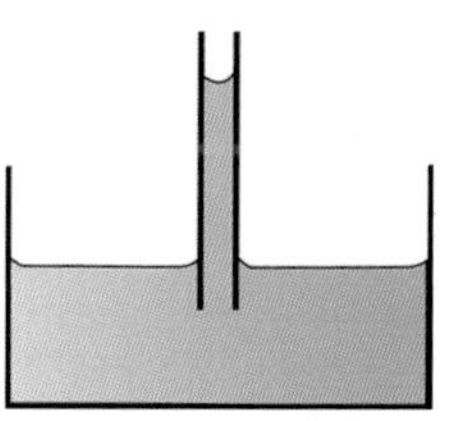

Special Guest

6.1 Fluids

6.1.1 Density, Specific Gravity

The *density* of an object is defined as the ratio of its mass to its volume.

$$density = mass / volume$$

This definition holds for solids, fluids and gases. From the definition, it is easy to see that solids are more dense than liquids which are in turn more dense than gases. This is true because for a given mass, the average distance between molecules of a given substance is bigger in the liquid state than in the solid state. Put simply, the substance occupies a bigger volume in the liquid state than in the solid state and a much bigger volume in gaseous state than in the liquid state.

At a given temperature, the *specific gravity* (SG) is defined as :

$$SG = \frac{\text{density of a substance}}{\text{density of water}}$$

The density of water is about 1 g/ml (= 1 g/cm^3 = 10^3 kg/m^3) over most common temperatures. So in most instances the specific gravity of a substance is the same as its density.

Note that the dimension of density is mass per unit volume, whereas the specific gravity is dimensionless. Density is one of the key properties of fluids (liquids or gases) and the other is pressure.

6.1.2 Hydrostatic Pressure, Buoyancy, Archimedes' Principle

Pressure (P) is defined as the force (F) per unit area (A):

$$P = F/A.$$

The force F is the normal (*perpendicular*) force to the area. The SI unit for pressure is the *pascal* (1 Pa = 1 N/m^2). Other units are: 1.00 atm = 1.01×10^5 Pa = 1.01 bar = 760 mmHg = 760 torr = 14.7 lb/in^2.

Pressure is also formulated as potential energy per unit volume as follows:

$$P = \frac{F}{A} = \frac{mg}{A} = \frac{(mg/A)}{(h/h)} = \frac{mgh}{v} = \rho gh$$

ρ = density and h = depth below surface; if the depth is changing we can write:

$$\Delta P = \rho g \Delta h.$$

We will now examine 6 key rules of incompressible fluids (liquids) that are not moving (*statics*).

1) In a fluid confined by solid boundaries, pressure acts perpendicular to the boundary – it is a normal force, sometimes called a *surface force*.

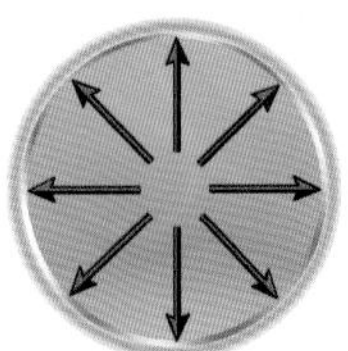

pipe or tube

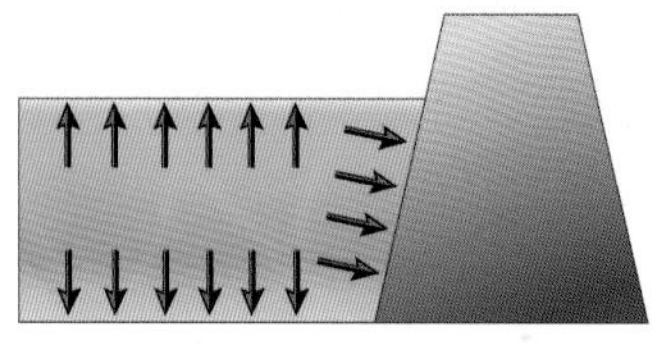

dam

2) At any particular depth, the pressure of the fluid is the same in all directions.

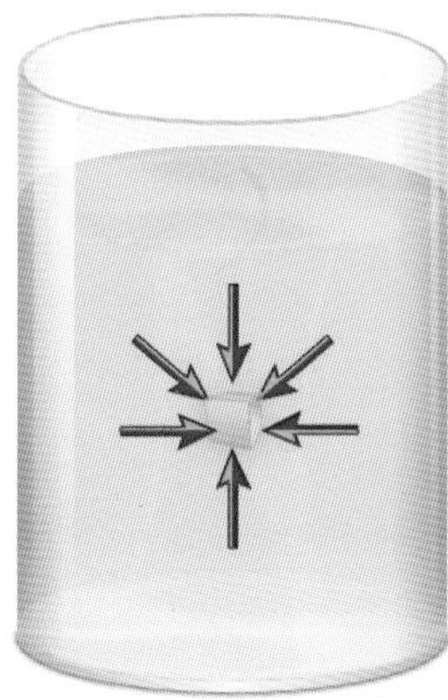

3) The fluid or *hydrostatic pressure* depends on the density and the depth of the fluid. So it is easy to calculate the change in pressure in an open container, swimming pool, the ocean, etc.:

P_1 = atmospheric pressure
h_1 = surface = a depth of 0
$P_2 - P_1 = \Delta P$
$h_2 - h_1 = \Delta h$

$\Delta P = \rho g \Delta h$

Vertical plane surfaces

We can now combine rules 1, 2 and 3 about fluids to examine a special case which is that of a vertical plane surface like a vertical wall that is underwater.

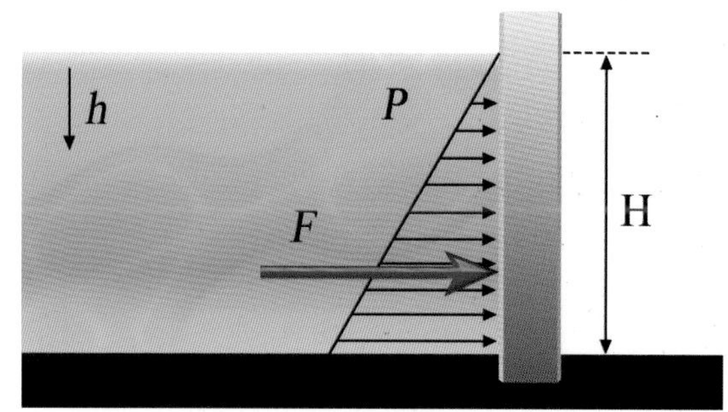

Of course pressure varies linearly with depth because $\Delta P = \rho g \Delta h$.

If the height of the vertical rectangular wall is H and the width W, with the help of calculus (which is *not* on the OAT!), the equation for the force on the wall, or vertical plane, at any depth can be determined to be:

$$F = 1/2\ \rho g W H^2$$

4) The size or shape of a container does not influence the pressure (= *hydrostatic paradox*). Note that the pressure is the same at the bottom of all 3 containers because the height h and fluid density are the same.

5) Pascal's Principle: If an external pressure is applied to a confined fluid, the pressure at every point within the fluid increases by that amount. This is the basis for hydraulic systems. Key points: (1) the pressure of the system is constant throughout and (2) by definition, P = F/A, so we get:

$$F_1/A_1 = F_2/A_2$$

Hydraulic systems, like the brakes in a car, can multiply the force applied. For example, if a 50 N force is applied by the left piston in the diagram and if the right piston has an area five times greater, then the force out at F_2 is 250 N (thus the force vector F_2 is 5 times longer).

$$F_2 = A_2(F_1/A_1) = 5A_1(F_1/A_1) = 5(F_1)$$

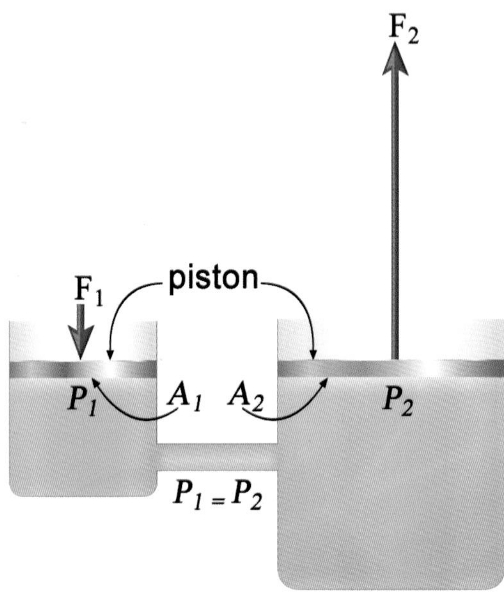

6) An object which is completely or partially submerged in a fluid experiences an upward force equal to the weight of the fluid displaced (*Archimedes' principle*).

This buoyant force F_b is :

$$F_b = V\rho g = mg$$

where ρ is the density of the fluid displaced. An object that floats must displace at most its own weight.

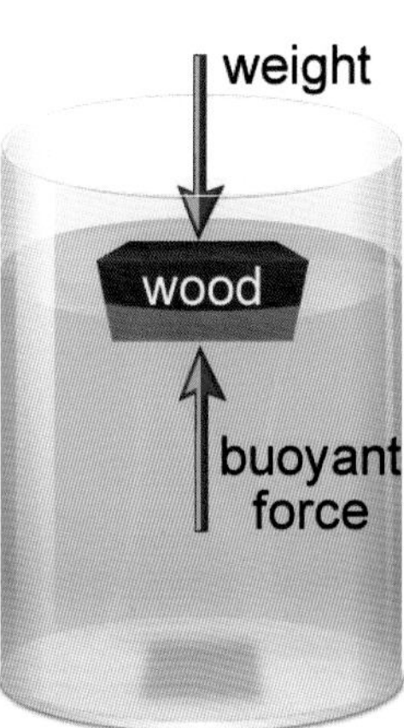

Archimedes' principle can be used to calculate specific gravity. And in turn, specific gravity is equivalent to the fraction of the height of a buoyant object below the surface of the fluid. Thus if SG = 0.90, then 90% of the height of the object would be immersed in water. Therefore, less dense objects float.

6.1.3 Atmospheric Pressure

Atmospheric pressure is the force per unit area exerted against a surface by the weight of the air above that surface. If the number of air molecules above a surface increases, there are more molecules to exert a force on that surface and thus, the pressure increases. On the other hand, a reduction in the number of air molecules above a surface will result in a decrease in pressure. Atmospheric pressure is measured with a "barometer", which is why atmospheric pressure is also referred to as *barometric* pressure.

Atmospheric pressure is often measured with a mercury (Hg) barometer, and a height of approximately 760 millimeters (30 in) of mercury represents atmospheric pressure at sea level (760 mmHg).

Unit	Definition or Relationship
SI Unit: 1 pascal (Pa)	$1\ kg\ m^{-1}\ s^{-2} = 1\ N/m^2$
1 bar	1×10^5 Pa
1 atmosphere (atm)	101,325 Pa = 101.3 kPa
1 torr	1 / 760 atm
760 mmHg	1 atm
14.7 pounds per sq. in. (psi)	1 atm

Units of Pressure

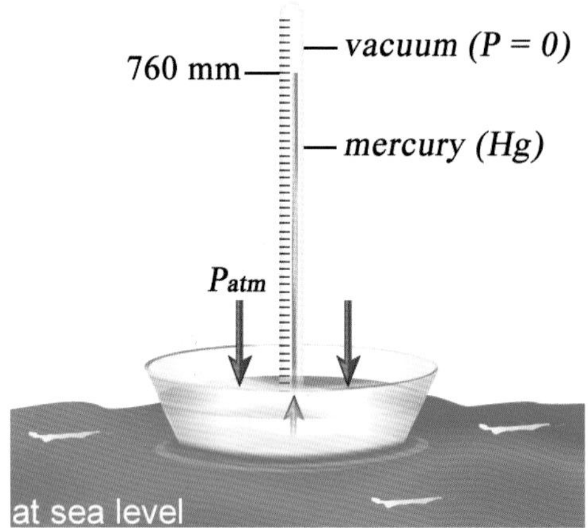

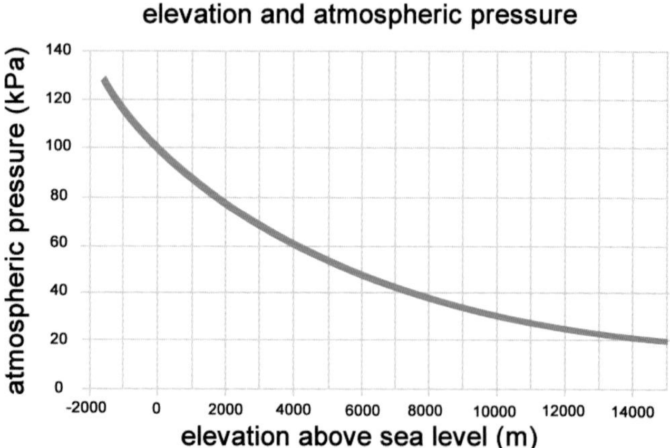

When the altitude or elevation increases, we get closer to "outer space" so there is less overlying atmospheric mass from gases, so that pressure decreases with increasing elevation.

Figure III.B.6.0: Atmospheric pressure decreases with elevation. Mount Everest is about 8,800 meters (m) and a 747 can cruise at an altitude of 10,000 m but requires increased cabin pressure to prevent passengers from having altitude sickness and low oxygen (hypoxia).

6.1.4 Gauge Pressure

When you measure the pressure in your tires, you are measuring the pressure difference between the tires and atmospheric pressure, which is the *gauge* (or *gage*) pressure.

Absolute pressure is the pressure of a fluid relative to the pressure in a vacuum. The absolute pressure is then the sum of the gauge pressure, which is what you measure, and the atmospheric pressure.

$$P_{abs} = P_{atm} + P_{gauge}$$

Pressure can be measured in devices in which one or more columns of a liquid (i.e. mercury or water) are used to determine the pressure difference between two points (i.e. U-tube manometer, inclined-tube manometer). Of course, electronic instruments for measurement are used more frequently.

6.1.5 Surface Tension

Molecules of a liquid exert attractive forces toward each other (cohesive forces), and exert attractive forces toward the surface they touch (adhesive forces). If a liquid is in a gravity free space without a surface, it will form a sphere (smallest area relative to volume).

If the liquid is lining an object, the liquid surface will contract (due to cohesive forces) to the lowest possible surface area. The forces between the molecules on this surface will create a membrane-like effect. Due to the contraction, a potential energy (PE) will present in the surface.

This PE is directly proportional to the surface area (A). An exact relation is formed as follows:

$$PE = \gamma A$$

γ = surface tension = PE/A = joules/m^2

An alternative formulation for the surface tension (γ) is:

$$\gamma = F/l$$

F = force of contraction of surface
l = length along surface

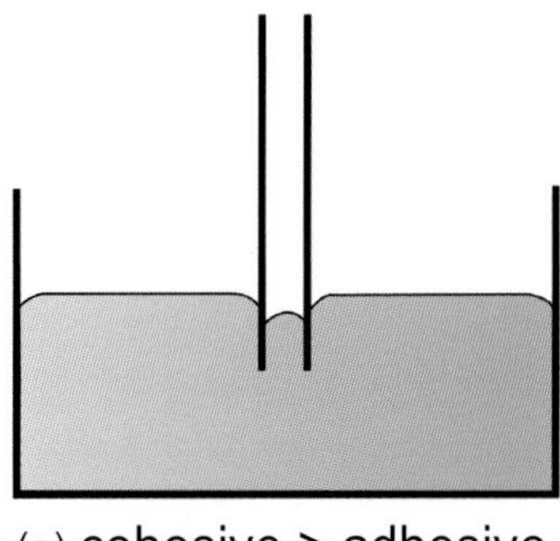

(a) cohesive > adhesive

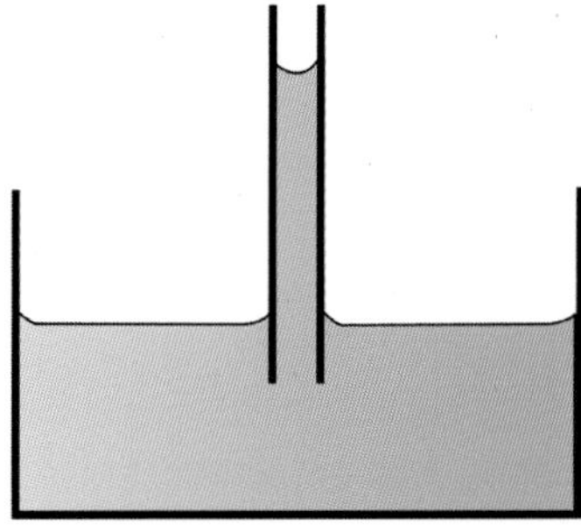

(b) adhesive > cohesive

Figure III.B.6.1: Effects of adhesive and cohesive forces.
The distance the liquid rises or falls in the tube is directly proportional to the surface tension γ and inversely proportional to the liquid density and radius of the tube. Examples of 2 liquids consistent with the illustrations include: (a) mercury; (b) water.

Because of the contraction, a small object which would ordinarily sink in the liquid may float on the surface membrane. For example, a small insect like a "water strider."

The liquid will rise or fall on a wall or in a capillary tube if the adhesive forces are greater than cohesive or vice versa (see Figure III.B.6.1).

6.2 Thermodynamics and Thermal Energy

The International System of Units (SI) defines seven units of measure as the basic set from which all other SI units are derived. These SI base units and their physical quantities are: (1) the meter for length; (2) the kilogram for mass (*not the gram*); (3) the second for time; (4) the ampere for electric current; (5) the kelvin for temperature (*not Celsius*); (6) the candela for luminous intensity (brightness); and (7) the mole for the amount of substance.

Because SI units are the units of choice for the OAT, it is important that you remember the conversion between kelvin and Celsius:

$$[K] = [°C] + 273$$

The Kelvin scale is an absolute, thermodynamic temperature scale. When K = 0, defined as absolute zero, all thermal motion stops. *Absolute zero* is the theoretical lowest possible temperature. It has never been achieved. {Incidentally: "kelvin units", "Kelvin scale", K with no little degrees symbol, might all look like typos but those are the rules for the Kelvin scale; fortunately, you won't be tested on semantics!}

Water boils at about 100 °C (212 °F; 373 K) at standard atmospheric pressure. The boiling point is defined as the temperature at which the vapor pressure is equal to the atmospheric pressure. Because of this, the boiling point of water is lower at lower pressure and higher at higher pressure. This is why cooking at elevations of more than 1,100 m (3,600 ft) above sea level is challenging because the water will boil at temperatures that are sometimes too low to properly cook the food.

This is not the end of your review of this topic!

There are areas where Physics and General Chemistry overlap and that includes Thermodynamics. We will not repeat content here. If you do not own our GS DAT Chemistry book then you can go to your OATbooks.com account and review the content there for free. If you own the GS DAT Chemistry book, then these are the sections that we suggest that you review as part of your OAT Physics preparation:

- 4.1.7 Combined Gas Law (Key: PV/T is constant)
- 4.3.2 Freezing Point, Melting Point, Boiling Point
- 7.2 1st Law of Thermodynamics
- 7.3 Thermal Units
- 7.4 Temperature Scales
- 7.5 Heat Transfer
- 7.6 State Functions
- 8.7 Calorimetry
- 8.8 2nd Law of Thermodynamics
- 8.9 Entropy

Our chapter review questions, our practice tests and the official OAT will include questions based on the assumption that you have an understanding of the basics of this material.

6.3 The Effect of Temperature on Liquids and Solids: Advanced OAT Topic

When substances gain or lose heat they usually undergo expansion or contraction. Expansion or contraction can be by linear dimension, by area or by volume.

Table III.B.6.1: Substance thermal expansion.

Type	Final	Original	Change caused by heat
(1) *Linear*	L $L = L_0 + \alpha\Delta T L_0$ $L = L_0(1 + \alpha\Delta T)$ α = *coefficient of linear thermal expansion* ΔT = *change in temperature*	L_0	$\alpha\Delta T L_0$
(2) *Area*	A $A = A_0 + \gamma\Delta T A_0$ $A = A_0(1 + \gamma\Delta T)$ γ = *coefficient of area thermal expansion* = 2α	A_0	$\gamma\Delta T A_0$
(3) *Volume*	V $V = V_0 + \beta\Delta T V_0$ $V = V_0(1 + \beta\Delta T)$ β = *coefficient of volume thermal expansion* = 3α	V_0	$\beta\Delta T V_0$

WAVE CHARACTERISTICS AND PERIODIC MOTION
Chapter 7

Memorize

ine: wavelength, frequency, velocity, plitude
ine: intensity, constructive/destructive erference, beat freq.
uation: relating velocity to frequency, elength
uation: Hooke's Law, work (periodic motion)

Understand

* SHM, transverse vs. longitudinal waves, phase
* Resonance, nodes, antinodes, pipes (standing waves)
* Harmonics, overtones
* Periodic motion: force, accel., vel., diplace., period
* The simple pendulum, theory and calculations

Importance

3 to 5 out of the 40 PHY

OAT questions are based on content in this chapter (in our estimation).

*Note that between 55% and 85% of the questions in OAT Physics are based on content from 6 chapters: 1, 2, 3, 6, 7 and 11.

Introduction

Wave characteristics and periodic motion describe the motion of systems that vibrate. Topics include transverse and longitudinal waves, interference, resonance, Hooke's law and simple harmonic motion (SHM). Some basic equations must be memorized but for most of the material, you must seek a comfortable understanding.

Additional Resources

Free Online Q&A + Forum

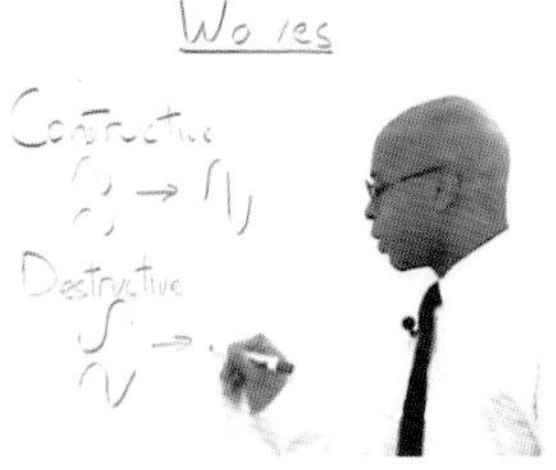

Video: Online or DVD

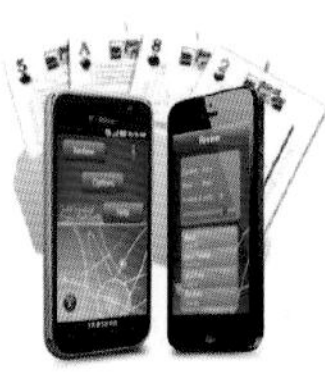

Flashcards

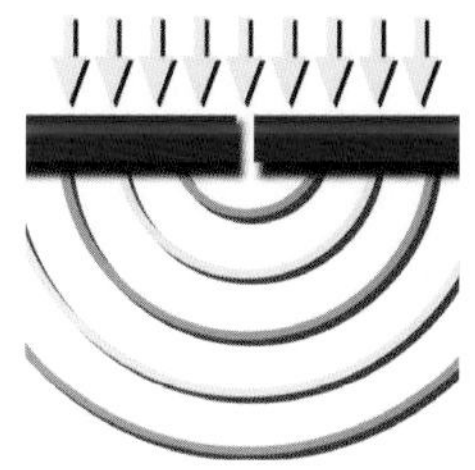

Special Guest

7.1 Wave Characteristics

7.1.1 Transverse and Longitudinal Motion

A wave is a disturbance in a medium such that each particle in the medium vibrates about an equilibrium point in a simple harmonic (*periodic*) motion. If the direction of vibration is perpendicular to the direction of propagation of the wave, it is called a transverse wave (e.g. light or an oscillating string under tension).

If the direction of vibration is in the same direction as the propagation of the wave, it is called a longitudinal wave (e.g. sound). Longitudinal waves are characterized by condensations (regions of crowding of particles) and rarefactions (regions where particles are far apart) along the wave in the medium.

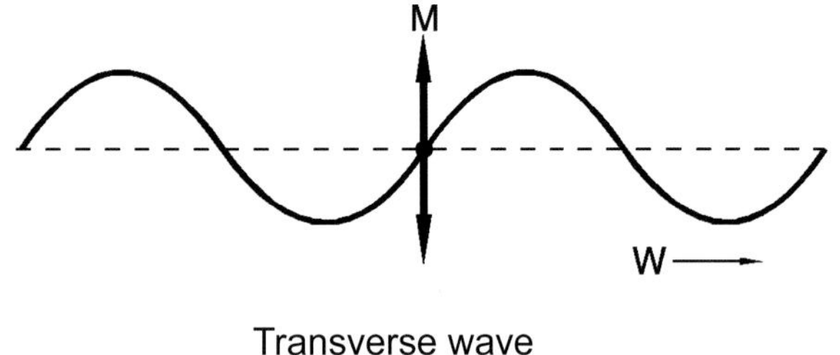

Transverse wave

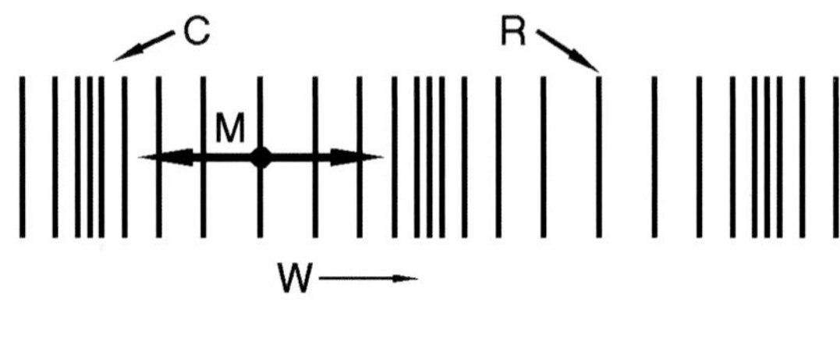

Longitudinal wave

Figure III.B.7.1: Transverse and longitudinal waves.
W = wave propagation, R = rarefaction, C = condensation, M = motion of particle.

7.1.2 Wavelength, Frequency, Velocity, Amplitude, Intensity

The wavelength (λ) is the distance from crest to crest (or valley to valley) of a transverse wave. It may also be defined as the distance between two particles with the same displacement and direction of displacement. In a longitudinal wave, the wavelength is the distance from one rarefaction (or condensation) to another. The *amplitude* (A) is the maximum displacement of a particle in one direction from its equilibrium point. The *intensity (I)* of a wave is the square of the amplitude.

Frequency (f) is the number of cycles per unit time (per second). *Period (T)* is the duration of one cycle, it is the inverse of the frequency. The *velocity (v)* of a wave is the velocity of the propagation of the disturbance that forms the wave through the medium.

The velocity is inversely proportional to the inertia of the medium. The velocity can be calculated according to the following important equation:

$$v = \lambda f$$

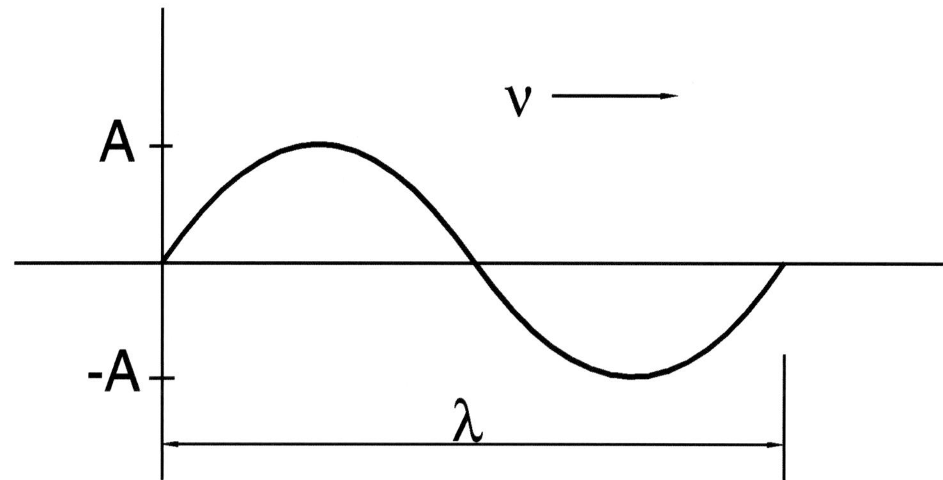

Figure III.B.7.2: Characteristics of waves.

7.1.3 Superposition of Waves, Phase, Interference, Addition

The superposition principle states that the effect of two or more waves on the displacement of a particle is independent. The final displacement of the particle is the resultant effect of all the waves added algebraically, thus the amplitude may increase or decrease. The *phase* of a particle under vibration is its displacement at the time of origin (t=0). The displacement can be calculated as follows:

$$x = A\sin(\omega t + \varphi)$$

where x is the displacement, A is the amplitude, ω is the angular velocity, t is the time, and φ is the phase.

Interference is the summation of the displacements of different waves in a medium. Certain criteria must first be established:

- *synchrony sources*: vibrations emitted by synchrony sources have the same phase.
- *coherent vibrations*: the phases of the vibrations are related, this means that the duration of the light impressions on the retina is much longer than the duration of a wave train between two emissions.
- *parallel vibrations*: the displacements of parallel vibrations keep parallel directions in space.

• *interference conditions*: two or more vibrations can interfere only when the are coherent, parallel and have the same period.

• *beat frequency*: the difference in frequency of two waves creates a new frequency (*see* Beats, PHY 8.4).

Given an elementary vibration $S_i = A_1\sin(w_t+\varphi_i)$ the composition of n vibrations that interfere is given by:

$$S_1 + S_2 + S_3 + \ldots + S_n = a_1\sin(wt+\varphi_1) + a_2\sin(wt+\varphi_2) + \ldots + a_n\sin(wt+\varphi_n) = A\sin(wt+\Phi)$$

where A is the resultant amplitude and Φ the resultant phase. Constructive interference (*see Figure III.B.7.4*) is when the waves add to a larger resultant wave than either original. This occurs maximally when the phase difference φ is a whole wavelength λ which corresponds to multiples of π.

This occurs at $\varphi = 0, 2\pi, 4\pi$, etc. Since $\varphi = 2\pi\Delta L/\lambda$, where ΔL equals the difference in path to a point of two waves of equal wavelength, these waves interfere constructively when $\Delta L = 0, \lambda, 2\lambda, 3\lambda$, *etc.* See Figure III.B.7.3 for the definition of ΔL.

Destructive interference (*see Figure III.B.7.5*) is when the waves add to a smaller resultant wave than either original wave. This occurs maximally when $\varphi = \pi, 3\pi, 5\pi$, *etc.*, which are multiples of one-half of a wavelength where $180^\circ = \pi$ which corresponds to ½λ. This occurs when $\Delta L = \lambda/2, 3\lambda/2, 5\lambda/2$, etc.

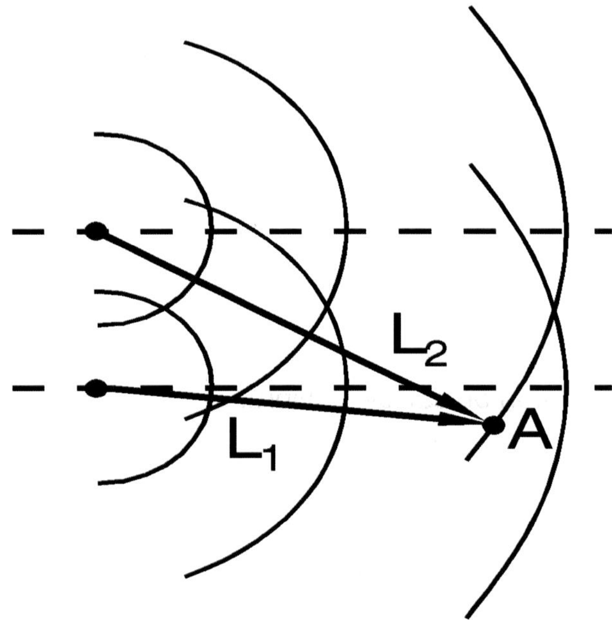

Figure III.B.7.3: Schematic for ΔL.
L_1 and L_2 are distances from the origins of the waves to point A. Thus $\Delta L = |L_2 - L_1|$ (absolute value).

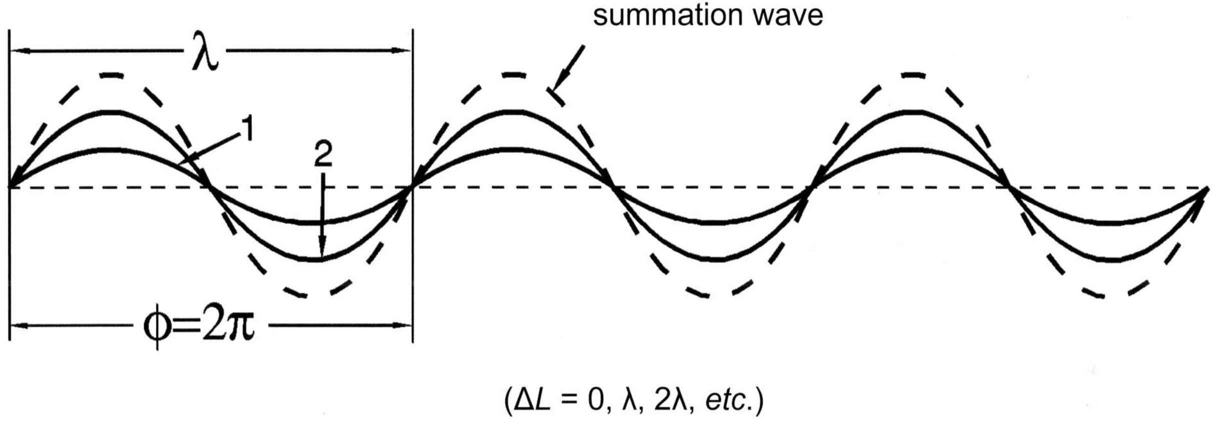

Figure III.B.7.4: Maximal constructive interference.
Waves (1) and (2) begin at the points shown, have the same λ but different amplitudes. The summation wave is maximal (i.e. highest amplitude but same wavelength) since ΔL = *λ in this example.*

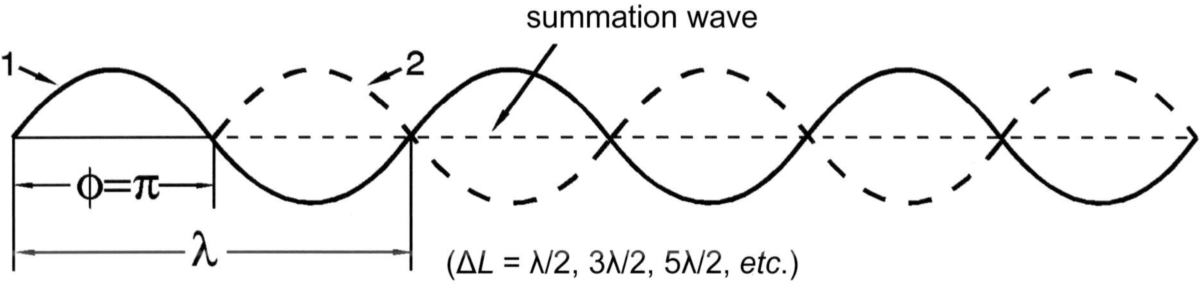

Figure III.B.7.5: Maximal destructive interference.

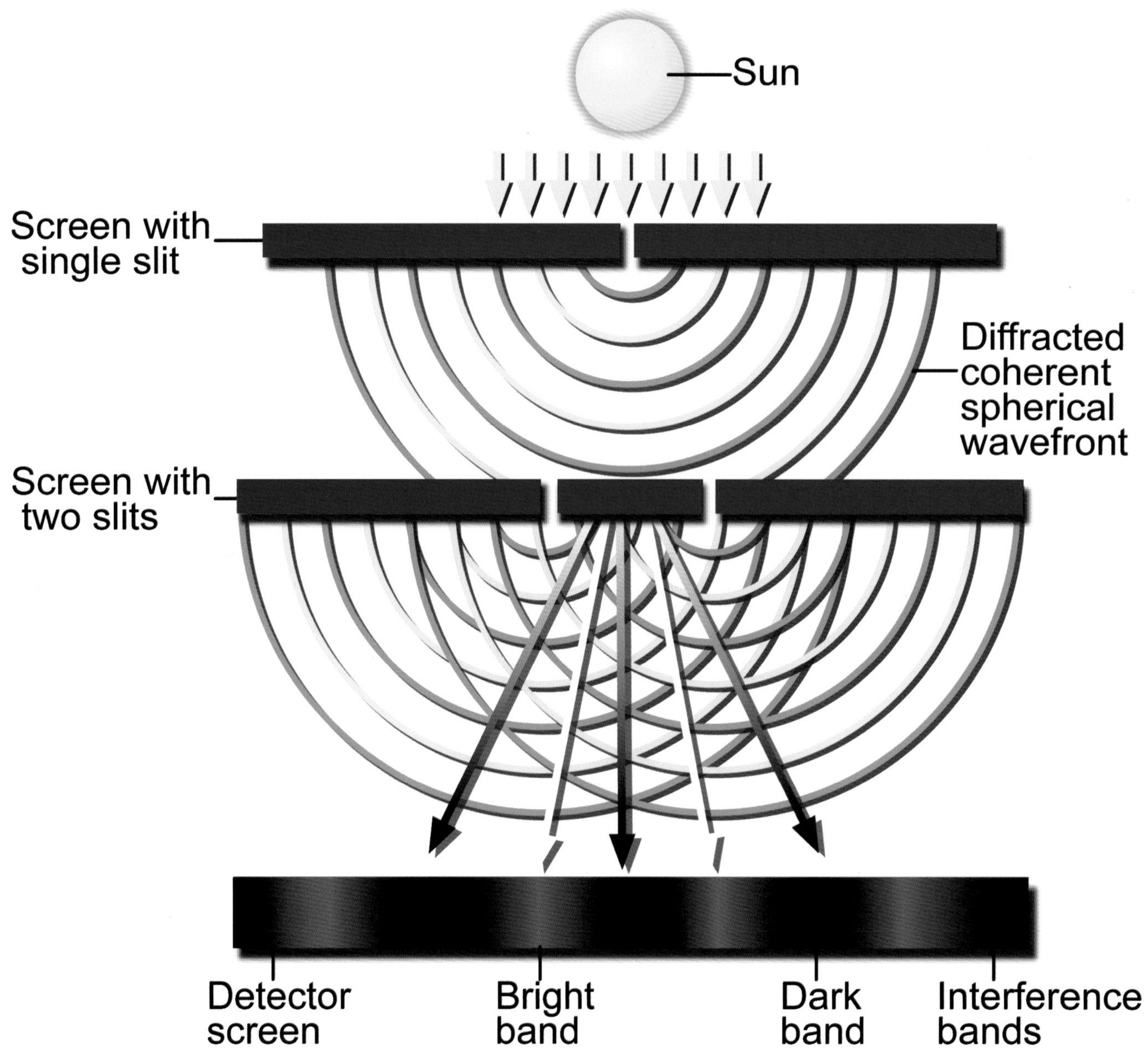

Figure III.B.7.5.1: Thomas Young's Double Slit Experiment Young's experiment demonstrates both the wave and particle natures of light. A coherent light source illuminates a thin plate with two parallel slits cut in it, and the light passing through the slits strikes a screen behind them. The wave nature of light causes the light waves passing through both slits to interfere, creating an interference pattern of bright and dark bands on the screen. However, at the screen, the light is always found to be absorbed as though it were made of discrete particles (photons). The double slit experiment can also be performed (using different apparatus) with particles of matter such as electrons with the same results. Again, this provides an additional circumstance demonstrating particle-wave duality. Diffraction is the apparent bending of a wave around a small obstacle. We see diffracted light waves through each of the slits above.

7.1.4 Resonance

Forced vibrations occur when a series of waves impinge upon an object and cause it to vibrate. Natural frequencies are the intrinsic frequencies of vibration of a system. If the forced vibration causes the object to vibrate at one of its natural frequencies, the body will vibrate at maximal amplitude. This phenomenon is called *resonance*. Since energy and power are proportional to the amplitude squared, they also are at their maximum.

7.1.5 Standing Waves, Pipes and Strings

Standing waves result when waves are reflected off a stationary object back into the oncoming waves of the medium and superposition results. *Nodes* are points where there is no particle displacement, which are similar to points of maximal destructive interference.

Nodes occur at fixed end points (points that cannot vibrate). Antinodes are points that undergo maximal displacements and are similar to points of maximal constructive interference. Antinodes occur at open or free end points (*see Figure III.B.7.6*).

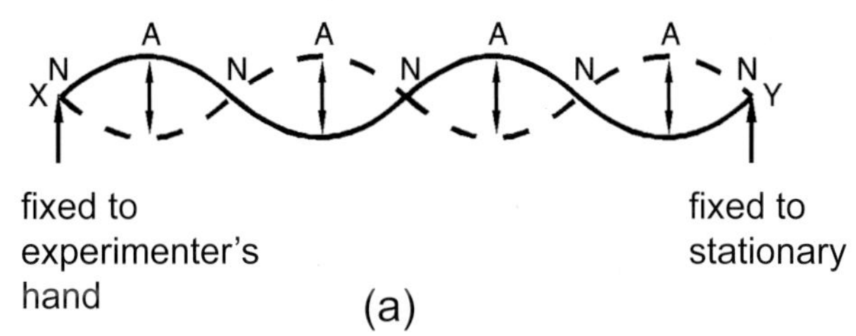

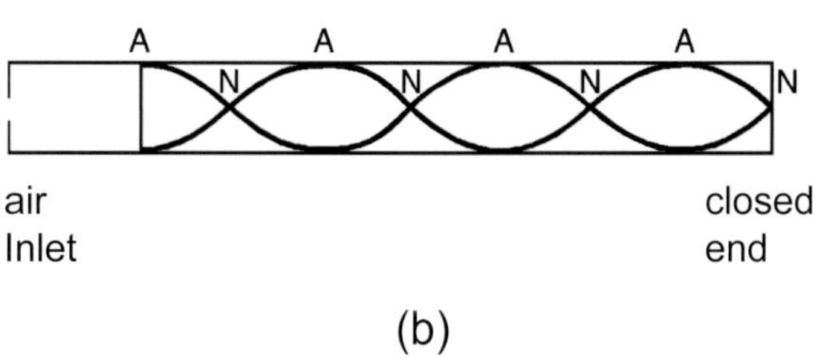

Figure III.B.7.6: Standing waves.
(a) String: Standing waves produced by an experimenter wiggling a string or rubber tube at point X towards a fixed point Y at the correct frequency. (b) Pipe: Standing wave produced in a pipe with a closed end point i.e. in a closed organ pipe where sound originates in a vibrating air column (A = *antinode* and N = *node*).

7.1.6 Harmonics

Consider a violin. A string is fixed at both ends and is bowed, transverse vibrations travel along the string; these disturbances are reflected at both ends producing a standing wave. The vibrations of the string give rise to longitudinal vibrations in the air which transmits the sound to our ears.

A string of length l, fixed at both ends, can resonate at frequencies f given by:

$$f_n = nv/(2l)$$

where the velocity v is the same for all frequencies and the number of antinodes $n = 1, 2, 3, \ldots$

The lowest frequency, $f_1 = v/(2l)$, is the *fundamental* frequency, and the others are called *overtones*. The fundamental is the first *harmonic*, the second harmonic $2f_1$ is the first overtone, the third harmonic $3f_1$ is the second overtone, etc. Overtones whose frequencies are integral multiples of the fundamental are called *harmonic series*.

7.2 Periodic Motion

7.2.1 Hooke's Law

The particles that are undergoing displacement when a wave passes through a medium undergo motion called simple harmonic motion (SHM) and are acted upon by a force described by Hooke's Law. SHM is caused by an inconstant force (called a *restoring force*) and as a result has an inconstant acceleration. The force is proportional to the displacement (*distance from the equilibrium point*) but opposite in direction,

$$F = -kx \text{ (Hooke's Law)}$$

where k = the spring constant, x = displacement from the equilibrium. The work W can be determined according to $W = ½kx^2$.

Notice that the equation for the work done by the spring is identical to the potential energy of a spring (PHY 5.4). This is because when an external force stretches the spring, this work is stored in the force field, which is said to be stored as potential energy. If the external force is removed, the force field acts on the body to perform the work as it moves the body back to the initial position, reducing the stretch of the spring. For example, an archer applies human force over a distance (= work; PHY 5.1) to pull an arrow back in the bow, elastic potential energy is now stored in the stretched bow, when the arrow leaves the bow, the potential energy turns into kinetic energy.

Examples of objects that have elastic potential energy include stretched or compressed elastic bands, springs, bungee cords, shock absorbers (cars, trucks, bicycles), trampolines, etc.

The work done in compressing or stretching a spring can be determined by taking the area under a Force vs. Displacement graph for the spring.

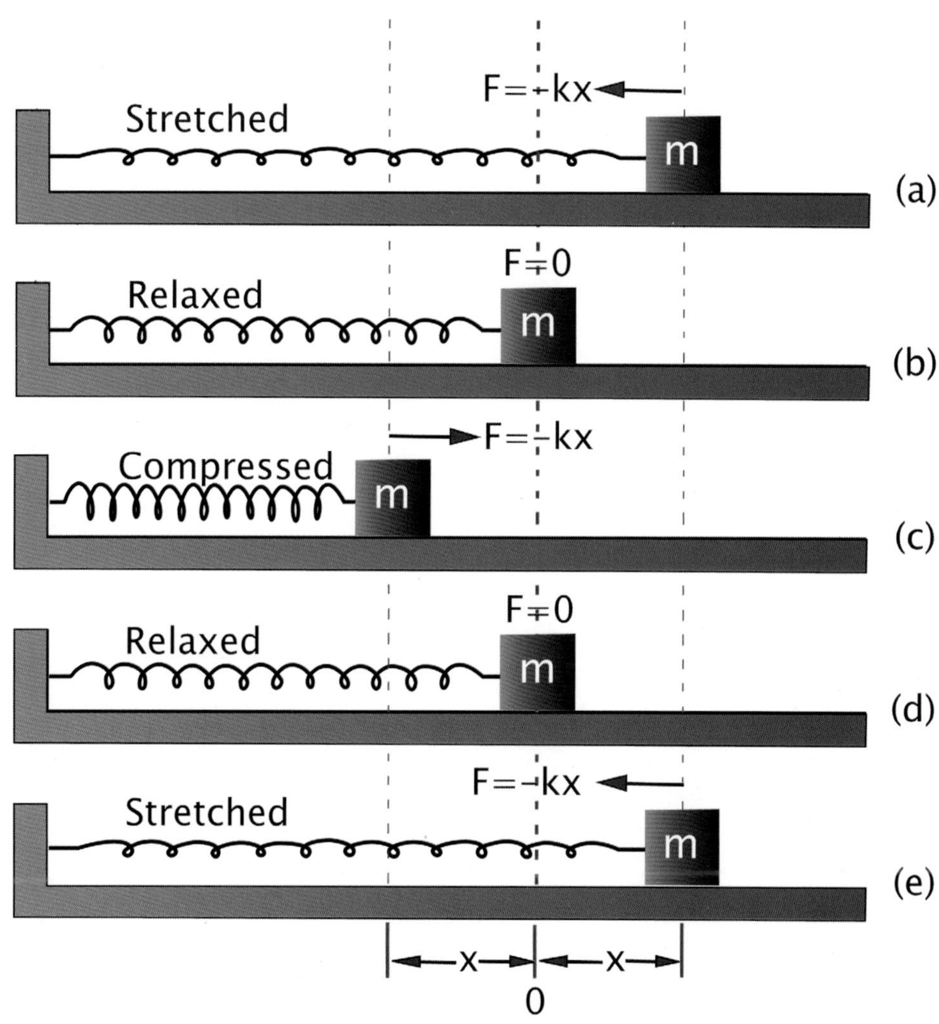

Figure III.B.7.7: Simple harmonic motion.

A block of mass m exhibiting SHM. The force F exerted by the spring on the block is shown in each case. Notice that the restoring force F is always pointing in the opposite direction to the direction of the displacement x. Because these two vectors are always opposite to each other, there is a negative sign built into the equation $F = -kx$.

7.2.2 Features of SHM and Hooke's Law

1) Force and acceleration are always in the same direction.
2) Force and acceleration are always in the opposite direction of the displace ment *(this is why there is a negative sign in the equation for force*).
3) Force and acceleration have their maximal value at +A and -A; they are zero at the equilibrium point (*the amplitude* A *equals the maximum displacement* x).
4) Velocity direction has no constant relation to displacement and acceleration.
5) Velocity is maximum at equilibrium and zero at A and -A.
6) The period *T* can be calculated from the mass *m* of an oscillating particle:

$$T = 2\pi\sqrt{m/k}$$

where k is the spring constant. The frequency *f* is simply $1/T$.

7.2.3 SHM Problem: The Simple Pendulum

A simple pendulum consists of a point mass *m* suspended by a light inextensible cord of length *l*. When pulled to one side of its equilibrium position, the pendulum swings under the influence of gravity producing a periodic, oscillatory motion (= *SHM*). Given that the angle θ with the vertical is small, thus $\sin\theta \approx \theta$, determine the general equation for the period *T*.

The tangential component of *mg* is the restoring force since it returns the mass to its equilibrium position. Thus the restoring force is:

$$F = -mg\sin\theta.$$

Recall $\sin\theta \approx \theta$, $x = l\theta$, and for SHM $F = -kx$:

$$F = -mg\theta = -mgx/l = -(mg/l)x = -kx.$$

Hence $mg/l = k$, thus the equation for the period *T* becomes:

$$T = 2\pi\sqrt{\frac{m}{k}} = 2\pi\sqrt{\frac{m}{mg/l}} = 2\pi\sqrt{\frac{l}{g}}$$

The equation for the period in the simple pendulum is therefore independent of the mass of the particle.

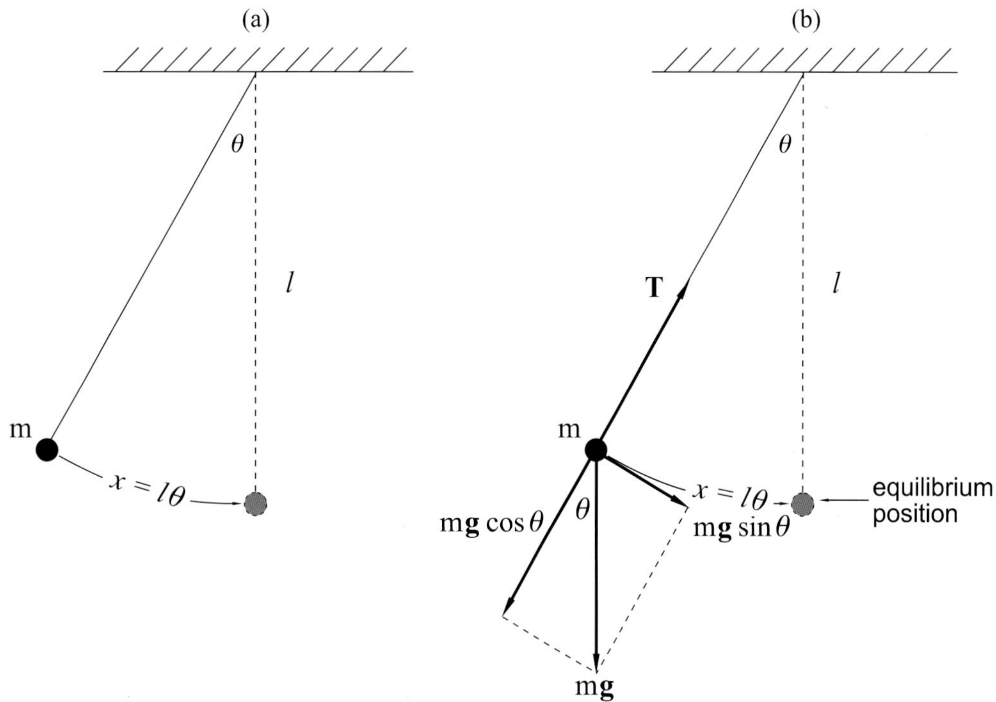

Figure III.B.7.8: The Simple Pendulum.
(a) The problem as it could be presented; the displacement x along the section of the circle (arc) is $l\theta$. (b) The vector components that should be drawn to solve the problem. The forces acting on a simple pendulum are the tension **T** in the string and the weight mg of the mass. The magnitude of the radial component of mg is mgcosθ and the tangential component is mgsinθ.

Go online to OATbooks.com for free chapter review Q&A and forum.

SOUND
Chapter 8

Memorize

* Sensory vs. physical correspondence of hearing

Understand

* Relative velocity of sound in solids, liquids and gases
* The relation of intensity to P, area, f, amplitude
* Calculation of the intensity level
* Rules of logarithms
* Doppler effect and calculations

Importance

0 to 2 out of the 40 PHY

OAT questions are based on content in this chapter (in our estimation).

*Note that between 55% and 85% of the questions in OAT Physics are based on content from 6 chapters: 1, 2, 3, 6, 7 and 11.

Introduction 

Sound waves are longitudinal waves which can only be transmitted in a material, elastic medium. Speed, intensity, resonance (Chapter 7) and the Doppler effect help to describe the behavior of sound in different media.

Additional Resources

Free Online Q&A + Forum

Video: Online or DVD

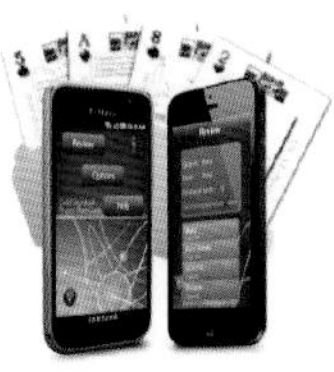

Flashcards

8.1 Production of Sound

Sound is a longitudinal mechanical wave which travels through an elastic medium. Sound is thus produced by vibrating matter. There is no sound in a *vacuum* because it contains no matter.

Compressions (condensations) are regions where particles of matter are close together; they are also high pressure regions. Rarefactions are regions where particles are sparse, they are low pressure regions of sound waves (PHY 7.1.1).

8.2 Relative Velocity of Sound in Solids, Liquids, and Gases

The velocity of sound is proportional to the square root of the elastic restoring force and inversely proportional to the square root of the inertia of the particles (e.g., density is a measure of inertia). Thus as a rule, the velocity of sound is higher in liquids as compared to gases, and highest in solids.

Furthermore, an increase in temperature increases the velocity of sound; conversely, a decrease in temperature decreases the velocity of sound in that medium.

8.3 Intensity, Pitch

Hearing is subjective but its characteristics are closely tied to physical characteristics of sound.

The quality depends on the number and relative intensity of the overtones of the waveform. Frequency, and therefore pitch are perceived by the ear from 20 to 20,000 Hz (hertz = cycles/second = s^{-1}). Frequencies below 20 Hz are called infrasonic. Frequencies above 20,000 Hz are called ultrasonic.

Sensory	*Physical*
loudness	intensity
pitch	frequency
quality	waveform

Table III.B.8.1:
Sensory and physical correspondence of hearing.

Sound intensity (I) is the rate of energy (power) propagation through space:

I = (*power/area*) which is proportional to ($f^2 A^2$)

where f = frequency, A = amplitude.

The loudness varies with the frequency. The ears are most sensitive (hears sounds of lowest intensity) at approximately 2,000 to 4,000 Hz. I_o is taken to be 10^{-12} *watts/cm*^{2}, is barely audible and is assigned a value of 0 dB (zero *decibels*). Then intensity level (I) of a sound wave in dB is,

$$dB = 10 \log_{10}(I/I_o)$$

where dB = the sound level, I = the intensity at a given level, I_o = the threshold intensity. {To calculate a change in the sound level or volume ΔV in units of dB, given two values for sound intensity, the given equation can be modified thus: $\Delta V = 10\log(I_{new}/I_{old})$}

Examples of some values of dB's are: whisper (20), normal conversation (60), subway car (100), pain threshold (120), and jet engine (160). Continual exposure to sound greater than 90 dB can lead to hearing impairment.

8.3.1 Calculation of the Intensity Level

What is the loudness or intensity level of Mr. Yell Alot's voice when he generates a sound wave ten million times as intense as I_0?

$$I = (10{,}000{,}000) \quad I_0 = (10^7)\, I_0$$

Thus

$$\begin{aligned} dB &= 10 \log_{10} (10^7\, I_0/I_0) \\ &= 10 \log_{10} 10^7 \\ &= 70 \log_{10} 10 = 70 \end{aligned}$$

{See chemistry section 6.5.1 for rules of logarithms. Question types involving logs including acids-bases (CHM Chapter 6) and rate law (CHM Chapter 9) are possible OAT question types.}

8.4 Beats

When sound of different frequencies are heard together, they interfere. Constructive interference results in beats. The number of beats per second is the absolute value of the difference of the frequencies ($|f_1 - f_2|$).

Hence, the new frequency heard includes the original frequencies and the absolute difference between them.

8.5 Doppler Effect

The Doppler effect is the effect upon the observed frequency caused by the relative motion of the observer (*o*) and the source (*s*). If the distance is decreasing between them, there is a shift to higher frequencies and shorter wavelengths (to higher pitch for sound and toward blue-violet for light, PHY 8.3 and 9.2.4). If the distance is increasing between them, there is a shift to longer wavelengths and lower frequencies (to lower pitch for sound and toward red for light). The summary equation of the above in terms of frequency (f) is :

$$f_o = f_s(V \pm v_o)/(V \pm v_s)$$

V = speed of the wave, v = speed of the observer (*o*) or the source (*s*).

Choose the sign such that the frequency varies consistently with the relative motion of the source and the observer. In other words, when the distance between the source and observer is *decreasing* use $+v_o$ and $-v_s$; if the distance is *increasing* use $-v_o$ and $+v_s$.

8.5.1 Doppler Effect Problem (SI units)

A car drives towards a bus stop with its car stereo playing opera. The opera singer sings the note middle C (= 262 Hz) loudly; however, the people waiting at the bus stop hear C sharp (= 277 Hz). Given that the speed of sound V in air is 331 m/s, how fast is the car moving?

{Remember the sign convention: since the distance between the source (the car) and the observer (people at the bus stop) is ***decreasing*** *we use $+v_o$ and $-v_s$}*

• the car (the *source* of the frequency) f_s = 262 Hz, v_s = unknown.

• the bus stop (where the *observers* are stationary) f_o = 277 Hz, v_o = 0 m/s.

$$f_o = f_s(V + v_o)/(V - v_s)$$

Thus

$$V - v_s = f_s(V + v_o)/f_o$$

Hence

$$v_s = -f_s(V + v_o)/f_o + V$$

Substitute

$$v_s = -262(331 + 0)/277 + 331 = 17.9 \text{ m/s.}$$

• Note that the answer contains three significant figures.

Go online to OATbooks.com for free chapter review Q&A and forum.

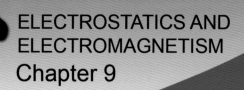

ELECTROSTATICS AND ELECTROMAGNETISM
Chapter 9

Memorize

uations: for charge Q, Coulomb's law, ctric field
uations: potential energy, absolute potential
uation relating energy, planck's constant, quency
uation: relating velocity to frequency, velength

Understand

* Conservation of charge, use of Coulomb's law
* Graphs/theory: electric field/potential lines, mag. induction
* Potential difference, electric dipoles, mag. induction
* Laplace's law, the right hand rule, magnetic field
* Direction of F in magn. field; electromagnetism

Importance

2 to 4 out of the 40 PHY

OAT questions are based on content in this chapter (in our estimation).

*Note that between 55% and 85% of the questions in OAT Physics are based on content from 6 chapters: 1, 2, 3, 6, 7 and 11.

Introduction

Electrostatics (statics = usu. at rest) refers to the science of stationary or slowly moving charges. Such charges can interact and behave in ways described by charge, electric force, electric field and potential difference. When a charge is in motion, it creates a magnetic field. Electromagnetism describes the relationship between electricity (moving electrical charge) and magnetism. The electromagnetic spectrum includes light and X-rays.

Additional Resources

Free Online Q&A + Forum

Video: Online or DVD

Flashcards

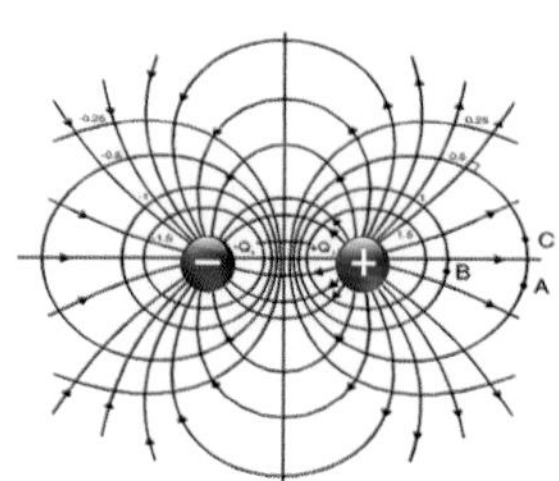

Special Guest

9.1 Electrostatics

9.1.1 Charge, Conductors, Insulators

By friction of matter we create between substances repulsive or attractive electric forces. These forces are due to two kinds of electric charges, distinguished by positive (+) and negative (-) signs. Each has a charge of 1.6×10^{-19} coulombs (C) but differ in sign. The electron is the negative charge carrier, and the proton is the positive charge carrier. Substances with an excess of electrons have a net negative charge. Substances with a deficiency of electrons have a net positive charge. The total amount of charge Q of matter depends on the number of particles n and the charge e on each particle, thus $Q = ne$.

The conservation of charge states that a net charge cannot be created but that charge can be transfered from one object to another. One way of charging substances is by rubbing them (i.e., by contact).

For example, glass rubbed on fur becomes positive and rubber rubbed on fur becomes negative. Objects can also be charged by induction which occurs when one charged object is brought near to another uncharged object causing a charge redistribution in the latter to give net charge regions. Conductors transmit charge readily. Insulators resist the flow of charge.

9.1.2 Coulomb's Law, Electric Force

Charges exert forces upon each other. Like charges repel each other and unlike charges attract. For any two charges q_1 and q_2 the force F is given by Coulomb's Law:

$$F = k\frac{q_1 q_2}{r^2} = \frac{1}{4\pi\varepsilon_o}\left(\frac{q_1 q_2}{r^2}\right)$$

where k = coulomb's constant = 9.0×10^9 N-m²/C², ε_o = permittivity constant = 8.85×10^{-12} C²/N-m², and r = the distance between the charges. Note that the relationship of force and distance follows an inverse square law. Thus if the distance r is doubled [$(2r)^2 = 4r^2$], the new force is quartered ($F_{new} = F/4$). {cf. Law of Gravity: PHY 2.4}

A charge generates an electric field (E) in the space around it. Fields (force fields) are vectors. A field is generated by an object and it is that region of space around the object that will exert a force on a second object brought into that field. The field exists independently of that second object and is not altered by its presence. The force exerted on the second object depends upon that object and the field. The electric field E is given by:

$$E = F/q = k\,Q/r^2$$

where E and F are vectors, Q = the charge generating the field, and q = the charge placed in the field.

Charges exert forces upon each other through fields. The direction of a field is the direction a positive charge would move if placed in it. *Electric field lines* are imaginary lines which are in the same direction as E at that point. The direction is away from positive charges and toward negative charges, or put another way, the electric field is directed toward the decreasing potentials.

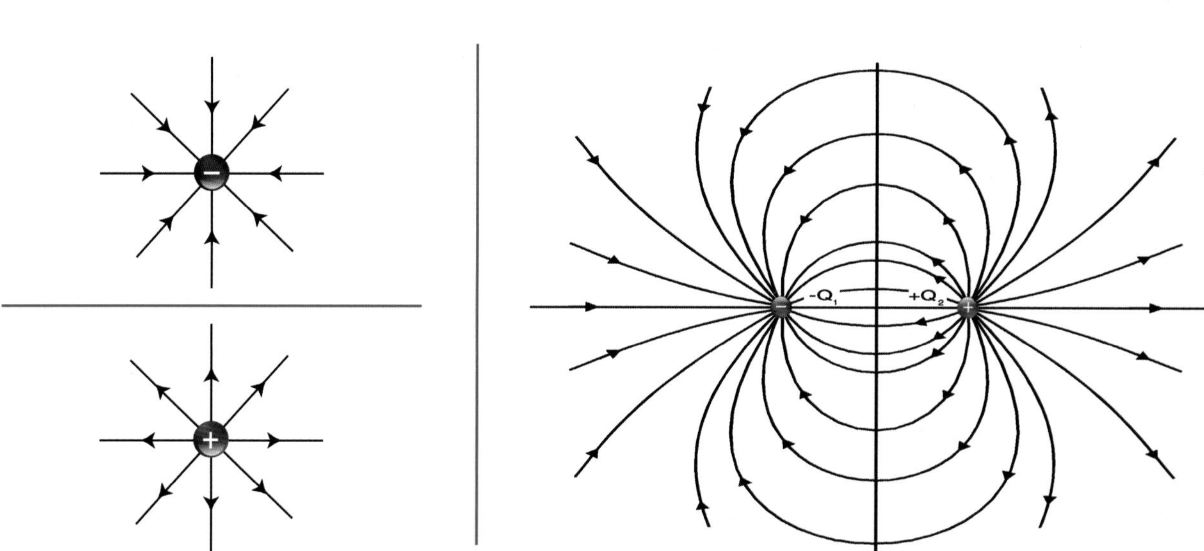

Figure III.B.9.1: Electric field lines.
The electric field is generated by the charges $-Q_1$ and $+Q_2$. The arrowheads show the direction of the electric field.

If an electric potential is applied between two plates in a vacuum, and an electron is introduced, the electron will experience an attractive force to the positive plate (*see Figure III.B.9.2*).

The force will cause the electron to accelerate towards the positive plate in a straight line. It suffers no collisions because the area between the plates is *in vacuo*. This effect is used in thermoionic valves.

If the electron is given some motion, and the electric field is applied perpendicular to the motion, interesting things happen (*see Figure III.B.9.3*). For example, a beam of electrons is emitted from a device called an electron gun. These electrons are moving in the *x* direction.

As the electrons pass between the plates they are accelerated in the *y* direction, as explained before, but their velocity in the *x* direction is unaltered. The electron beam is thus deflected as shown.

By varying the potential applied to the plates, the angle of deflection can be controlled. This effect is the basis of the cathode ray oscilloscope.

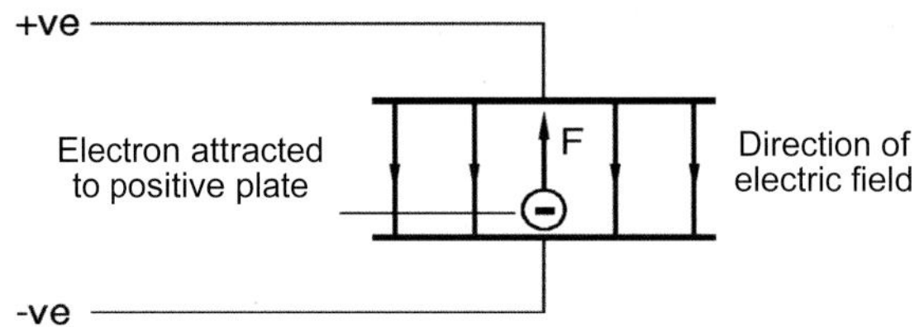

Figure III.B.9.2:
Electric field between parallel plates.

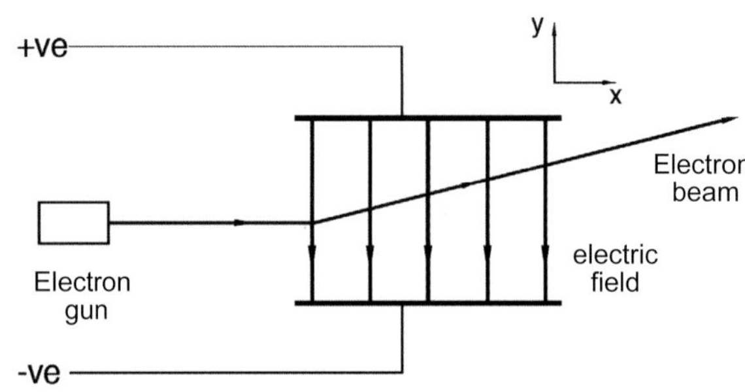

Figure III.B.9.3:
Electrostatic deflection of an electron beam.

9.1.4 Potential Energy, Absolute Potential

The *potential energy* (E_p) of a charged object in a field equals the work done on that object to bring it from infinity to a distance (r) from the charge setting up the electric field,

$$E_p = work = Fr = (qE)r = kQq/r$$

where Q = the charge setting up field, and *q* = the charge brought in to a distance r.

When a +q moves against E, its E_p increases. When a -q moves against the electric field E, its E_p decreases. If two positive or negative charges were brought together, work would have to be done to the system (and E_p would increase), and vice versa for charges of opposite charges.

The *absolute potential* (V) is a scalar, and it is defined at each distance (r) from a charge (Q) generating an electric field. It represents the negative of the work per unit charge in bringing a +q from infinity to r:

• $V = E_p/q = kQ/r$ in volts where 1 volt = 1 joule/coulomb.

• $V = Ed$ for a parallel plate capacitor where *d* = distance between the plates (PHY 10.4).

Equipotential lines are lines (and surfaces) of equal V and are *perpendicular* to electric field lines. Work can only be done when moving between surfaces of equal V and is, therefore, independent of the path taken. No work is done when a charge (q) is moved along an equal potential (*equipotential*) surface (or line), because the component of force is zero along it. Potential (V) is defined in terms of positive charges such that V is positive when due to a +Q and negative when due a -Q. Potential (V) is added algebraically at a point (because it is a scalar).

See Figure III.B.9.4:

1) V_1, V_2 are two potentials perpendicular to the electric field E and the force *F*;
2) $V_2 - V_1$ is the potential difference (*PD*);
3) charge (*q*) moved from A ($V_1 = 0.5$) to B ($V_2 = 1$) has work (*W*) done on it:

$$W = q(V_2 - V_1) = q(PD)$$

4) charge (*q*) moved from A to C has no work done on it because this is along an equipotential surface ($V = 0.5$) and the non-zero component of force (*F*) is perpendicular to it;
5) the lines of *F* are along the lines of *E*.

The *potential difference* (*PD*) is the difference in V between two points, or it is the work per unit positive charge done by electric forces moving a small test charge from the point of higher potential to the point of lower potential:

$$PD = V_a - V_b = volts = work/charge$$

$$work = q(V_a - V_b) = q(PD).$$

An *electric dipole* consists of two charges separated by some finite distance (d). Usually the charges are equal and opposite. The laws of forces, fields, etc., apply to dipoles. A dipole is characterized by its *dipole moment* which is the product of the charge (q) and d.

Dipoles tend to line up with the electric field (Fig. III.B.9.5). Motion of dipoles against an electric field requires energy as discussed above.

If you consider a single isolated point charge and the circular equipotential line produced, in 3 D, it is a sphere where each point on the surface of the sphere has the same potential because it is the same distance from the charge. This imaginary 3 D shape is called a *gaussian* surface.

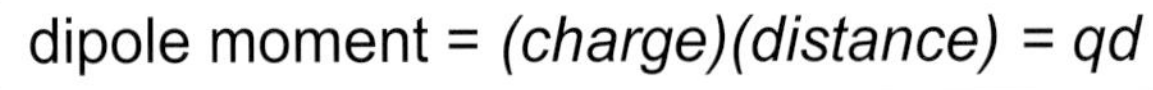

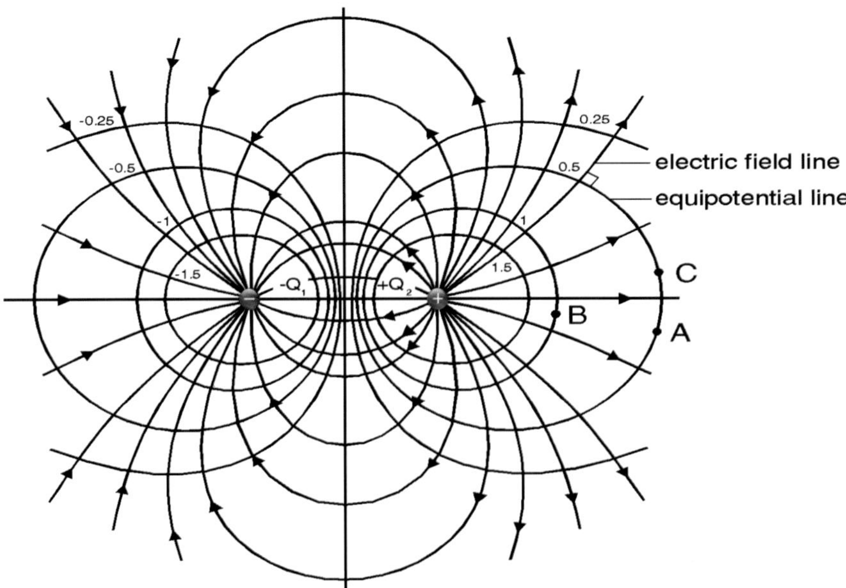

Figure III.B.9.4: Equipotential lines.
The circle-like curves around each charge $-Q_1$ and $+Q_2$ are the equipotential lines corresponding to each charge. The numbers represent the electric potential value (i.e. in millivolts) of the respective equipotential lines. Note the electric field lines as in Figure III.B.9.1.

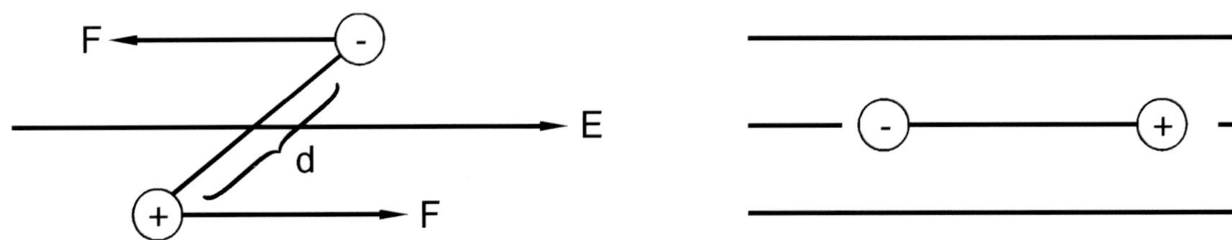

Dipole with equal and opposite charges

Alignment of dipole with E

Figure III.B.9.5: Dipole and electric field.
E = electric field, *F* = forces exerted by E on the dipole

9.2.1 Notion of Electromagnetic Induction

Coulomb's Law in electrostatics gives the nature of the forces acting upon electric charges at rest, but when the charges are moving, new forces appear.

They are not of the same nature as the electrostatic forces and they act differently on the electric charges. They are called electromagnetic forces.

9.2.2 Magnetic Induction Vector

Experiments have shown that two straight conductors (e.g. copper wires) traversed by electric currents of intensities I and I′ in the same direction are acted upon by an attractive force proportional to the product of the intensities and inversely proportional to the distance between the two conductors. It can be demonstrated that when the electric current in one of the conductors disappears, the force also disappears.

Therefore, the force is due to the motion of the electric charges in both conductors.

We decompose the phenomenon by introducing a new physical quantity: the magnetic induction vector *B*, also created by magnets.

The SI unit for *B* is the tesla where 1 T = 1 N/(A·m) = 10^4 gauss.

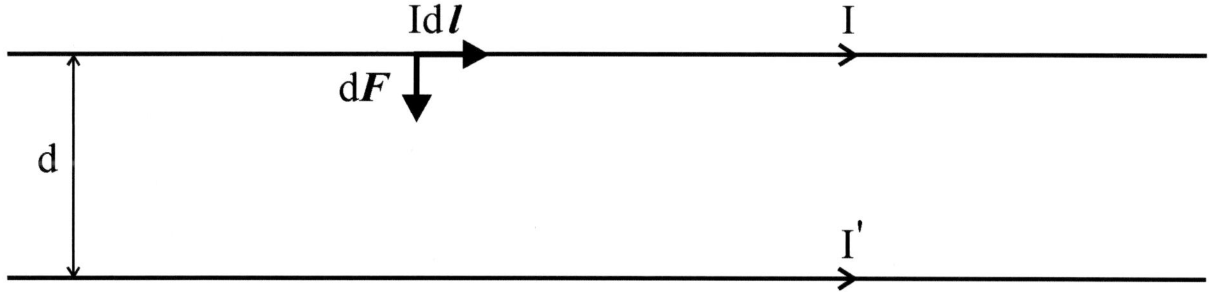

Figure III.B.9.6: Magnetic induction.
Two conductors a distance d apart; the current element *Idl* and the perpendicular force *dF* associated with the magnetic induction vector *B* are both shown. Vector B, which is not shown, has a direction perpendicular to both Idl and dF, pointing out of the page.

Thus, two effects have been shown by the preceding experiment:

1) a moving charge produces a magnetic induction.

2) a magnetic induction exerts a force on any nearby moving charge.

9.2.3 Laplace's Law

A test particle with charge *dq* moving at a velocity *v* in a magnetic induction field B is acted upon by a force *dF* given by the following formula:

$$dF = dq\ v \times B = dq\ v(B\sin\alpha)$$

where α is the angle formed by the direction of *v* with that of *B* (= the cross product).

The force *dF* is perpendicular to the magnetic induction vector and also to the displacement velocity vector of the charge (*see Figure III.B.9.6*).

When many charges are in motion so as to produce an electric current of intensity $I = dq/dt$ the force acting upon an elemental length of conductor *dl* traversed by that electric current is :

$$dF = I\ dl \times B = I\ dl(B\sin\alpha)$$

where α is the angle formed by the direction of the current element of conductor with that of *B* (= the cross product).

In order to determine the direction of a cross (= *vector*) product we can use the right-hand rule. If $c = a \times b$ then the right hand is held so that the curled fingers follow the rotation of *a* to *b*, the extended right thumb will point in the direction of *c* (*dF* in the preceding example). {Student's trick: "Grab the Wire!" Examine Fig. III.B.9.6. Turn the book around such that with your right hand open and thumb extended, the fingers point in the direction of *dF* and your thumb points in the direction *Idl*. As you begin to grab the wire, the initial direction of the tips of your fingers move perpendicular to both *dF* and *Idl*. Now the tips of your fingers make a circular motion around the wire. Those fingers have just described the direction of the magnetic induction vector *B*!}

9.2.4 Electromagnetic Spectrum, Radio, Infrared, X Rays

An electromagnetic field is described as having at every point of the field, two perpendicular vectors: *the electric field* vector E and the magnetic induction field vector B.

Radar (= *radio detection* and ranging) is an example of a radio wave.

Visible light can be broken down into colors remembered by the mnemonic (*from highest to lowest wavelength*), Roy G. BIV: Red, Orange, Yellow, Green, Blue, Indigo, Violet.

The separation of white light into these colors can occur as a result of refraction through a prism (PHY 11.4) or through water (i.e. mist or rain resulting in a rainbow).

Planck developed the relation between energy (E) and the frequency f of the electromagnetic radiation,

$$E = hf$$

where h = planck's constant. Thus high frequency or short wave length corresponds to high energy and vice versa.

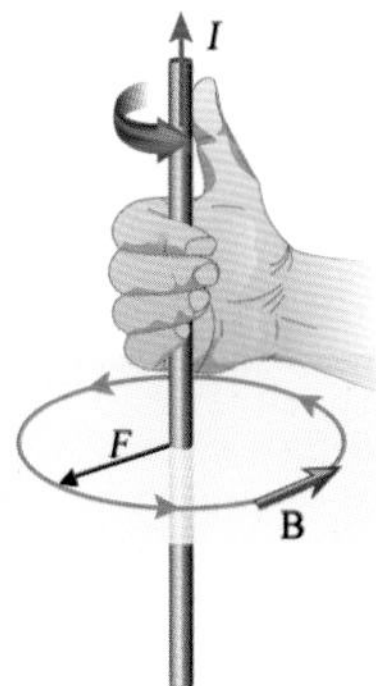

Figure III.B.9.6b: Right-hand rule.

The speed of light (= electromagnetic radiation), given by c, can be measured from the wavelength λ and the frequency f of an electromagnetic wave in a vacuum (= in vacuo = no pressure/no particles approximated by outer space). Recall that $v = \lambda f$ (PHY 7.1.2), and so we have the special case for the speed of light,

$$c = \lambda f$$

The result is the constant $c = 3 \times 10^8$ m/s which is normally given at the beginning of the OAT test. The speed at which light propagates through transparent materials, such as glass, water or air, is less than c, given by the refractive index n of the material ($n = c/v$; PHY 9.2.4). The change in c in different materials (refraction) is responsible for the colors of a rainbow.

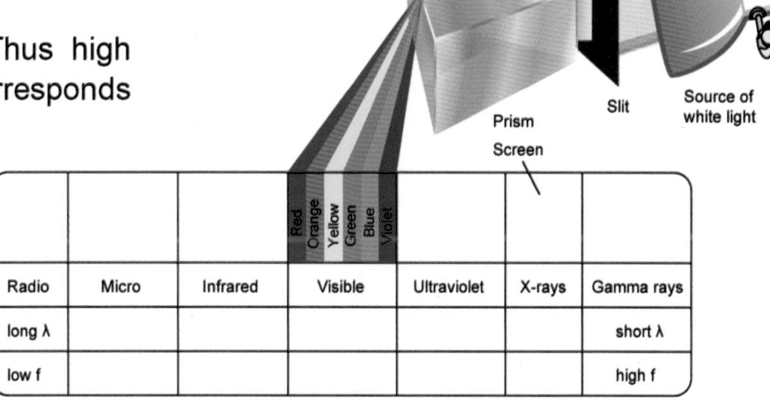

Radio	Micro	Infrared	Visible	Ultraviolet	X-rays	Gamma rays
long λ						short λ
low f						high f

Figure III.B.9.7: The complete electromagnetic spectrum.

Go online to OATbooks.com for free chapter review Q&A and forum.

ELECTRIC CIRCUITS
Chapter 10

Memorize

inition/equation/units: current, resistance
n's law, resistors in series/parallel
:hoff's laws

Understand

* Battery, emf, voltage, terminal potential
* Internal resistance of the battery, resistivity
* Ohm's law, resistors in series/parallel
* Parallel plate capacitor, series, parallel
* Conductivity, power in circuits, Kirchoff's laws

Importance

2 to 4 out of the 40 PHY

OAT questions are based on content in this chapter (in our estimation).

*Note that between 55% and 85% of the questions in OAT Physics are based on content from 6 chapters: 1, 2, 3, 6, 7 and 11.

OATbooks.com

Introduction 

Electric circuits are closed paths which includes electronic components (i.e. resistors, capacitors, power supplies) through which a current can flow. There are 3 basic laws that govern the flow of current in an electrical circuit: Ohm's law and Kirchoff's first and second laws.

Additional Resources

Free Online Q&A + Forum

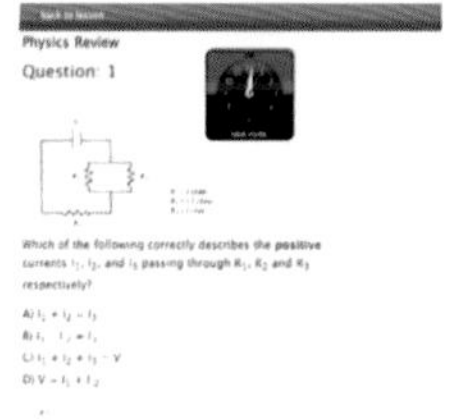

Video: Online or DVD

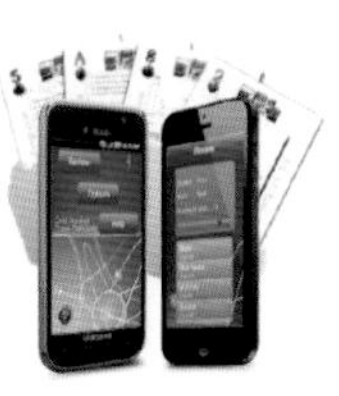

Flashcards

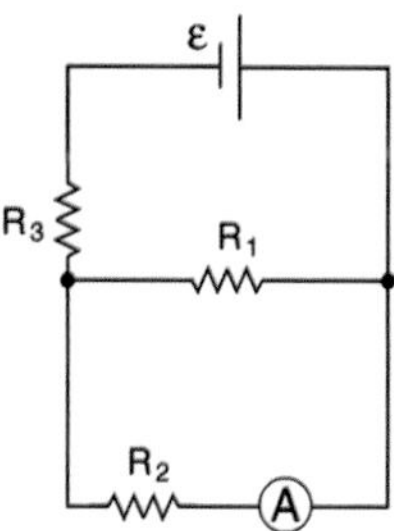

Special Guest

10.1 Current

The current (I) is the amount of charge (Q) that flows past a point in a given amount of time (t),

$$I = Q/t = amperes = coulombs/sec.$$

Current is caused by the movement of electrons between two points of significant potential difference of an electric circuit. Free electrons will accelerate towards the positive connection. As they move they will collide with atoms in the substance, losing energy which we observe as heat. The net effect is a drift of electrons at a roughly constant speed towards the positive connection. The motion of electrons is an *electric current*. As electrons are removed by the electric potential source at the positive connection, electrons are being injected at the negative connection. The potential can be considered as a form of *electron pump.*

This model explains many observed effects.

If the magnitude of the electric potential is increased, the electrons will accelerate faster and their mean velocity will be higher, i.e., the current is increased. The collisions between electrons and atoms transfer energy to the atoms. The collisions manifest themselves as heat. This effect is known as *Joule heating*. Materials such as these are termed ohmic conductors, since they obey the well-known Ohm's Law:

$$V = IR$$

where V is the voltage, I is the current, and R is the resistance.

The potential difference is maintained by a voltage source (emf). The direction of current is taken as the direction of positive charge movement, by convention. It is represented on a circuit diagram by arrows. Ammeters are used to measure the flow of current and are symbolized as in Figure III.B.10.1.

Figure III.B.10.1: Symbol of an ammeter.

Resistance (R) is the measure of opposition to the flow of electrons in a substance. Resistivity (ρ) is an inherent property of a substance. It varies with temperature. For example, the resistivity of metals increases with increasing temperature.

Resistance is directly proportional to resistivity and length l but inversely proportional to the cross-sectional area A.

$$R = \rho l/A$$

Resistance increases with temperature because the thermal motion of molecules increases with temperature and results in more collisions between electrons which impede their flow.

The units of resistance are ohms, symbolized by Ω (omega). From Ohm's Law, 1 ohm = 1 volt/ampere.

When a positive current flows across a resistor, there is a voltage decrease and an energy loss:

$$\text{energy loss} = Vq = VIt = \textit{joules}$$

$$\text{power loss } (P) = VIt/t = VI = \textit{watts}$$

$$\textit{watts} = \textit{volts} \times \textit{amperes} = \textit{joules/sec.}$$

The energy loss may be used to perform work. These relations hold for power (P),

$$P = VI = (IR)(I) = I^2R = V(V/R) = V^2/R.$$

constant (normal) resistance
"classic" image of resistor

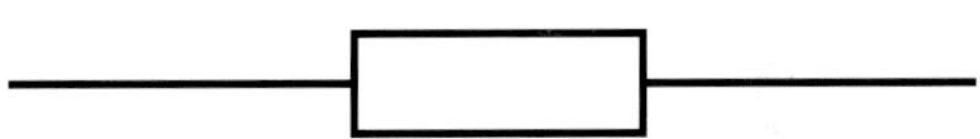

"modern" image of resistor

variable resistance (rheostat)

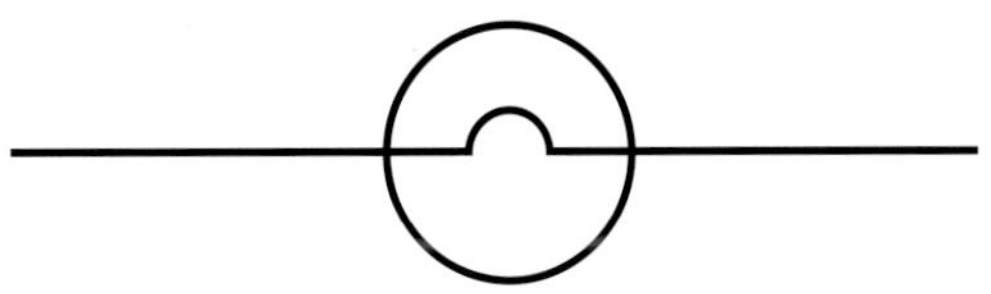

incandescent light bulb
treated like resistor

Figure III.B.10.2: Representations of resistors. Note that the filament inside of a light bulb (= *incandescent lamp* or *globe*) is a resistor. Because it resists the flow of current, it becomes hot and glows providing light. This is why a light bulb in a circuit is treated exactly like a resistor. The brightness of a light bulb depends on how much power it loses (= *dissipates*; $P = VI$) .

Circuit elements are either in series or in parallel. Two components are in series when they have only one point in common; that is, the current travelling from one of them back to the emf source must pass through the other. In a complete series circuit, or for individual series loops of a larger mixed circuit, the current (I) is the same over each component and the total voltage drop in the circuit elements (resistors, capacitors, inductors, internal resistance of emf sources, etc.) is equal to the sum V_t of all the emf sources. The value of the equivalent resistance R_{eq} in a series circuit is:

$$R_{eq} = R_1 + R_2 + R_3 + \ldots$$

Two components are in parallel when they are connected to two common points in the circuit; that is, the current travelling from one such element back to the emf source need not pass through the second element because there is an alternate path.

In a parallel circuit, the total current is the sum of currents for each path and the voltage is the same for all paths in parallel. The equivalent resistance in a parallel circuit is:

$$1/R_{eq} = 1/R_1 + 1/R_2 + 1/R_3 + \ldots$$

10.2.1 Resistance Problem in Series and Parallel

Determine the equivalent resistance between points A and B in Figure III.B.10.3.

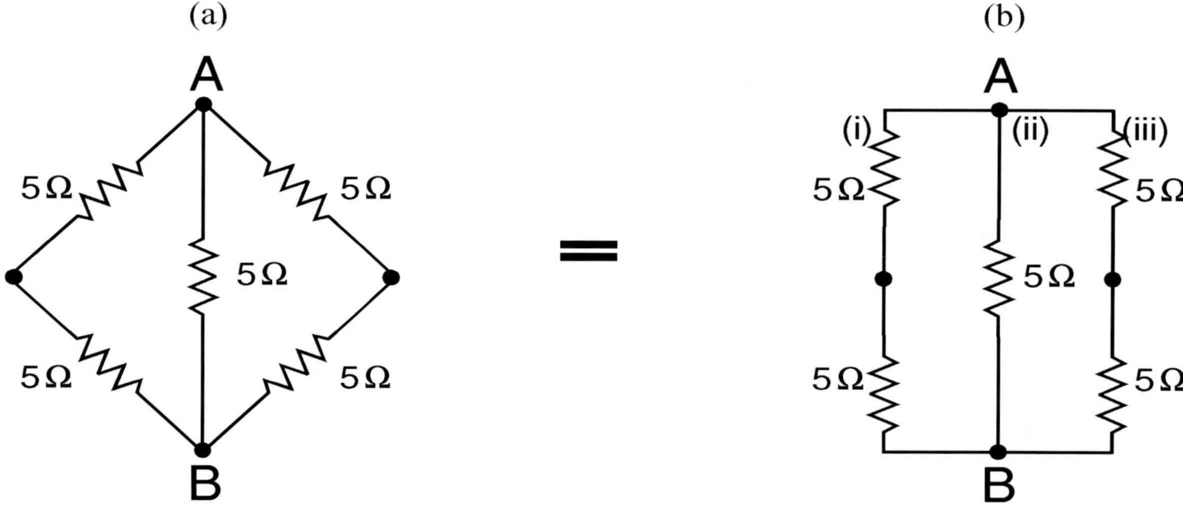

Figure III.B.10.3: Equivalent resistance.
(a) The problem as it could be presented; (b) the way you should interpret the problem.

- Wire (i) has two resistors in a row (*in series*): $R_{(i)} = 5 + 5 = 10\ \Omega$

- Wire (ii) has only one resistor: $R_{(ii)} = 5\ \Omega$

- Wire (iii) has two resistors in series: $R_{(iii)} = 5 + 5 = 10\ \Omega$

Between *A* and *B* we have three resistor systems in parallel: (i), (ii) and (iii), thus

$$1/R_{eq} = 1/R_{(i)} + 1/R_{(ii)} + 1/R_{(iii)}$$
$$= 1/10 + 1/5 + 1/10 = 4/10$$

multiply through by $10R_{eq}$ to get: $10 = 4R_{eq}$

thus $R_{eq} = 10/4 = 2.5\ \Omega$.

10.3 Batteries, Electromotive Force, Voltage, Internal Resistance

An *electromotive force (emf)* source maintains between its terminal points, a constant potential difference. The emf source replaces energy lost by moving electrons. Sources of emf are batteries (conversion of chemical energy to electrical energy) and generators (conversion of mechanical energy to electrical energy).

The source of emf does work on each charge to raise it from a lower potential to a higher potential.

Then as the charge flows around the circuit (naturally from higher to lower potential) it loses energy which is replaced by the emf source again.

energy supplied = energy lost

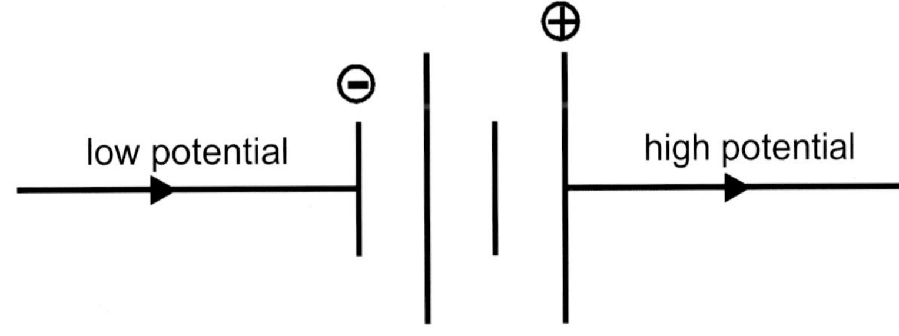

Figure III.B.10.4: Symbol of an emf source. Arrows show the normal direction of current.

Energy is lost whenever a charge (as current) passes through a resistor. The units of emf are volts. The actual voltage delivered to a circuit is not equal to the value of the source. This is reduced by an internal voltage lost which represents the voltage loss by the *internal resistance (r)* of the source itself. The net voltage is called the terminal voltage or *terminal potential* V_t.

Figure III.B.10.5:
Simplified symbol of an emf source.

$$V_t = V - Ir = IR_t$$

I, R_t = totals for the circuit; V = maximal voltage output of the emf source.

When two emf sources are connected in opposition, (positive pole to positive pole) the charge loses energy when passing in the second emf source.

Therefore, if there is more than one emf source in a circuit, the total emf is the sum of the individual emf sources not in opposition reduced by the sum of individual sources in opposition in a given direction.

10.3.1 Kirchoff's Laws and a Multiloop Circuit Problem

Given that the emf of the battery ε = 12 volts and the resistors R_1 = 12 Ω, R_2 = 4.0 Ω, and R_3 = 6.0 Ω, determine the reading in the ammeter (*see Figure* III.B.10.6).

Ignore the internal resistance of the battery.

{*The ammeter will read the current which flows through it which is i_2*}

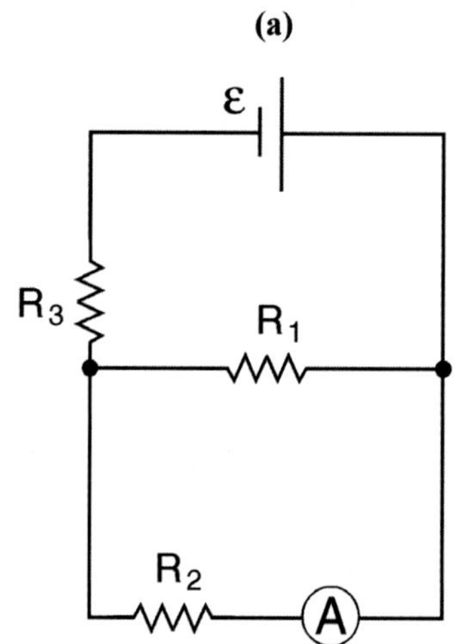

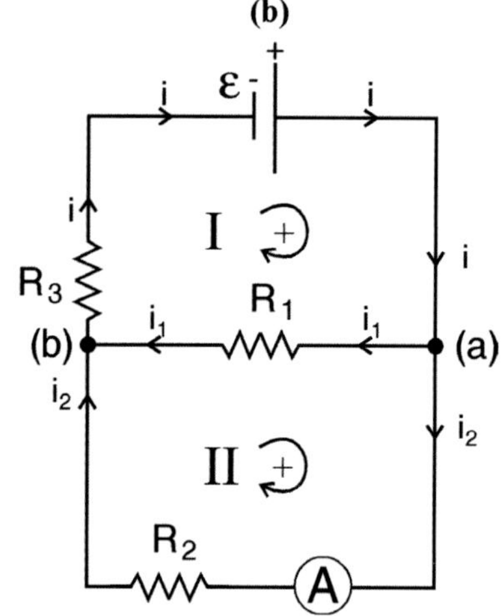

Figure III.B.10.6: A multiloop circuit.
(**a**) The problem as it could be presented; (**b**) the way you should label the diagram. Note that the current emanates from the positive terminal and is the same current i which returns to the emf source.

Kirchoff's Law I (*the junctional theorem*): when different currents arrive at a point (= *junction*, as in points (*a*) and (*b*) in the labelled diagram) the sum of current equals zero.

We can arbitrarily define all current *arriving* at the junction as positive and all current *leaving* as negative.

Kirchoff's Law I	$\Sigma i = 0$ at a junction

Thus at junction (a) $i - i_1 - i_2 = 0$

And for junction (b) $i_1 + i_2 - i = 0$

Both (a) and (b) reduce to equation (c):

$$i = i_1 + i_2$$

Kirchoff's Law II (*the loop theorem*): the sum of voltage changes in one continous loop of a circuit is zero. A single loop circuit is simple since the current is the same in all parts of the loop hence the loop theorem is applied only once.

In a multiloop circuit (loops *I* and *II* in the labelled diagram), there is more than one loop thus the current in general will not be the same in all parts of any given loop. We can arbitrarily define all voltage changes around the loop in the *clockwise* direction as positive and in the *counterclockwise* direction as negative.

Thus if by moving in the clockwise direction we can move from the battery's negative terminal (*low potential*) to its positive terminal (*high potential*), the value of the emf ε is negative.

Kirchoff's Law II	$\Sigma\Delta V = 0$ in a loop

Thus in loop *I* (*recall: V=IR*)

$$i_1R_1 + iR_3 - \varepsilon = 0$$

And in loop II

$$i_2R_2 - i_1R_1 = 0$$

We now have simultaneous equations. There are three unknowns (i, i_1, i_2) and three equations (c, loop *I*, and loop *II*). We need only solve for the current i_2 which runs through the ammeter.

Substitute (c) into loop I

$$i_1R_1 + (i_1 + i_2)R_3 - \varepsilon = 0$$

Thus

$$i_1R_1 + i_1R_3 + i_2R_3 - \varepsilon = 0$$

Substitute i_1 from loop *II* where $i_1 = i_2R_2/R_1$, hence

$$i_2R_2 + i_2R_2R_3/R_1 + i_2R_3 = \varepsilon$$

Begin isolating i_2

$$i_2(R_2 + R_2R_3/R_1 + R_3) = \varepsilon$$

Isolate i_2

$$i_2 = \varepsilon(R_2 + R_2R_3/R_1 + R_3)^{-1}$$

Substitute

$$i_2 = 12[4 + (4)(6)/(12) + 6]^{-1} = 12/12 = 1.0$$ ampere.

10.4 Capacitors and Dielectrics

Capacitors can store and separate charge. Capacitors can be filled with dielectrics which are materials which can increase capacitance. The capacitance (C) is an inherent property of a conductor and is formulated as:

C = charge/electric potential = Q/V = farad = coulomb/volt

The capacitance is the number of coulombs that must be transferred to a conductor to raise its potential by one volt.

The amount of charge that can be stored depends on the shape, size, surroundings and type of the conductor.

The higher the dielectric strength (i.e., the electric field strength at which a substance ceases to be an insulator and becomes a conductor) of the medium, the greater the capacitance of the conductor.

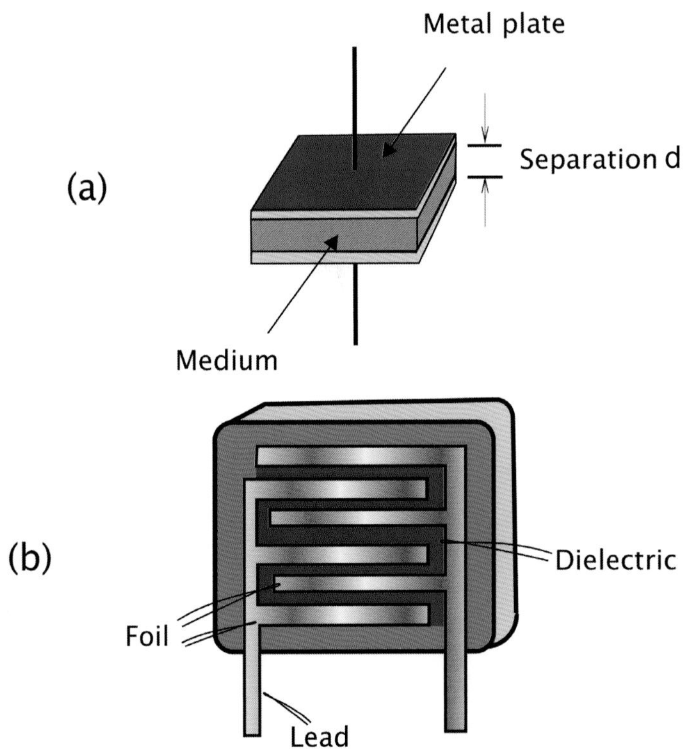

Figure III.B.10.7: (a) Parallel plate capacitor; (b) Ceramic capacitor.

A capacitor is made of two or more conductors with opposite but equal charges placed near each other.

A common example is the parallel plate capacitor. The important formulas for capacitors are:

1) C = Q/V where V = the potential between the plates
2) V = Ed where E = electric field strength, and d = distance between the plates
3) C is directly proportional to the surface area *A* of the plates and inversely proportional to the distance between the plates

$$C = \varepsilon_o A/d$$

for air as a medium between the plates. If the capacitor contains a dielectric, the above equation would by multiplied by the factor κ (= *dielectric constant*) whose value depends on the dielectric being used.

4) The equivalent capacitance C_{eq} for capacitors arranged in series and in parallel is:

$$\text{Series: } 1/C_{eq} = 1/C_1 + 1/C_2 + 1/C_3 \ldots$$

$$\text{Parallel: } C_{eq} = C_1 + C_2 + C_3 \ldots$$

The dielectric substances set up an opposing electric field to that of the capacitor which decreases the net electric field and allows the capacitance of the capacitor to increase ($C = Q/Ed$). The molecules of the dielectric are dipoles which line up in the electric field.

{cf. Fig. III.B.9.5 from PHY 9.1.4 and Fig. III.B.10.8 in this section}

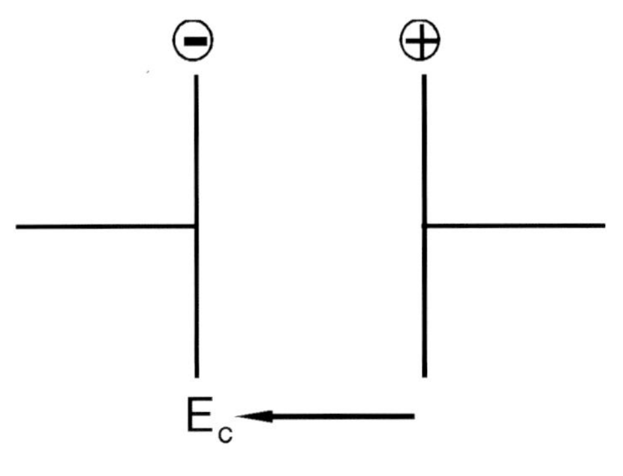

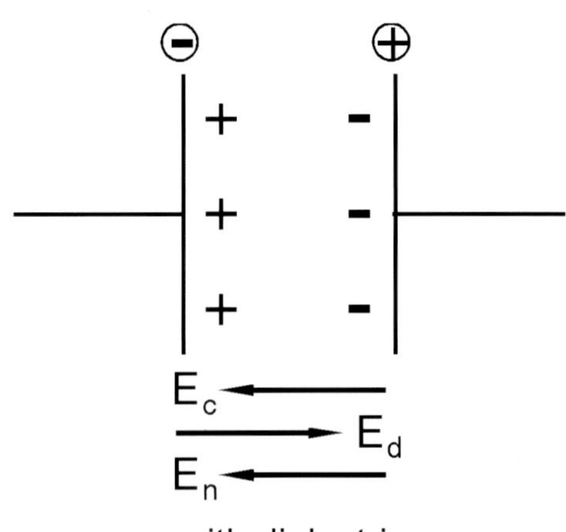

Figure III.B.10.8: Capacitors and dielectrics.
Note that the capacitor is symbolized by two parallel lines of equal length. The electric fields: E_c generated by the capacitor, E_d generated by the dielectric, and E_n is the resultant electric field.

The energy associated with each charged capacitor is:

Potential Energy (PE) = $W = (1/2V)(Q) = 1/2QV$

also

$$W = 1/2(CV)(V) = 1/2CV^2$$

and

$$W = 1/2Q(Q/C) = 1/2Q^2/C.$$

10.5 Root-Mean-Square Current and Voltage

DC (*direct current*) circuits contain a continuous current. Thus calculating power output is quite simple using $P = I^2R = IV$. However, AC (*alternating current*) circuits pulsate; consequently, we must discuss the average power output P_{av} where

$$P_{av} = (I_{rms})^2R = (I_{rms})(V_{rms})$$

which is true for a purely resistive load where the root-mean-square (*rms*) values are determined from their maximal (*max*) values:

$$I_{rms} = I_{max}/\sqrt{2} \quad \text{and} \quad V_{rms} = V_{max}/\sqrt{2}.$$

Thus by introducing the *rms* quantities the equations for DC and AC circuits have the same forms. The OAT only uses DC circuits so you do not need to memorize any equations in this section, and the content is only presented here for perspective.

LIGHT AND GEOMETRICAL OPTICS
Chapter 11

Memorize

* Equations: PHY 11.3, 11.4, 11.5
* Rules for drawing ray diagrams

Understand

* Rules/equations: reflection, refraction, Snell's law
* Dispersion, total internal reflection
* Mirrors, lenses, real/virtual images
* Ray diagrams
* Lens strength, aberration

Importance

3 to 5 out of the 40 PHY

OAT questions are based on content in this chapter (in our estimation).

*Note that between 55% and 85% of the questions in OAT Physics are based on content from 6 chapters: 1, 2, 3, 6, 7 and 11.

Introduction 

To be honest, not every Physics chapter will last you for a lifetime, but this one can! Optometry requires an understanding of optics. We hope this chapter will help both for the OAT test and as a small contribution to your future knowledge as a professional.

Geometrical optics describes the propagation of light in terms of "rays". Rays are then bent at the interface of 2 rather different substances (i.e. air and glass) thus the ray may curve. A basic understanding of the equations and the geometry of light rays is necessary for solving problems in geometrical optics. Discrete questions regarding total internal reflection are frequent.

Additional Resources

Free Online Q&A + Forum

Video: Online or DVD

Flashcards

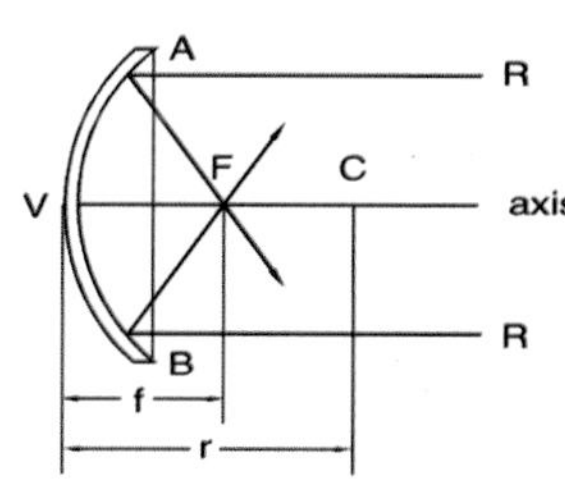

Special Guest

11.1 Visual Spectrum, Color

Geometrical optics is a first approximation of physical optics, which by its wavy nature, is part of the electromagnetic wave theory. The theory of light has a dualistic aspect:

• *particulate*: referring to a packet of energy called a photon when one wants, for example, to explain the photoelectric effect.

• *wavy* : when one wants to explain, for example, light interference and diffraction. Diffraction occurs when waves of light bend at the interface between two different media.

The optics domain of the electromagnetic wave theory corresponds to the following range of wavelengths of the electromagnetic spectrum (expressed in microns 1μ $=10^{-6}\,m$):

$$0.4\mu < \lambda < 0.8\mu$$

or

$$0.4\mu < \textit{visible} < 0.8\mu.$$

See PHY 9.2.4 for the colors in the visual spectrum. See PHY 9.2.4, 11.4 and 12.3 for the speed of light in a vacuum.

11.2 Polarization

An electromagnetic field is described as having at every point of the field two perpendicular vectors: *the electric field vector E* and *the magnetic induction field vector B.*

The electromagnetic wave front is polarized in a straight line when *E* and *B* are fixed at all times. Thus polarized light is light that has waves in only one plane.

11.3 Reflection, Mirrors

Reflection is the process by which light rays (= *imaginary lines drawn perpendicular to the advancing wave fronts*) bounce back into a medium from a surface with another medium (*versus being refracted or absorbed*). The ray that arrives is the *incident* ray while the ray that bounces back is the *reflected* ray. The laws of reflection are:

1) the angle of incidence (I) equals the angle of reflection (R) at the normal (*N*, the line perpendicular to the surface)

2) the I, R, N all lie in the same plane.

After a ray strikes a mirror or a lens it forms an image. A <u>virtual image</u> has no light rays passing through it and cannot be projected upon a screen.

A real image has light rays passing through it and can be projected upon a screen.

Mirrors have a plane surface, like an ordinary household mirror, or a non-plane surface. For a plane mirror, all incident light is reflected in parallel off the mirror and therefore all images seen are virtual, erect, left-right reversed and appear to be just as far (perpendicular distance) behind the mirror as the object is in front of the mirror.

In other words, the object (*o*) and the image (*i*) distances have the same magnitudes but have opposite directions (*i* = -*o*).

Spherical mirrors are non-plane mirrors which may have the reflecting surface convex (*diverges light*) or concave (*converges light*). Note the images formed by a converging mirror (concave) are like those for a converging lens (convex); and diverging mirrors (convex) and a diverging lens (concave) also form similar images. The terminology for spherical mirrors is :

r = radius of curvature
C = center of curvature
F = focal point

V = vertex (center of the mirror itself)
axis = line through C and V
f = focal length (distance from F to V)

i = image distance (distance from V to image along the axis)
o = object distance (distance from V to object along the axis)
AB = linear aperture (cord connecting the ends of the mirror; the larger the aperture, the better the resolution).

As a rule, capital letters refer to a point (*or position)* and small case letters refer to a distance.

Concave (converging)

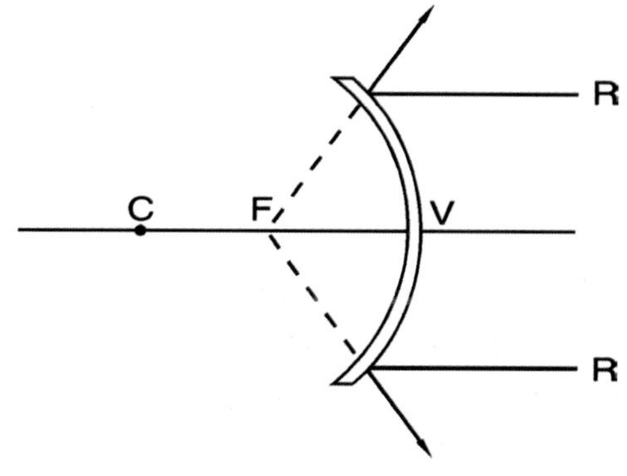

Convex (diverging)

Figure III.B.11.1: Reflection by spherical mirrors. R = the light rays.

With concave (spherical) mirrors the incident light is converged toward the axis. The path of light rays is as follows:

1)
if o < f, then the image is virtual and erect;
if o > f, then the image is real and inverted;
if o = f, then no image is formed;
2)
if o < r, then the image is enlarged in size;
if o > r, then the image is reduced in size;
if o = r, then the image is the same.

The relations are similar to those for a converging lens (convex). With convex (spherical) mirrors, the incident light is diverged from the axis after reflection. It is the backward extension (dotted lines in the diagram) that may pass through the focal point F. The path of light rays are as follows:

1) Incident rays parallel to the axis have backward extension of their reflections through F (*see Figure III.B.11.1*);
2) incident rays along a radius (that would pass C if extended) reflect back along themselves;
3) incident rays that pass through F (if extended) reflect parallel to the axis.

The image formed for a convex mirror is always virtual, erect and smaller than the object. The mirror equation and the derivations from it allow the above relations between object and image to be calculated instead of memorized. The equation is valid for convex and concave mirrors:

$$1/i + 1/o = 1/f$$

$$f = r/2$$

$$M = magnification = -i/o.$$

Convention:
- for i and o, *positive* values mean real, *negative* values mean virtual;
- for r and f, *positive* values mean converging, *negative* values mean diverging;
- for M, a *positive* value means erect, *negative* is inverted;
- for M > 1 the image is enlarged, M < 1 the image is diminished.

11.4 Refraction, Dispersion, Refractive Index, Snell's Law

Refraction is the bending of light as it passes from one transparent medium to another and is caused by the different speeds of light in the two media.

If θ_1 is taken as the angle (to the normal) of the incident light and θ_2 is the angle (to the normal) of the refracted light, where 1 and 2 represent the two different media, the following relations hold (Snell's Law):

where v = velocity and λ = wavelength.

$$\frac{\sin \theta_1}{\sin \theta_2} = \frac{v_1}{v_2} = \frac{n_2}{n_1} = \frac{\lambda_1}{\lambda_2}$$

$$n = \frac{\text{speed of light in vacuum}}{\text{speed of light in medium}} = \frac{c}{v}$$

$c = 3 \times 10^8$ *m/sec* or 181,000 *mi/sec*
n = 1.0 for air, n = 1.33 for H_2O
n = 1.5 for glass (at λ = 589 *nm*)
n = *the refractive index which is a property of the medium*
n_1 = *refractive index of medium 1*
n_2 = *refractive index of medium 2*
N = *normal line to the surface*
S = *surface line, represents the separation between the two media*
I = *incident light*
R = *refracted light*

The speed at which light propagates through transparent materials, such as glass, water or air, is less than c, as you can tell from index of refractions above.

The angle θ is smaller (closer to the normal, e.g. θ_1) in the more optically dense (higher n) medium.

Also the smaller wavelength of the incident light (i.e. toward the violet end), the closer θ_2 is to the normal (i.e. it is smaller than θ_1).

This means longer wavelengths travel faster in a medium than shorter wavelengths (i.e. longer wavelengths are more subject to refraction).

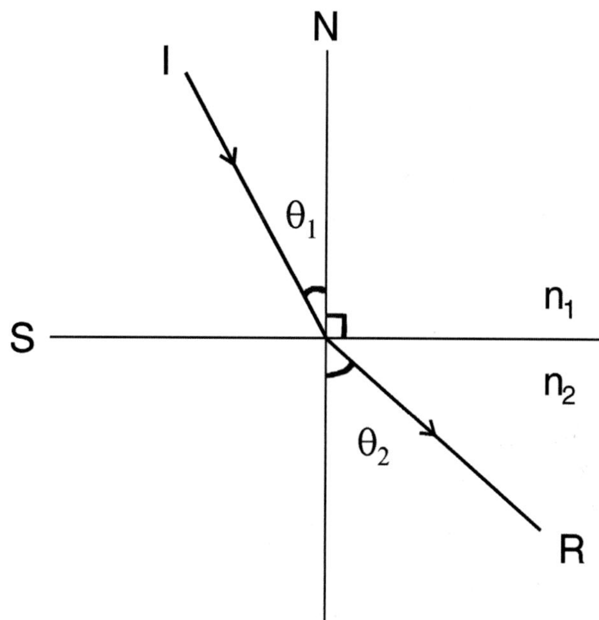

Figure III.B.11.2: Refraction.

This leads to *dispersion* which is the separation of white light (= *all colors together*) into individual colors by this differential refraction. For example, a prism disperses white light. See PHY 9.2.4.

The laws of refraction are:

1) The incident ray, the refracted ray and the normal ray all lie in the same plane.
2) The path of the ray (incident and refracted parts) is reversible.

When light passes from a more optically dense (higher n) medium into a less optically dense medium, there exists an angle of incidence such that the angle of refraction θ_2 is 90°.

This special angle of incidence is called the critical angle θ_c.

This is because when the angle of incidence is less then θ_c refraction occurs. If the angle of incidence is equal to θ_c, then neither refraction nor reflection occur.

And if $\theta_1 > \theta_c$, then total internal reflection (*ray is reflected back into the more optically dense medium*) occurs. The θ_c is found from Snell's Law:

$$n_1 \sin\theta_c = n_2 \sin\theta_2$$

$$\text{and } \theta_2 = 90^0 \Rightarrow \sin\theta_2 = 1$$

$$\text{giving } n_1 \sin\theta_c = n_2 \times 1$$

$$\text{finally } \sin\theta_c = n_2/n_1$$

$$\text{where } n_2 < n_1.$$

When looking at an object under water from above the surface, the object appears closer than it actually is. This is due to refraction. In general:

$$\textit{apparent depth/actual depth} = n_2/n_1$$

where n_2 = the medium of the observer, and n_1 = the medium of the object.

11.5 Thin Lens, Diopters

A lens is a transparent material which refracts light. Converging lenses refract toward the axis, and diverging lenses refract the light away from the axis.

A converging lens is wider at the middle than at the ends, and the diverging lens is thinner at the middle than at the ends.

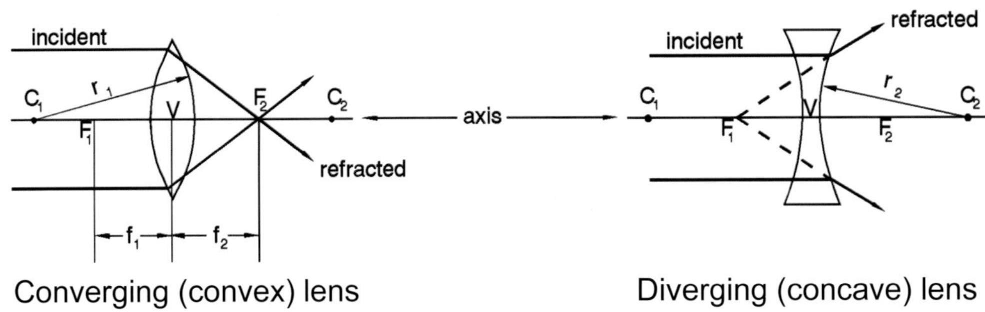

Figure III.B.11.3: Refraction by spherical lenses; *r = the radius of curvature.*

If the surface is convex, r is positive (e.g., r_1). If the surface is concave, r is negative (e.g., r_2).
Subscript 1 refers to the incident side, 2 refers to the refracted side.

C = center of curvature, F = focal point
V = the optical center of the lens or vertex
axis = line through C and V

f = focal length is the distance between V and F
i = image distance (from V to the image)
o = object distance (from V to the object).

The path rays through a lens are:

1) incident rays parallel to the axis refract through F_2 of the converging lens, and appear to come from F_1 of a diverging lens (backward extensions of the refracted ray, see dotted line on diverging diagram);

2) an incident ray through F_1 of a converging lens or through F_2 of a diverging lens (if extended) are refracted parallel to the axis;

3) incident rays through V are deviated (refracted).

For a converging lens (e.g., convex) the image formed depends on the object distance relative to the focal length (f). The relations (note similarity with a converging mirror) are:

1) if $o < f_1$, then image is virtual and erect;
if $o > f_1$, the image is real and inverted;
if $o = f_1$, then no image is formed;

2) if $o < 2f_1$, then the image is enlarged is size;
if $o > 2f_1$, then the image is reduced in size;
if $o = 2f_1$, then the image is the same.
remember $2f_1 = r$.

For a diverging lens (e.g., concave), the image is always virtual, erect and reduced in size as for a diverging mirror.

The above relations can be calculated rather than memorized by use of the lens equation (similar to the mirror equation) and derivations from it,

1) $1/o + 1/i = 1/f$ (lens equation, same as mirror equation)

2) $D = 1/f = (n-1)\,(1/r_1 - 1/r_2)$, (lens maker's equation, n = index of refraction)

A magnifying glass (or "hand lens") is a convex lens that is used to produce a magnified image of an object. The lens is usually mounted in a frame with a handle. You can determine from the preceding rules that, in order to have an image that is erect (upright) and magnified for easier viewing, the object distance must be less than the focal length of the convex lens.

3) diopters (D) = $1/f$ where f is in meters, measures the refractive *power* of the lens; the larger the diopters, the stronger the lens. The diopters has a positive value for a converging lens and a negative value for a diverging lens.

To get the refractive power (D) of lenses in series just add the diopters which can then be converted into focal length:

$$D_T = D_1 + D_2 = 1/f_T \ (T = total).$$

4) Note that you can add only inverses of focal lengths :

$$1/f_T = 1/f_1 + 1/f_2 \ . \ . \ .$$

5) M = *Magnification* = $-i/o = M_1 M_2$ for lenses in series.

See BIO 1.5 for a description of light microscopy.

Convention:

- for i and o, positive values mean real, negative values mean virtual;
- for r and f, positive values mean converging, negative values mean diverging;
- for M, a positive value means erect, negative is inverted.

The lens equation holds only for thin lenses (the thickness is small relative to other dimensions). For combination of lenses not in contact with each other, the image is found for the first lens (nearer the object) and then this image is used as the object of the second lens to find the image formed by it.

It should be noted that since concave lenses are concave on both sides they are sometimes called *biconcave.* Likewise, convex lenses may be called *biconvex.*

11.5.1 Lens Aberrations

In practice, the images formed by various refracting surfaces, as described in the previous section, fall short of theoretical perfection. Imperfections of image formation are due to several mechanisms or *aberrations.*

For example a nick or cut in a convex lens might create a microscopic area of concavity. Thus the light ray which strikes the aberration diverges instead of converging. Therefore the image will be less sharp or clear as the number or sizes of the aberrations increase.

MODERN PHYSICS

Chapter 12

Memorize

uation relating energy and mass; half-life
pha, beta, gamma particles
uation for maximum number of electrons
a shell
uation relating energy to frequency
uation for the total energy of the electrons
in atom

Understand

* Basic atomic structure, amu
* Fission, fusion; the Bohr model of the atom
* Problem solving for half-life
* Quantized energy levels for electrons
* Fluorescence

Importance

0 to 2 out of the 40 PHY

OAT questions are based on content in this chapter (in our estimation).

*Note that between 55% and 85% of the questions in OAT Physics are based on content from 6 chapters: 1, 2, 3, 6, 7 and 11.

Introduction 

"Modern Physics" is one of the topics that you must cover for OAT Physics and it really means physics "after" Newton. It implies that classical descriptions are lacking in some way, and that an accurate, "modern" description of reality is needed. Small velocities and large distances is usually dealt with using classical Newtonian mechanics which we have already reviewed. Modern physics often deals with extreme conditions like distances comparable to atoms and velocities that compare to the speed of light (3×10^8 m/s). You will find that GS General Chemistry Chapter 11 is a more detailed review of this topic but that is because less detail is required for OAT Physics.

Additional Resources

Free Online Q&A + Forum

Video: Online or DVD

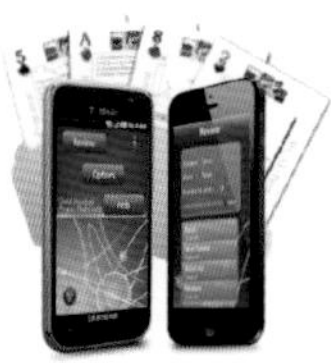

Flashcards

12.1 Protons, Neutrons, Electrons

Only recently, with high resolution electron microscopes, have large atoms been visualized. However, for years their existence and properties have been inferred by experiments. Experimental work on gas discharge effects suggested that an atom is not a single entity but is itself composed of smaller particles. These were termed elementary particles. The atom appears as a small solar system with a heavy nucleus composed of positive particles and neutral particles: *protons* and *neutrons.* Around this nucleus, there are clouds of negatively charged particles, called *electrons.* The mass of a neutron is slightly more than that of a proton (both ≈ 1.7×10^{-24} g); the mass of the electron is considerably less (9.1×10^{-28} g).

Since an atom is electrically neutral, the negative charge carried by the electrons must be equal in magnitude (but opposite in sign) to the positive charge carried by the protons.

Experiments with electrostatic charges have shown that opposite charges attract, so it can be considered that electrostatic forces hold an atom together. The difference between various atoms is therefore determined by their *composition.*

A hydrogen atom consists of one proton and one electron; a helium atom of two protons, two neutrons and two electrons. They are shown in diagram form in Figure III.B.12.1.

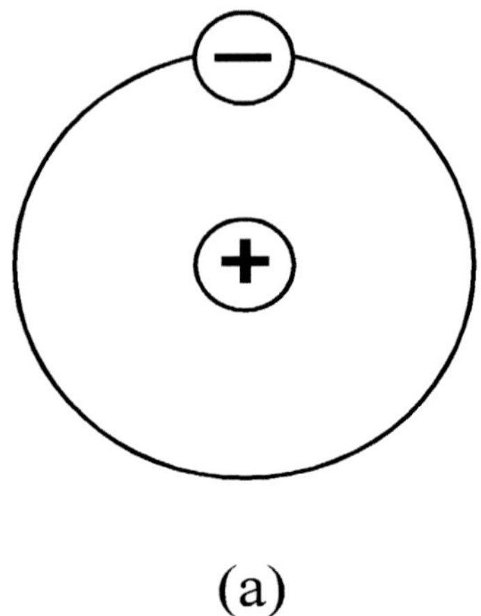

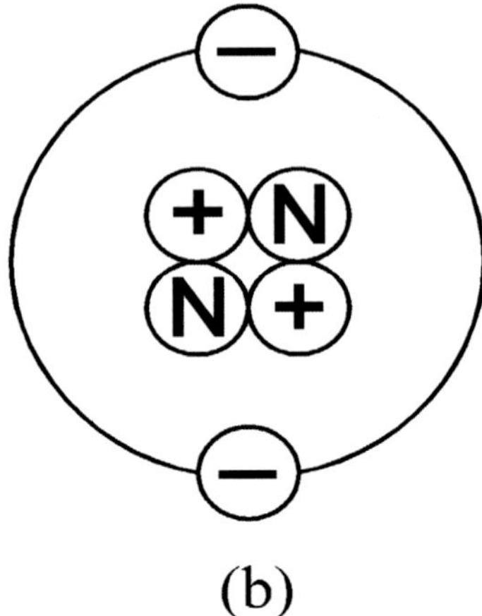

Figure III.B.12.1: Atomic structure simplified: (a) hydrogen atom; (b) helium atom.

12.2 Isotopes, Atomic Number, Atomic Weight

A proton has a mass of 1 a.m.u. (*atomic mass unit*) and a charge of +1, whereas, a neutron has a mass of 1 a.m.u. and no charge. The *atomic number* (*AN*) of an atom is the number of protons in the nucleus.

An *element* is a group of atoms with the same AN. *Isotopes* are elements which have the same AN (= protons) but different numbers of neutrons. It is the number of protons that distinguishes elements from each other.

The *mass number* (*MN*) of an atom is the number of protons and neutrons in an atom. The *atomic weight* (*AW*) is the weighted average of all naturally occurring isotopes of an element.

It is also important to note that as the number of protons distinguishes *elements* from each other, it is their electronic configuration (CHM 2.1, 2.2, 2.3) that determines their *reactivity*.

12.3 Nuclear Forces, Nuclear Binding Energy, Stability, Radioactivity

Coulomb repulsive force (between protons) in the nuclei are overcome by nuclear forces. The nuclear force is a non-electrical type of force that binds nuclei together and is equal for protons and neutrons. The nuclear binding energy (E_b) is a result of the relation between energy and mass changes associated with nuclear reactions,

$$\Delta E = \Delta mc^2$$

in ergs in the CGS system, i.e. m = grams and c = cm/sec; ΔE = energy released or absorbed; Δ*m* = mass lost or gained, respectively; c = velocity of light = 3.0×10^{10} cm/sec.

Conversions:

1 *gram* = 9×10^{20} *ergs*

1 *a.m.u.* = 931.4 *MeV* (*Mev* = 10^6 electron volts)

1 *a.m.u.* = 1/12 the mass of ${}_6C^{12}$.

The preceding equation is a statement of the law of conservation of mass and energy.The value of E_b depends upon the mass number (MN) as follows, (*see Figure III.B.12.2*):

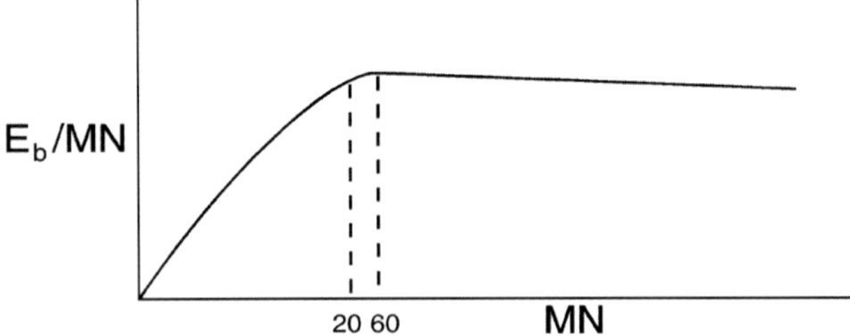

Figure III.B.12.2: Binding Energy per Nucleus. *E_b/MN = binding energy per nucleus; this is the energy released by the formation of a nucleus.*

The peak E_b/MN is at MN=60. Also, E_b/MN is relatively constant after MN=20. Fission is when a nucleus splits into smaller nuclei. Fusion is when smaller nuclei combine to form a larger nucleus. Energy is released from a nuclear reaction when nuclei with MN >> 60 undergo fission or nuclei with MN << 60 undergo fusion.

Not all combinations of protons are stable. The most stable nuclei are those with an even number of protons and an even number of neutrons. The least stable nuclei are those with an odd number of protons and an odd number of neutrons. Also, as the atomic number (AN) increases, there are more neutrons (N) needed for the nuclei to be stable.

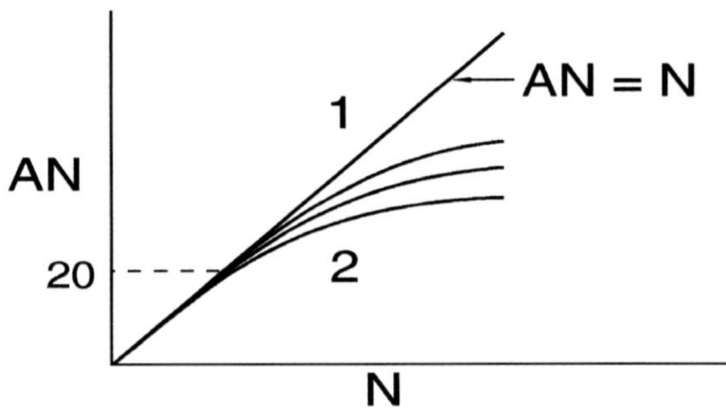

Figure III.B.12.3: Stability of Atoms.
AN = atomic number and N = number of neutrons.

Up to AN = 20 (Calcium) the number of protons is equal to the number of neutrons, after this there are more neutrons. If an atom is in region #1 in Figure III.B.12.3, it has too many protons or too few neutrons and must decrease its protons or increase its neutrons to become stable. The reverse is true for region #2. All nuclei after AN = 84 (Polonium) are unstable.

Unstable nuclei become stable by fission to smaller nuclei or by absorption or emission of small particles. Spontaneous fission is rare. Spontaneous radioactivity (emission of particles) is common. The common particles are:

1) alpha (α) particle = ${}_{2}He^{4}$ (helium nucleus);

2) beta (β) particle = ${}_{-1}e^{0}$ (an electron);

3) a positron ${}_{+1}e^{0}$ (same mass as an electron but opposite charge);

4) gamma (γ) ray = no mass and no charge, just electromagnetic energy;

5) orbital electron capture - nucleus takes electrons from K shell and converts a proton to a neutron. If there is a flux of particles such as neutrons (${}_{0}n^{1}$), the nucleus can absorb these also.

12.4 Nuclear Reaction, Radioactive Decay, Half-Life

Nuclear reactions are reactions in which changes in nuclear composition occur. An example of a nuclear reaction which involves uranium and hydrogen:

$${}_{92}U^{238} + {}_{1}H^{2} \longrightarrow {}_{93}Np^{238} + 2\,{}_{0}n^{1}$$

for ${}_{92}U^{238}$: 238 = mass number, 92 = atomic number. The sum of the lower (or higher) numbers on one side of the equation equals the sum of the lower (or higher) numbers on the other side of the equation. Another way of writing the preceding reaction is: ${}_{92}U^{238}({}_{1}H^{2}, 2\,{}_{0}n^{1}){}_{93}Np^{238}$. {# neutrons (i.e. ${}_{92}U^{238}$)= superscript (238) - subscript (92) = 146}

Spontaneous radioactive decay is a first order process. This means that the rate of decay is *directly* proportional to the amount of material present:

$$\Delta m/\Delta t = \text{rate of decay}$$

where Δm = change in mass, Δt = change in time.

The preceding relation is equalized by adding a proportionality constant called the decay constant (k) as follows,

$$\Delta m/\Delta t = -km.$$

The minus sign indicates that the mass is decreasing. Also, $k = -(\Delta m/m)/\Delta t$ = fraction of the mass that decays with time.

The *half-life* $(T_{1/2})$ of a radioactive atom is the time required for one half of it to disintegrate. The half-life is related to k as follows,

$$T_{1/2} = 0.693/k.$$

If the number of half-lifes n are known we can calculate the percentage of a pure radioactive sample left after undergoing decay since the fraction remaining = $(1/2)^n$.

For example, given a pure radioactive substance X with $T_{1/2}$ = 9 years, calculating the percentage of substance X after 27 years is quite simple,

$$27 = 3 \times 9 = 3\ T_{1/2}$$

Thus

$$n = 3,\ (1/2)^n = (1/2)^3 = 1/8 \text{ or } 13\%.$$

After 27 years of disintegration, 13% of pure substance X remains. {Similarly, note that *doubling time* is given by $(2)^n$; *see* BIO 2.2}

12.5 Quantized Energy Levels For Electrons, Emission Spectrum

Work by Bohr and others in the early part of the present century demonstrated that the electron orbits are arranged in shells, and that each shell has a defined maximum number of electrons it can contain.

For example, the first shell can contain two electrons, the second eight electrons (*see* CHM 2.1, 2.2). The maximum number of electrons in each shell is given by:

$$N_{electrons} = 2n^2$$

$N_{electrons}$ designates the number of electrons in shell n.

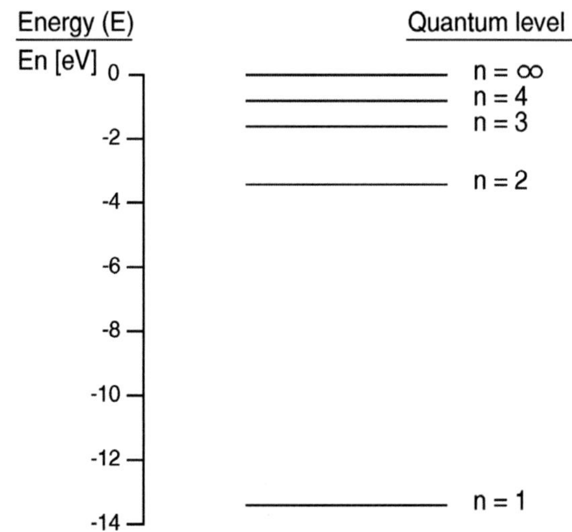

Figure III.B.12.4: Energy levels. The energy E_n in each shell n is measured in electron volts.

The state of each electron is determined by the four quantum numbers:

• *principal quantum number n* determines the number of shells, possible values are: 1 (K), 2 (L), 3 (M), etc...
• *angular momentum quantum number l*, determines the subshell, possible values are: 0 (s), 1 (p), 2 (d), 3 (f), n-1, etc...
• *magnetic momentum quantum number* m_l, possible values are: $\pm l, \ldots, 0$
• *spin quantum number* m_s, determines the direction of rotation of the electron, possible values are: ±1/2.

Chemical reactions and electrical effects are all concerned with the behavior of electrons in the outer shell of any particular atom. If a shell is full, for example, the atom is unlikely to react with any other atom and is, in fact, one of the noble (inert) gases such as helium.

The energy that an electron contains is not continuous over the entire range of possible energy. Rather, electrons in a atom may contain only discrete energies as they occupy certain orbits or shells. Electrons of each atom are restricted to these discrete energy levels. These levels have an energy below zero.

This means energy is released when an electron moves from infinity into these energy levels.

If there is one electron in an atom, its ground state is n = 1, the lowest energy level available. Any other energy level, n = 2, n = 3, etc., is considered an excited state for that electron. The difference in energy (*E*) between the levels gives the absorbed (or emitted) energy when an electron moves to a higher orbit (or lower orbit, respectively) and therefore, the frequency (*f*) of light necessary to cause excitation.

$$E_2 - E_1 = hf$$

where E_1 = energy level one, E_2 = energy level two, h = planck's constant, and f = the frequency of light absorbed or emitted.

Therefore, if light is passed through a substance (e.g., gas), certain wavelengths will be absorbed, which correspond to the energy needed for the electron transition. An *absorption* spectrum will result that has dark lines against a light background. Multiple lines result because there are possible transitions from all quantum levels occupied by electrons to any unoccupied levels.

An *emission* spectrum results when an electron is excited to a higher level by another particle or by an electric discharge, for example. Then, as the electron falls from the excited state to lower states, light is emitted that has a wavelength (which is related to frequency) corresponding to the energy difference between the levels since: $E_1 - E_2 = hf$.

The resulting spectrum will have light lines against a dark background. The absorption and emission spectrums should have the same number of lines but often will not. This is because in the absorption spectrum, there is a rapid radiation of the absorbed light in all directions, and transitions are generally from the ground state initially.

These factors result in fewer lines in the absorption than in the emission spectrum.

The total energy of the electrons in an atom can be given by:

$$E_{total} = E_{emission} \text{ (or } E_{ionization}) + KE$$

12.6 Fluorescence

Fluorescence is an emission process that occurs after light absorption excites electrons to higher electronic and vibrational levels. The electrons spontaneously lose excited vibrational energy to the electronic states. There are certain molecular types that possess this property, e.g., some amino acids (tryptophan).

The fluorescence process is as follows:

- step 1 - absorption of light;
- step 2 - spontaneous deactivation of vibrational levels to zero vibrational level for electronic state;
- step 3 - fluorescence with light emission (longer wavelength than absorption).

Figure III.B.12.5 shows diagrammatically the steps described above. Step 2 which is not shown in the figure is the intermediate step between light absorption and light emission.

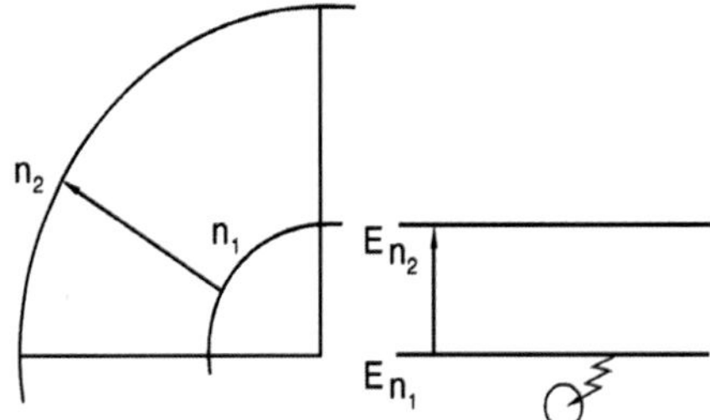

Step 1: light absorption

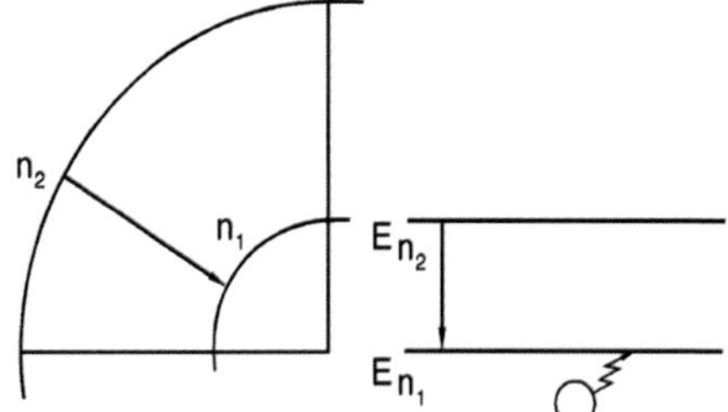

Step 3: light emission

Figure III.B.12.5: The fluorescence process. Represented is an atom with shells n_1, n_2 and their respective energy levels E_n.

www.oatbooks.com

Gold Standard OAT PRACTICE TEST 2013-2014

GS-1

THE GOLD STANDARD OAT

Introduction

Prior to attempting this practice test, section 2.3 from this book - Understanding the OAT - should be reviewed.

The following full length practice Gold Standard (GS) OAT is designed to challenge you and to teach you at a whole new level. You will need to take the tools you have learned and build new structures and create new paths to solving problems. **Please consider using your computer's on screen default calculator (with the same four basic functions described in QR 1.2).** The problems will range from very simple to very challenging, but they will all be very helpful for your OAT preparation. Do not be afraid of making mistakes - it is part of the learning process. The student who makes the most mistakes has the greatest learning potential!

Timing is critical. Many students do not complete various sections of the exam. If you decide to do a few problems from time to time then you have never practiced for the OAT. An almost five hours exam is a rigorous event. It requires practice that simulates exam conditions. An important aspect of the latter is timing. Practice according to the prescribed exam schedule.

Upon finishing the exam, the next challenge is the equally important thorough review. Mistakes, and even correct answers for which some doubt existed, should be examined without time restrictions for maximum learning benefit.

You are not alone! You have access to a free interactive forum at oatbooks.com/forum so you can discuss any question from your practice exam with other students or even with the authors. You can share your experience, learn, complain, contribute or gain some new tips.

Optometry Admission Test	
Survey of Natural Sciences	90 minutes
Reading Comprehension Test	50 minutes
Physics Test	50 minutes
Quantitative Reasoning Test	45 minutes

Notice about RC: We have kept the longer version of RC in this paper version of GS-1 with 50 questions in 60 minutes. If you want to do the shorter version with 40 questions in 50 minutes (which is a bit easier because of shorter passages as well), go online to oatbooks.com and you can do the shorter version for free (original book owner only).

Preparing the Tests

You will need a watch or timer for this practice test. During the actual administration, a basic calculator will be provided on-screen during the Quantitative Reasoning section. Any calculations or notations can also be made on the laminated note boards using fine-tip permanent markers, both of which will be provided by the testing center upon request (scrap paper is not permitted).

These exam sheets are perforated so that you can tear your sheets out gently and systematically. Place the front of the book flat on a table and open to the pages just after the full length exam and Answer Documents. Tear along the perforation.

The page numbers reflect the exam section to which the page belongs. For example, GS-NAT SCI-3 is the 3rd page of the Natural Sciences Test of the GS OAT. Begin pulling out pages while paying close attention to the page numbers. Once the complete exam is removed, you will require a stapler. Now you can use the Answer Document.

PERIODIC TABLE OF THE ELEMENTS

1 H 1.008																	2 He 4.003
3 Li 6.941	4 Be 9.012											5 B 10.81	6 C 12.011	7 N 14.007	8 O 15.999	9 F 18.998	10 Ne 20.179
11 Na 22.990	12 Mg 24.305											13 Al 26.982	14 Si 28.086	15 P 30.974	16 S 32.06	17 Cl 35.453	18 Ar 39.948
19 K 39.098	20 Ca 40.08	21 Sc 44.956	22 Ti 47.90	23 V 50.942	24 Cr 51.996	25 Mn 54.938	26 Fe 55.847	27 Co 58.933	28 Ni 58.70	29 Cu 63.546	30 Zn 65.38	31 Ga 69.72	32 Ge 72.59	33 As 74.922	34 Se 78.96	35 Br 79.904	36 Kr 83.80
37 Rb 85.468	38 Sr 87.62	39 Y 88.906	40 Zr 91.22	41 Nb 92.906	42 Mo 95.94	43 Tc (98)	44 Ru 101.07	45 Rh 102.906	46 Pd 106.4	47 Ag 107.868	48 Cd 112.41	49 In 114.82	50 Sn 118.69	51 Sb 121.75	52 Te 127.60	53 I 126.905	54 Xe 131.30
55 Cs 132.905	56 Ba 137.33	57 *La 138.906	72 Hf 178.49	73 Ta 180.948	74 W 183.85	75 Re 186.207	76 Os 190.2	77 Ir 192.22	78 Pt 195.09	79 Au 196.967	80 Hg 200.59	81 Tl 204.37	82 Pb 207.2	83 Bi 208.980	84 Po (209)	85 At (210)	86 Rn (222)
87 Fr (223)	88 Ra 226.025	89 **Ac 227.028	104 Unq (261)	105 Unp (262)	106 Unh (263)												

*	58 Ce 140.12	59 Pr 140.908	60 Nd 144.24	61 Pm (145)	62 Sm 150.4	63 Eu 151.96	64 Gd 157.25	65 Tb 158.925	66 Dy 162.50	67 Ho 164.930	68 Er 167.26	69 Tm 168.934	70 Yb 173.04	71 Lu 174.967
**	90 Th 232.038	91 Pa 231.036	92 U 238.029	93 Np 237.048	94 Pu (244)	95 Am (243)	96 Cm (247)	97 Bk (247)	98 Cf (251)	99 Es (254)	100 Fm (257)	101 Md (258)	102 No (259)	103 Lr (260)

Survey of the Natural Sciences

Time limit: 90 minutes

This GS-1 exam has 100 multiple choice questions.
Biology: 1-40; General Chemistry: 41-70; and Organic Chemistry: 71-100

Please do not begin until your timer is ready.

1. Which of the following represents a genetic mutation in which bases are added or deleted in numbers other than multiples of three?

A. Inversion
B. Duplication
C. Frame shift
D. Translocation
E. Point mutation

2. All of the following are functions of the human spleen EXCEPT one. Which one is the EXCEPTION?

A. Produces platelets.
B. Filters damaged red blood cells.
C. Filters bacteria.
D. Stores erythrocytes.
E. Stores antigen presenting cells.

3. Which of the following statements is true concerning inspiration?

A. The internal pressure is positive with respect to the atmosphere.
B. The diaphragm and accessory muscles relax.
C. It is a passive process.
D. The thoracic cage moves inward, while the diaphragm moves downward.
E. The phrenic nerve is stimulated.

4. PKU disease is a recessive autosomal genetic condition. DNA isolated from parents reacted with normal specific and abnormal specific probes in the following manner:

	normal specific	abnormal specific
mother	reaction	reaction
father	no reaction	reaction

A male offspring of the couple represented in the table above could potentially be which of the following?
I. PKU disease positive
II. PKU disease negative, PKU gene carrier
III. PKU disease negative, PKU gene non-carrier

A. I only
B. I and II only
C. I and III only
D. II and III only
E. I, II and III

5. A conjoint and open vascular bundle will be observed in the transverse section of which of the following?

A. Monocot twig
B. Monocot root
C. Monocot stem
D. Dicot root
E. Dicot stem

6. Match and choose the correct option:

I. Cuticle	i. guard cells
II. Bulliform cells	ii. single layer
III. Stomata	iii. waxy layer
IV. Epidermis	iv. empty colorless cell

A. I-i, II-iv, III-iii, IV-ii
B. I-i, II-ii, III-iii, IV-iv
C. I-iii, II-iv, III-i, IV-ii
D. I-iii, II-ii, III-i, IV-iv
E. I-iii, II-ii, III-iv, IV-i

7. The mechanism by which blastomeres differentiate into germ cells is referred to as:

A. induction.
B. determination.
C. specialization.
D. differentiation.
E. neurulation.

8. Prokaryotic organisms make up the:

A. Protists.
B. Protists and Eubacteria.
C. Archaebacteria and Protists.
D. Archaebacteria, Eubacteria, and Protists.
E. Eubacteria and Archaebacteria.

9. Calcitonin lowers calcium levels in blood by inhibiting the action of:

A. osteoclasts.
B. osteoblasts.
C. osteocytes.
D. osteons.
E. osteomeres.

10. All of the following are characteristics of most enzymes EXCEPT one. Which one is the EXCEPTION?

A. They affect the equilibrium of reaction.
B. They affect the rate of reaction.
C. They are specific to particular substrates.
D. They lower the energy of activation of a chemical reaction.
E. They are composed of simple or complex proteins.

11. Implantation of the developing embryo into the uterine lining occurs during:

A. fertilization.
B. cleavage.
C. blastulation.
D. gastrulation.
E. neurulation.

12. The antarctic tundra:

A. is characterized by deciduous needleleaf trees.
B. is characterized by evergreen needleleaf trees.
C. is divided by the tree line.
D. contains numerous species of reptiles.
E. is unforested because it is both cold and dry.

13. In which of the following blood vessels would pO_2 be the highest?

A. Hepatic portal system
B. Left pulmonary artery
C. Renal vein
D. Inferior vena cava
E. Pulmonary vein

14. Filtration of plasma occurs in the Bowman's capsule of the nephron. What is the driving force for this initial filtration step in the kidney?

A. An ionic gradient formed by a countercurrent multiplier system
B. Blood pressure
C. A chemiosmotic gradient across the semipermeable tubular membrane
D. Contraction of smooth muscles surrounding the Bowman's capsule
E. Vacuoles in the podocytes

15. Consider the following table.

Table 1: Experimental data presenting the rates of protein degradation (Rxn rate) with varying concentration of trypsin and the enzyme inhibitor inhibitin.

Trial#	[trypsin] mmol/L	Rxn rate $mmol(Ls)^{-1}$	[inhibitin] mmol/L
1	5.6×10^{-4}	5.40	0
2	7.4×10^{-3}	5.45	3.6×10^{-6}
3	5.6×10^{-4}	1.98	7.2×10^{-6}
4	7.4×10^{-3}	2.02	1.1×10^{-5}
5	8.3×10^{-5}	0.04	1.4×10^{-5}

On statistical analysis, researchers confirmed that there was no significant difference between the rate of reaction determined for Trial # 1 and Trial # 2. The most likely explanation is:

A. the concentration of inhibitin was 0.
B. the concentration of inhibitin was significantly elevated.
C. the concentration of trypsin was significantly elevated.
D. the concentration of trypsin was significantly decreased.
E. the concentration of trypsin was 0.

16. Which of the following statements could be used to correctly describe the overall polymerase chain reaction (PCR)?

A. It is an anabolic reaction that breaks down new DNA strands.
B. It is an anabolic reaction that synthesizes new DNA strands.
C. It is a catabolic reaction that breaks down new DNA strands.
D. It is a catabolic reaction that synthesizes new DNA strands.
E. It is neither anabolic nor catabolic.

17. The medication AZT is an analog of thymidine which has an $-N_3$ group in the place of an $-OH$ at the 3' position of the sugar. Thus AZT will act to disrupt which process of the retrovirus HIV?

A. Transcription
B. Reverse transcription
C. Translation
D. Endocytosis
E. Exocytosis

18. The genetic basis of human blood types includes recessive (Z^O) and codominant alleles (Z^A and Z^B). Determine which of the following genotypes produce blood that agglutinates when combined with type O serum.

I. Z^AZ^A
II. Z^AZ^B
III. Z^AZ^O

A. I only
B. III only
C. I and II only
D. I and III only
E. I, II and III

19. Which of the following structures of the ear is responsible for maintaining a sense of equilibrium?

A. The organ of Corti
B. The vestibulo-cochlear apparatus
C. The semicircular canals
D. The Eustachian tube
E. The ossicles

20. Plasmodesmata:

A. are considered to be the desmosomes of plant cells.
B. connect to intermediate fibers of the cytoskeleton.
C. encircle cells like a belt.
D. connect actin fibers of one cell to the extracellular matrix of another.
E. connect the cytoplasm of one plant cell to that of another.

21. Exocytosis is directly associated with all of the following EXCEPT one. Which one is the EXCEPTION?

A. Porosomes
B. Chloride and calcium channels
C. Clathrin-coated vesicles
D. "Kiss-and-run" fusion
E. SNARE proteins

22. Which of the following observations would support the hypothesis that the movement of dopamine into a cell is mediated by a transporter protein in the plasma membrane?

A. A hypotonic cell bathed in dopamine leads to increased dopamine uptake by the cell.
B. A cell bathed in an isotonic dopamine solution has no net uptake of dopamine.
C. The rate of dopamine influx increases proportionally with the extracellular dopamine concentration.
D. The rate of dopamine influx reaches a plateau, despite increasing extracellular concentration.
E. Cyclic AMP concentration remains steady.

23. The early earth was a harsh environment. The present day organisms that could possibly have survived that type of environment are:

A. eubacteria.
B. protobionts.
C. blue-green algae.
D. archeabacteria.
E. eukaryotic organisms.

24. A time versus population-size graph with exponential growth may be graphed with what shaped curve?

A. S
B. k
C. C
D. J
E. N

25. Consider the diagram below.

Prot = proteins which are the only ions which cannot cross the membrane *m*. Thus the membrane is semipermeable.

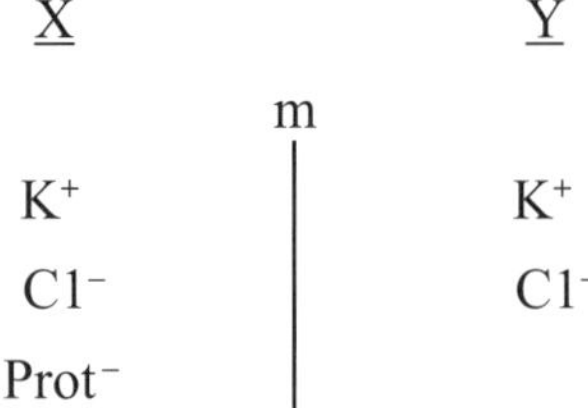

Assuming that the total concentrations of anions and cations on both sides of the membrane are initially equal, how would Cl^- ions be expected to act?

A. They would not move at all because no electro chemical gradient exists.
B. They would diffuse across the membrane from Y to X along its chemical gradient.
C. They would diffuse across the membrane from X to Y along the electrochemical gradient.
D. They would diffuse across the membrane from Y to X along its electrical gradient.
E. Cl^- ions from both sides of the membrane would diffuse across the membrane, but would stop net movement once the electrochemical gradient no longer existed.

26. After sexual maturation, the primordial germ cells in the testes are initially called:

A. spermatids and are haploid.
B. primary spermatocytes and are diploid.
C. primary spermatocytes and are haploid.
D. spermatogonia and are diploid.
E. spermatogonia and are haploid.

27. In which order of priority are the human body's nutrient stores utilized for energy production during fasting and subsequent starvation?

A. Glycogen, protein, fat
B. Fat, glycogen, protein
C. Glycogen, fat, protein
D. Fat, protein, glycogen
E. Protein, fat, glycogen

28. Which of the following hormones, found in the human menstrual cycle, are produced in the ovary?

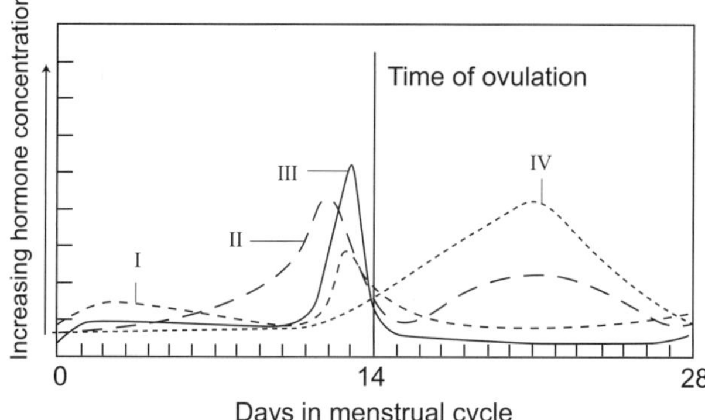

A. I and II
B. II and III
C. III and IV
D. I and III
E. II and IV

29. The K_m is the substrate concentration at which an enzyme-catalyzed reaction occurs at half its maximal velocity, $V_{max}/2$. What effect would a competitive reversible inhibitor be expected to have on V_{max} and K_m?

A. V_{max} would stay the same, but K_m would decrease.
B. V_{max} would stay the same, but K_m would increase.
C. K_m would stay the same, but V_{max} would decrease.
D. Both V_{max} and K_m would decrease.
E. Both V_{max} and K_m would increase.

30. Down's syndrome, in which 2N = 47, is one of the most common forms of chromosomal abnormalities. This results from the failure of one pair of homologous chromosomes to separate during meiosis. During which of the meiotic phases would this likely occur?

A. Metaphase I
B. Metaphase II
C. Anaphase I
D. Anaphase II
E. Telophase

31. What sequence of bases would tRNA have, in order to recognize the mRNA codon CAG?

A. GTC
B. UAG
C. CAG
D. GCU
E. GUC

32. The difference between the bacterium Lactobacillus and the eukaryote Trichomonas is that Lactobacillus has no:

A. ribosomes.
B. cell wall.
C. plasma membrane.
D. lysosomes.
E. RNA.

33. Bile, a chemical which emulsifies fat, is produced by the:

A. liver.
B. gallbladder.
C. common bile duct.
D. pancreas.
E. duodenum.

34. During the dark phase of photosynthesis, the molecule that is oxidized and the molecule that is reduced, respectively, are:

A. NADP and water.
B. water and CO_2.
C. water and NADP.
D. $NADPH_2$ and CO_2.
E. CO_2 and water.

35. Which of the following are LEAST appropriately matched?

A. Reduction - gain of electrons
B. Anabolic reactions - expend energy
C. Exergonic reaction-catabolism
D. Endergonic reaction - anabolism
E. Activation energy - entropy

36. At what level(s) of protein structure could you expect to find hydrogen bonds?

A. Primary
B. Secondary
C. Tertiary
D. Only A and B
E. Only B and C

37. In cardiovascular physiology, ejection fraction (EF) represents which of the following?

A. Blood pressure / heart rate
B. Stroke volume × heart rate
C. Stroke volume / heart rate
D. Stroke volume × end diastolic volume
E. Stroke volume / end diastolic volume

38. Assuming that parasites and their hosts coevolve in an "arms race," we might deduce that the parasite is "ahead" if local populations are more capable of attacking the host population with which they are associated than other populations. Whereas the host may be "ahead" if local populations are more resistant to the local parasite than to other populations of the parasite. The preceding suggests that one result of interspecific interactions might be:

A. genetic drift within sympatric populations.
B. genetic drift within allopatric populations.
C. genetic mutations within sympatric populations.
D. genetic mutations within allopatric populations.
E. genetic mutations within migrating populations.

39. Each of the following statements are true regarding evidence consistent with the endosymbiotic theory EXCEPT one. Which one is the EXCEPTION?

A. Mitochondria and chloroplasts reproduce independently of their eukaryotic host cell.
B. Mitochondria and chloroplasts possess their unique DNA which is circular like prokaryotic DNA.
C. The thylakoid membranes of chloroplasts resemble the photosynthetic membranes of cyanobacteria.
D. The ribosomes of mitochondria and chloroplasts resemble those of prokaryotes in both size and sequence.
E. Animal cells do not have chloroplasts and plant cells do not have mitochondria.

40. The wrist bones are also referred to as which of the following?

A. Carpals
B. Metacarpals
C. Phalanges
D. Tarsals
E. Metatarsals

41. Using the information in the table, calculate the enthalpy change for the following process:

$$C_{graphite} \rightarrow C_{diamond}$$

Table 1

	Graphite	Diamond
Enthalpy of combustion to yield oxide (ΔH_c) kJ mol^{-1}	-393.3	-395.1

A. 1.8 kJ mol^{-1}.
B. −1.8 kJ mol^{-1}.
C. 1.0 kJ mol^{-1}.
D. −1.0 kJ mol^{-1}.
E. 0 kJ mol^{-1}.

42. H_2SO_3 acts as a Lewis acid probably because sulfurous acid:

A. is a proton donor.
B. donates a pair of electrons from another species.
C. reacts with NaOH which is a strong base.
D. possesses oxygen atoms.
E. accepts a pair of electrons from another species.

43. What is the percent by mass of oxygen in sulfurous acid (H_2SO_3)?

A. 31.9%
B. 19.7%
C. 39.0%
D. 58.5%
E. 68.8%

44. 20 mL of 0.05 M Mg^{2+} in solution is desired. It is attempted to achieve this by adding 5 mL of 0.005 M $MgCl_2$ and 15 mL of $Mg_3(PO_4)_2$. What is the concentration of $Mg_3(PO_4)_2$?

A. $$\frac{(0.015)}{[(.05)(.02)-(.005)(.005)]}$$

B. $$(0.015)[(0.05)(.02)\ -\ (.005)(.005)]$$

C. $$\left[\frac{(.05)(.02)-(.005)(.005)}{(0.015)}\right]$$

D. $$\frac{(0.045)}{[(.05)(.02)-(.005)(.005)]}$$

E. $$\frac{[(.05)(.02)-(.005)(.005)]}{(0.045)}$$

45. What would be the pH of a 1.0 M solution of an unknown salt hydroxide given that the metal is monovalent and the K_b of the salt is 1.0×10^{-6}?

A. 11
B. 8.0
C. 7.5
D. 13.0
E. 14.0

46. A sample of white phosphorus (P_4) was reacted with excess Cl_2 gas to yield 68.75 grams of phosphorus trichloride. How many discrete P_4 molecules were there in the sample?

A. $$\left[\frac{\left(\frac{69}{138}\right)}{4}\right](6.0\times10^{23})$$

B. $$\frac{\left[\frac{\left(\frac{69}{138}\right)}{4}\right]}{(6.0\times10^{23})}$$

C. $$\left[\frac{\left(\frac{69}{138}\right)}{8}\right](6.0\times10^{23})$$

D. $$\frac{(6.0\times10^{23})}{\left[\frac{\left(\frac{69}{138}\right)}{4}\right]}$$

E. $$\frac{(6.0\times10^{23})}{\left[\frac{\left(\frac{69}{138}\right)}{8}\right]}$$

47. Which of the following is the strongest reducing agent?

Electrochemical reaction	E° value (V)
$MnO_2 + 4H^+ + 2e^- \rightleftharpoons Mn^{2+} + 2H_2O$	+1.23
$Fe^{3+} + e^- \rightleftharpoons Fe^{2+}$	+0.771
$Cr^{3+} + e^- \rightleftharpoons Cr^{2+}$	−0.410

A. Cr^{3+}
B. Cr^{2+}
C. Mn^{2+}
D. MnO_2
E. Fe^{3+}

48. As the atomic number increases as one moves across the periodic table, the numerical value for electron affinity generally:

A. remains neutral though the electron affinity increases.
B. becomes more positive because of the decreasing effective nuclear charge.
C. becomes more negative because of the increasing effective nuclear charge.
D. becomes more positive because of the increasing atomic radius.
E. becomes more negative because of the increasing atomic radius.

49. HCl has a higher boiling point than either H_2 or Cl_2. The likely reason is that HCl:

A. exhibits weak dipole-dipole interactions, unlike H_2 and Cl_2.
B. has a greater molecular mass than either H_2 or Cl_2.
C. is less polar than either H_2 or Cl_2.
D. is a smaller molecule than H_2 and Cl_2.
E. is a strong acid.

50. Which of the following molecules can be involved in hydrogen bond formation but cannot form hydrogen bonds with molecules of its own kind?

A. C_2H_5OH
B. HCOOH
C. CH_3OCH_3
D. HF
E. H_3O^+

51. Reaction I was carried out in the dark and stopped before equilibrium was reached. The partial pressure of Cl_2 was found to be 35 atm and the mole fraction of HCl found to be 0.40. If the total pressure of the system is 100 atm, what is the partial pressure of H_2?

Reaction I

$H_2 + Cl_2 \rightleftharpoons 2HCl$

A. 10 atm
B. 25 atm
C. 65 atm
D. 75 atm
E. 85 atm

52. A fossil was discovered in the forests of Africa and when examined, it was found that it had a carbon-14 activity of 10.8 disintegrations per minute per gram (dpm g^{-1}). If the average activity of carbon-14 in a living organism is 43.0 dpm g^{-1}, approximately how many half-lives have passed since the death of the organism?

A. 8
B. 6
C. 4
D. 3
E. 2

53. Uranium ^{238}U is radioactive. One of the intermediates in its decay is obtained via 3 alpha emissions, 2 beta emissions and 3 gamma emissions. What is the identity of this intermediate?

A. $^{238}_{84}Po$

B. $^{232}_{88}Ra$

C. $^{226}_{84}Po$

D. $^{226}_{88}Ra$

E. $^{238}_{86}Po$

54. Given the following information:

$2Fe \rightleftharpoons 2Fe^{2+} + 4e^-$ $E^o = +0.440$ V

$O_2 + 2H_2O + 4e^- \rightleftharpoons 4OH^-$ $E^o = +0.401$ V

Determine the E° for the overall reaction:

$2Fe(s) + O_2(g) + 2H_2O(l) \rightarrow 2Fe^{2+}(aq) + 4OH^-(aq)$

A. +0.382 V
B. +0.841 V
C. −0.058 V
D. −1.702 V
E. −0.673 V

55. Given that the K_{sp} of FeX_2 is 5.0×10^{-16} where "X" is an unknown anion, what is its solubility in moles per liter?

A. 1.0×10^{-2}
B. 2.1×10^{-3}
C. 3.4×10^{-3}
D. 5.0×10^{-6}
E. 6.1×10^{-3}

56. Which of the following is a plausible structure for white phosphorus (P_4)?

A. 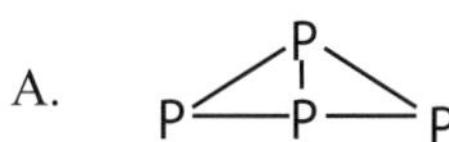

B. 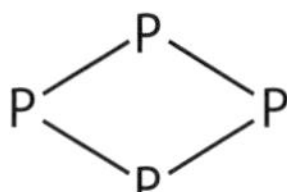

C. 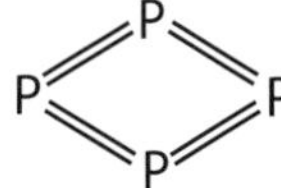

D. 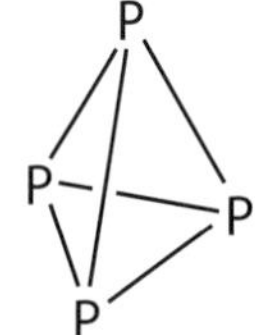

E. 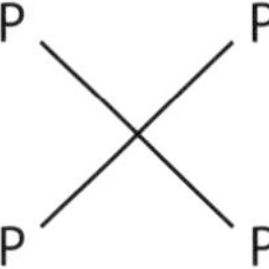

57. All of the following can be used to describe metals EXCEPT one. Which one is the EXCEPTION?

A. Excellent conductors of heat
B. Form positive ions by losing electrons
C. Ductile and malleable
D. Low ionization energy
E. Good conductors of electricity, but less well than metalloids

58. When s-block carbonates decompose, a gas is obtained which is heavier than air and does not support a lighted splint. What gas is it?

A. O_2
B. CO
C. CO_2
D. CO_3
E. C

59. Li_2O is often considered to be covalent in nature because of the unusually high electronegativity of lithium. Which of the following would be a plausible Lewis dot structure for the compound?

A. 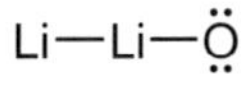 Li—Li—Ö (with lone pairs on O)
B. Li—Ö—Li (with lone pairs on O)
C. Li=O=Li
D. ·Li—Ö—Li· (with lone pairs on O)
E. ·Li—O—Li·

60. In the following electrolytic cell, which solution(s) could be used such that the electrode at A is the anode?

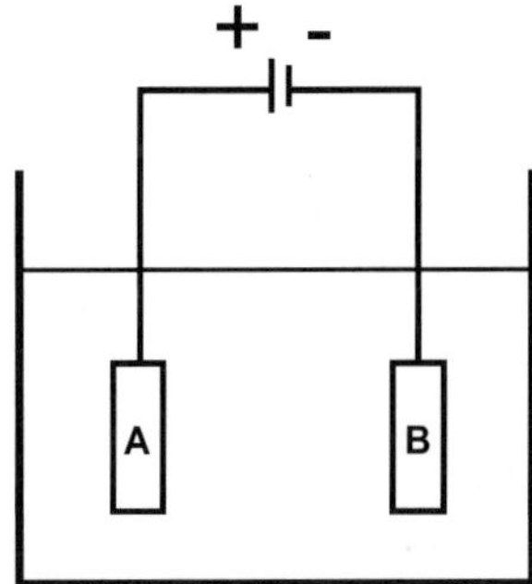

A. Molten NaCl
B. $CuSO_4$
C. $FeBr_2$
D. All of the above
E. None of the above

61. Given that the K_a of the indicator methyl-orange (HMe) is 4.0×10^{-4}, a solution of pH = 2 containing methyl-orange would be what color?

$$\underset{\text{Red}}{\text{HMe}} \rightleftharpoons \underset{\text{Colorless}}{H^+} + \underset{\text{Yellow}}{Me^-}$$

A. Orange
B. Yellow
C. Colorless
D. Pink
E. Red

62. Consider the following reaction:

$FeCl_2(aq) + H_2S(g) \rightarrow FeS(s) + 2HCl(aq)$

When sulfur is precipitated, what type of reaction has occurred?

A. Oxidation-reduction
B. Neutralization
C. Disproportionation
D. Displacement
E. Double replacement

63. Which of the following electron configurations of atoms in neutral form corresponds to that of a Group II metal?

A. $1s^2, 2s^3$
B. $1s^2$
C. $1s^2, 2s^2, 2p^6, 3s^2$
D. $1s^2, 2s^2, 2p^2$
E. $1s^2, 2s^2, 2p^6, 3s^2, 3p^6, 3d^4, 4s^2$

64. What is the K_{a2} expression for hydrogen sulfide (H_2S) as an acid?

A. $[H^+][S^{2-}]$

B. $$\frac{[H^+][S^{2-}]}{[HS^-]}$$

C. $[H^+]^2[S^{2-}]$

D. $$\frac{[H^+]^2[S^{2-}]^2}{[HS^-]}$$

E. $$\frac{[2H^+]^2[2S^{2-}]}{[HS^-]}$$

65. At a given temperature T in kelvin, the relationship between the three thermodynamic quantities including the change in Gibbs free energy (ΔG), the change in enthalpy (ΔH) and the change in entropy (ΔS), can be expressed as follows:

$\Delta G = \Delta H - T\Delta S$

The sublimation of carbon dioxide occurs quickly at room temperature. What might be predicted for the three thermodynamic quantities for the reverse reaction?

A. Only ΔS would be positive.
B. Only ΔS would be negative.
C. Only ΔH would be negative.
D. Only ΔG would be positive.
E. All 3 would be negative.

66. Water has a specific heat of 4.18 J/g•°C while glass (Pyrex) has a specific heat of 0.78 J/g•°C. If 40.0 J of heat is added to 1.00 g of each of these, which will experience the larger temperature increase?

A. They both will experience the same change in temperature because only the mass of a substance relates to the increase in temperature.
B. Neither would necessarily experience a temperature increase.
C. It would depend on the source of the heat added.
D. Water
E. Glass

67. 50 grams of glucose ($C_6H_{12}O_6$) and 50 grams of sucrose ($C_{12}H_{22}O_{11}$) were each added to beakers of water (beaker 1 and beaker 2, respectively). Which of the following would be true?

A. Boiling point elevation for beaker 1 would be greater than the boiling point elevation for beaker 2.
B. Boiling point elevation for beaker 1 would be less than the boiling point elevation for beaker 2.
C. The same degree of boiling point elevation will occur in both beakers.
D. No boiling point elevation would be observed in either of the beakers.
E. Boiling point depression would occur in both beakers but to different degrees.

68. Which of the following would cause a gas to more closely resemble an ideal gas?

A. Decreased pressure
B. Decreased temperature
C. Decreased volume
D. Increased pressure
E. Increased volume

69. The data in Table 1 were collected for Reaction I:

Reaction I

2X + Y → Z

Table I

Exp.	[X] in M	[Y] in M	Initial rate of reaction
1	0.050	0.100	2×10^{-4}
2	0.050	0.200	8×10^{-4}
3	0.200	0.100	8×10^{-4}

What is the rate law expression for Reaction I?

A. Rate = $k[X]^2[Y]$
B. Rate = $k[X]^2[Y]^2$
C. Rate = $k[X][Y]^2$
D. Rate = $k[X][Y]$
E. Rate = $k[2X][Y]$

70. What piece of laboratory equipment is best for accurately measuring the volume of a liquid?

A. Graduated cylinder
B. Erlenmeyer flask
C. Beaker
D. Evaporating dish
E. More than one of the above

71. Morphine is illustrated below.

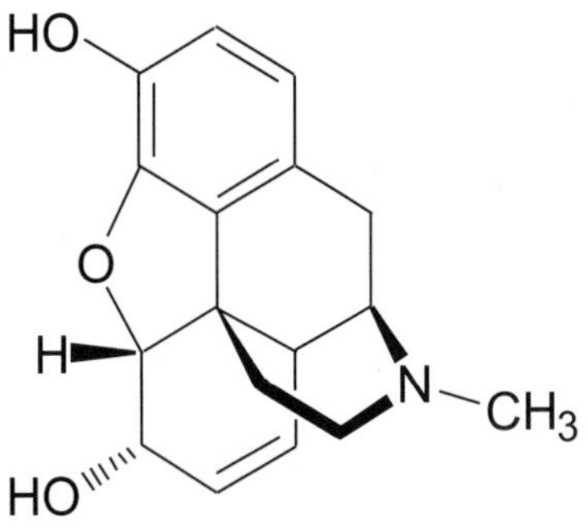

How many chiral carbons are there in morphine?

A. 5
B. 6
C. 7
D. 8
E. More than 8

72. Using 2 equivalents of the first and 1 equivalent of the second, respectively, which of the following pairs of compounds can be used to form the following tertiary alcohol?

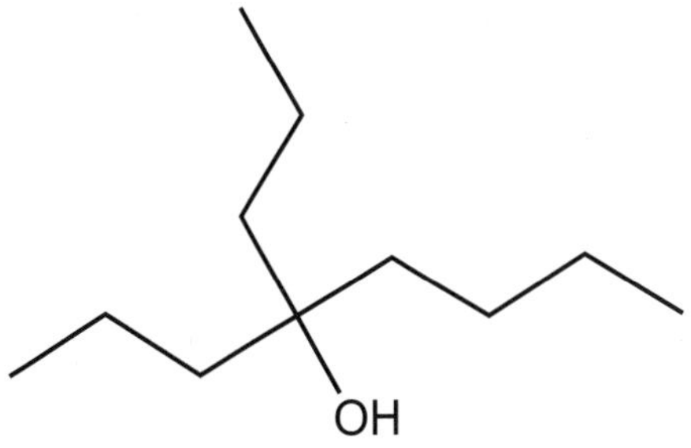

A. Propyl lithium and methyl butanoate
B. Butyl magnesium bromide and propyl butanoate
C. Butyl lithium and pentyl pentanoate
D. Pentyl magnesium chloride and propyl propanoate
E. Propyl magnesium bromide and hexyl pentanoate

73. Rank the following compounds from most to least basic:

I. $CH_3CH_2^-$
II. $CH_3CH_2O^-$
III. $CH_3CH_2NH_2$

A. I > II > III
B. II > III > I
C. III > II > I
D. II > I > III
E. I > III > II

74. Four compounds – allyl alcohol, benzoic acid, 2-butanone and butyraldehyde - were identified and stored in separate bottles. By accident, the labels were lost from the sample bottles. The following information was obtained via infrared spectroscopy and was used to identify and relabel the sample bottles.

Infrared absorption peaks (cm^{-1})

Bottle I	Bottle II	Bottle III	Bottle IV
1700 (sharp)	1710	1730 (sharp)	3333 (broad)
–	3500 – 3333 (broad)	2730	1030 (small)

Which of the following most accurately represents the contents of bottles I, II, III, and IV, respectively?

A. Butyraldehyde, 2-butanone, benzoic acid, allyl alcohol
B. Benzoic acid, butyraldehyde, allyl alcohol, 2-butanone
C. 2-Butanone, butyraldehyde, allyl alcohol, benzoic acid
D. 2-Butanone, benzoic acid, butyraldehyde, allyl alcohol
E. Benzoic acid, allyl alcohol, butyraldehyde, 2-butanone

75. What is the structure of formic acid?

A. H — C (= O — O — H)

B. H — O (= C = O — H)

C. O = C = O, with H above and H below C

D. H — C (= O)(— O — H)

E. C (= O)(— O (— H)(— H))

76. Phenols are soluble in a strongly basic sodium hydroxide solution, and insoluble in dilute sodium bicarbonate. Phenol has a pKa = 10.0. The introduction of an ortho bromine atom into the phenol would have the effect of:

A. lowering the pKa and thus decreasing the acidity of the phenol.
B. lowering the pKa and thus increasing the acidity of the phenol.
C. increasing the pKa and thus decreasing the acidity of the phenol.
D. increasing the pKa and thus increasing the acidity of the phenol.
E. no effect on the pKa nor the acidity of the phenol.

77. What is the product of the following acid catalyzed reaction?

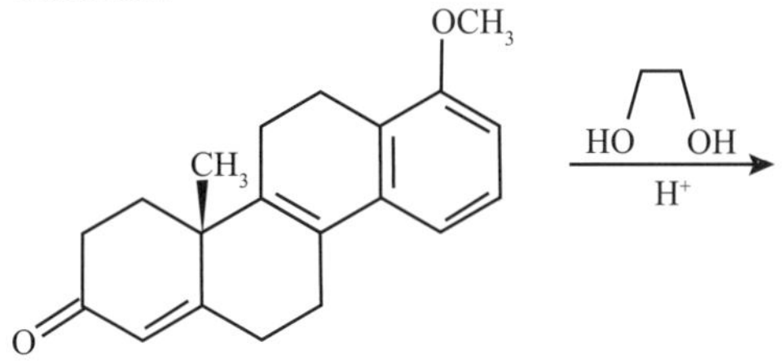

[Reactant structure: steroid with OCH_3 on aromatic ring, CH_3, ketone (O=); reagent: HO–CH₂CH₂–OH, H^+]

A. 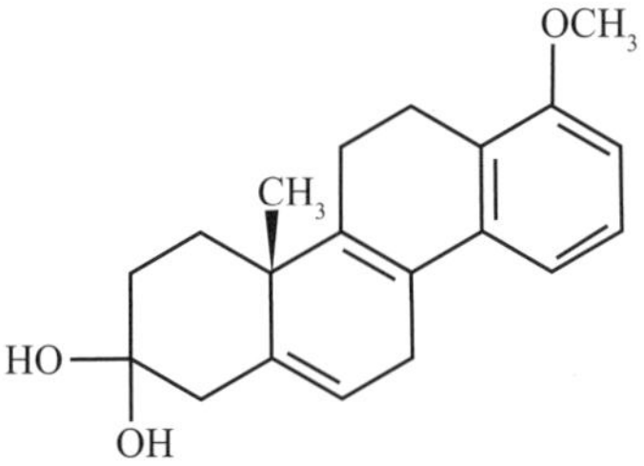 [Structure with OCH_3, CH_3, HO and OH on same carbon]

B. 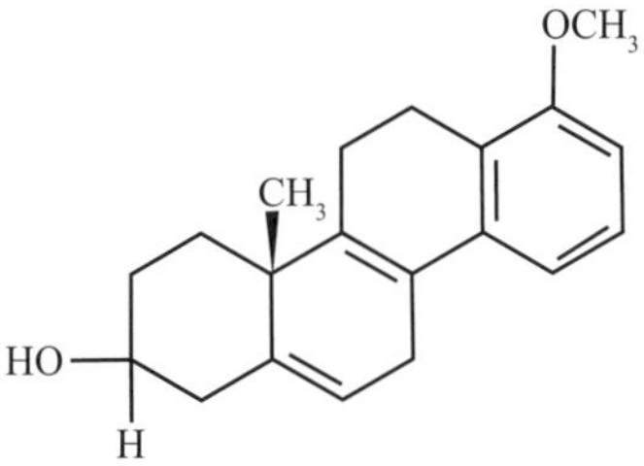 [Structure with OCH_3, CH_3, HO and H]

C. 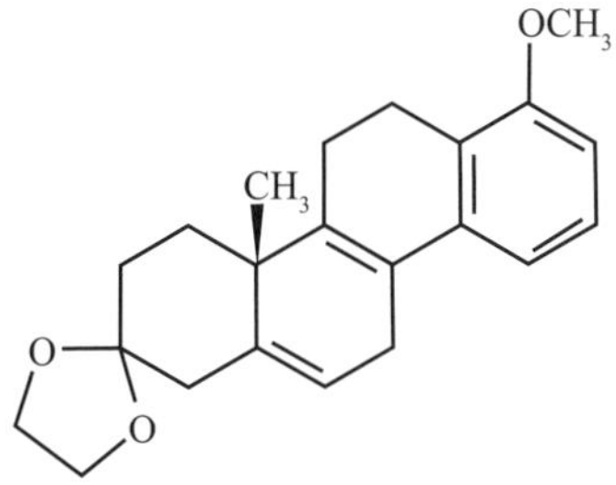 [Structure with OCH_3, CH_3, cyclic ketal (O, O)]

D. 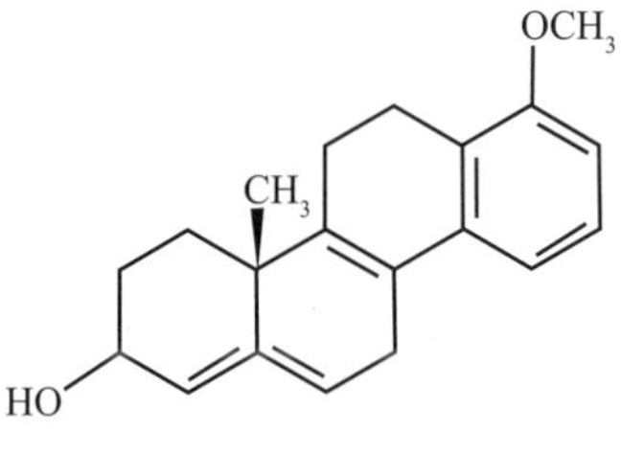 [Structure with OCH_3, CH_3, HO]

78. The efficiency of the distillation process in producing a pure product is improved by repeating the process, increasing the length of the column and avoiding overheating. All of the following can prevent overheating EXCEPT one. Which one is the EXCEPTION?

A. Boiling chips
B. Boiling slowly
C. Adding a vacuum
D. Adding a nucleophile
E. Decreasing the vapor pressure

79. Cyclic ethers, or epoxides, are important chemical compounds that are composed of a 3–membered ring containing an oxygen atom and 2 carbon atoms. What are the bond angles in the epoxide ring?

A. 109.5°
B. 60°
C. 108°
D. 110°
E. 120°

80. Which hydrogen(s) labeled below – directly bonded to a carbon – is (are) most acidic?

$NH_2CH_2CH_2CH_2COOH$
1 2 3 4

A. 1
B. 2
C. 3
D. 4
E. 1, 2 and 3 are equally acidic.

81. Which of the following would explain the non-separation of cortisol from cortisone by gas-liquid chromatography (GLC)?

A. The solid material in the column of the GLC,
through which substances pass in their mobile phase, absorbs cortisol and cortisone equally well.
B. Cortisol and cortisone have relatively high boiling points.
C. Cortisol and cortisone have very similar melting points.
D. Cortisol moves through the column of the GLC, through which substances pass in their mobile phase, at a much quicker rate than cortisone.
E. Cortisone moves through the column of the GLC at a much quicker rate than cortisol.

82. Which of the following represents the amino acid methionine at its isoelectric point?

A. 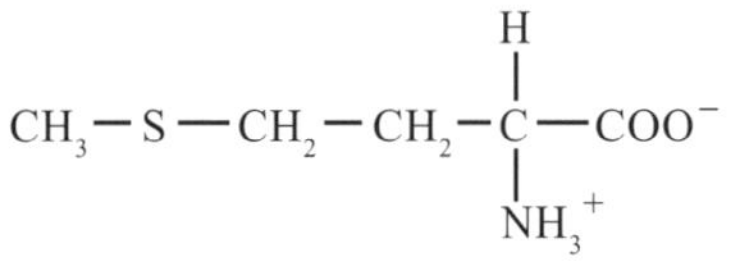 $CH_3-S-CH_2-CH_2-C(H)(NH_3^+)-COO^-$

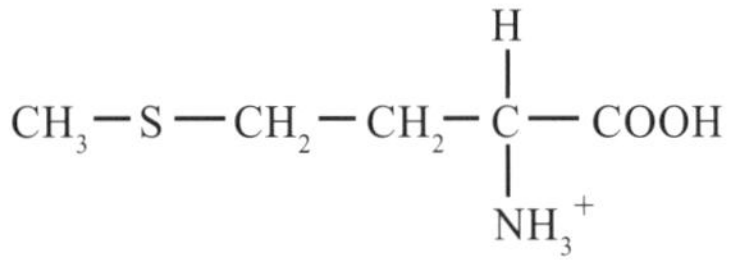

B. $CH_3-S-CH_2-CH_2-C(H)(NH_3^+)-COOH$

C. $CH_4^+-S-CH_2-CH_2-C^-(NH_2)-COOH$

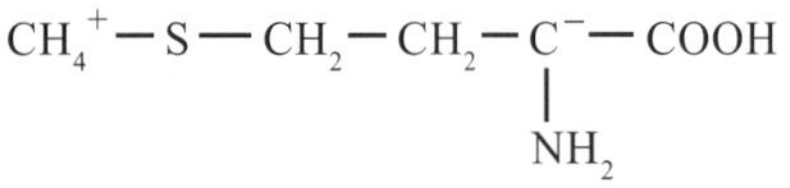

D. 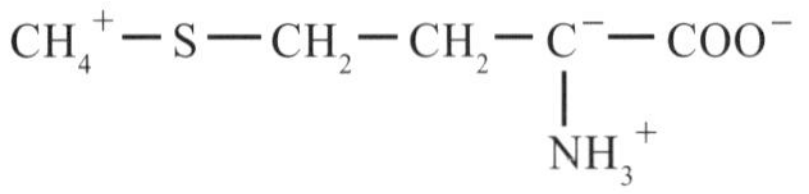 $CH_4^+-S-CH_2-CH_2-C^-(NH_3^+)-COO^-$

83. Consider the following schematic of a ¹H NMR:

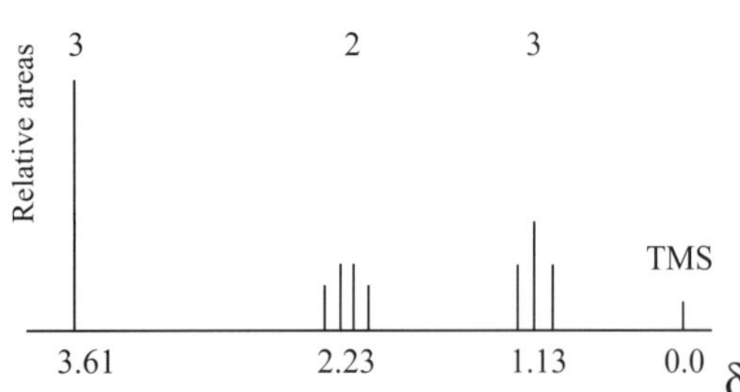

Which of the following compounds is most consistent with the ¹H NMR above?

A. C_4H_6O
B. $CH_3COCH_2OCH(CH_3)_2$
C. $CH_3CH_2COOCH_3$
D. $CH_3CH_2OCH_2CH_2CH_3$
E. $CH_3COCH_2OCH_3$

84. Choose the correct structure for:

$CH_3CH_2CH(CH_3)CH(CH(CH_3)_2)CH_2CH = C(CH_3)_2$

A.

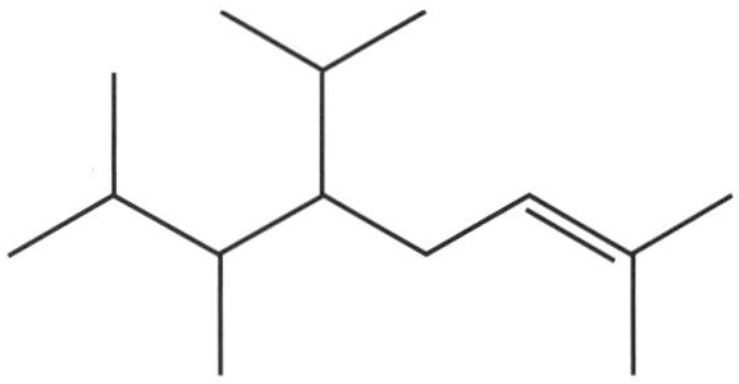

B.

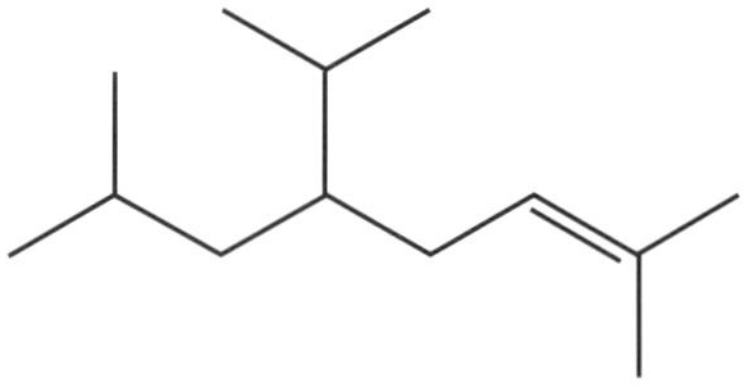

C.

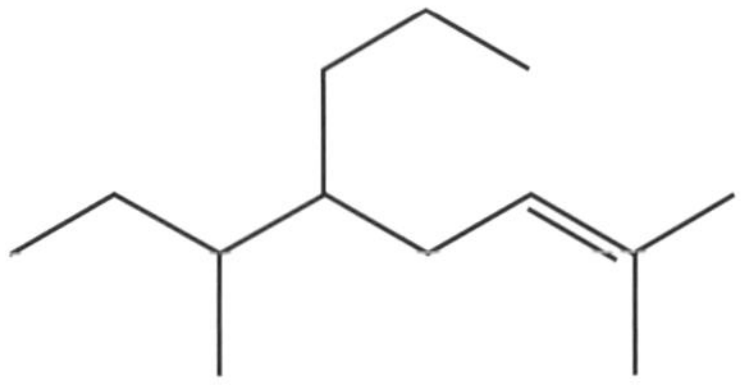

D.

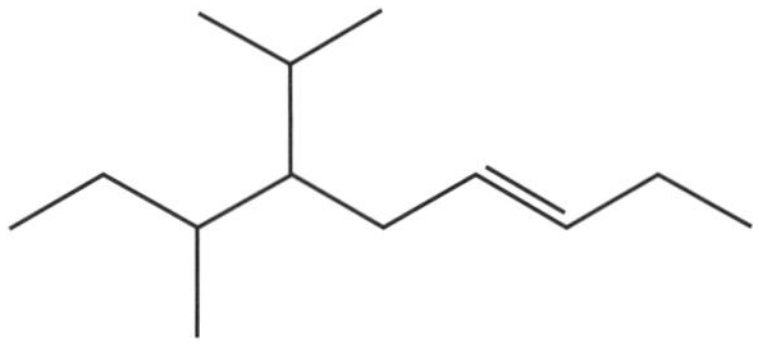

E.

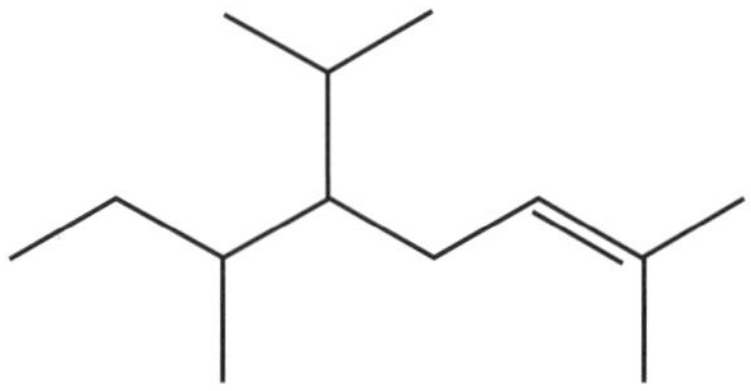

85. The solvent used to do an extraction should do all of the following EXCEPT one. Which one is the EXCEPTION?

A. It must be sparingly soluble in the liquid from which the solute is to be extracted.
B. It must readily dissolve the substance to be extracted.
C. It must react chemically with the solute to form a product.
D. It must be easily separated from the solute after extraction.
E. None of the above.

86. How many possible structural isomers are there for C_4H_8?

A. 2
B. 4
C. 5
D. 6
E. 16

87. Which of the following statements is consistent with the acid-catalyzed dehydration of tertiary alcohols?

A. Formation of the carbocation is a slow step.
B. Protonation of the OH functional group is rapid and reversible.
C. Deprotonation of the carbocation is a fast step.
D. Cleavage of the C–O bond occurs in the rate determining step.
E. All of the above

88. Consider the following reaction:

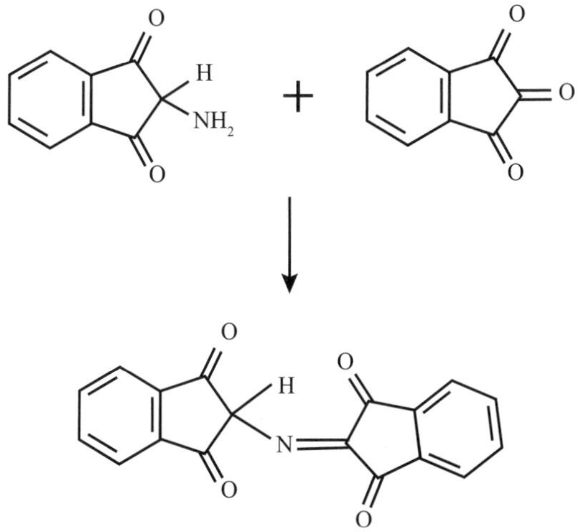

The preceding reaction can be classified most closely as which of the following?

A. Enamine formation
B. Decarboxylation reaction
C. Enzymatic cleavage
D. Sp-sp hybridization
E. Imine formation

89. How many of the following compounds contain at least 1 chiral carbon and how many exhibit optical activity, respectively?

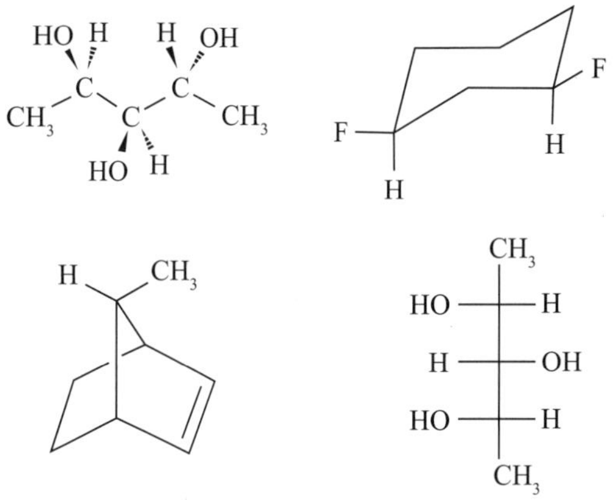

A. 4 compounds possess at least 1 chiral carbon; 1 compound is optically active.
B. 4 compounds possess at least 1 chiral carbon; 2 compounds are optically active.
C. 2 compounds possess at least 1 chiral carbon; 1 compound is optically active.
D. 2 compounds possess at least 1 chiral carbon; 2 compounds are optically active.
E. 3 compounds possess at least 1 chiral carbon; 3 compounds are optically active.

90. Consider the following reaction:

$(CH_3)_2C = CH_2 + HCl \rightarrow$ Product

Which of the following compounds best exemplifies the major organic product of the above reaction?

A. $(CH_3)_2CHCH_2Cl$
B. $(CH_3)_2CClCH_3$
C. $CH_2{=}CCl{-}CH_2CH_3$
D. $CH_3{-}CCl_2{-}CH_2CH_3$
E. $(ClCH_2)_2CHCH_3$

91. Acid catalysts such as *p*–toluensulfonic acid are often used to dehydrate alcohols. The role of the acid catalyst is to:

A. increase ΔG° and increase the activation energy for the dehydration reaction.
B. increase ΔG° and lower the activation energy for the dehydration reaction.
C. maintain ΔG° at the same value and lower the activation energy for the dehydration reaction.
D. lower ΔG° and increase the activation energy for the dehydration reaction.
E. lower ΔG° and lower the activation energy for the dehydration reaction.

92. Which of the following is the most accurate representation of the reaction coordinate diagram for the solvolysis of t–butyl bromide?

Note that [ ]* represents the intermediate.

A.

Potential energy
$(CH_3)_3C\,Br + C_2H_5OH$
$(CH_3)_3COC_2H_5 + HBr$
[ ]*
Reaction coordinate

B.

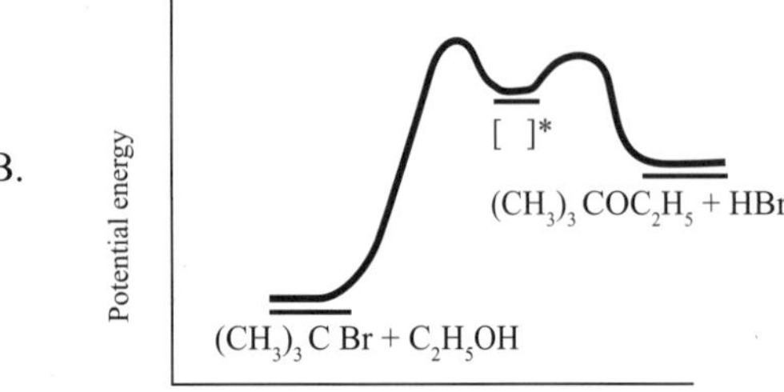

C.

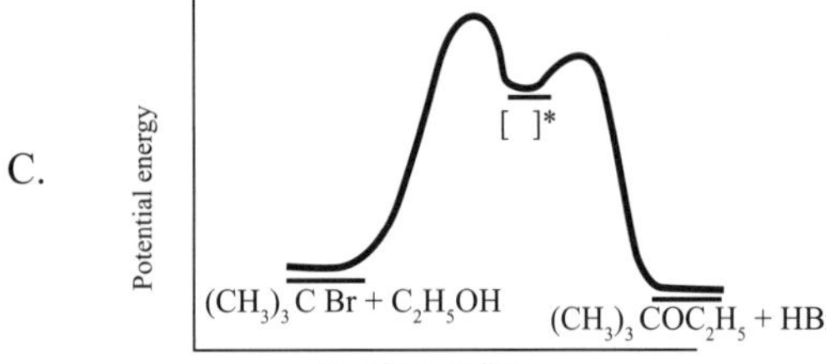

D.

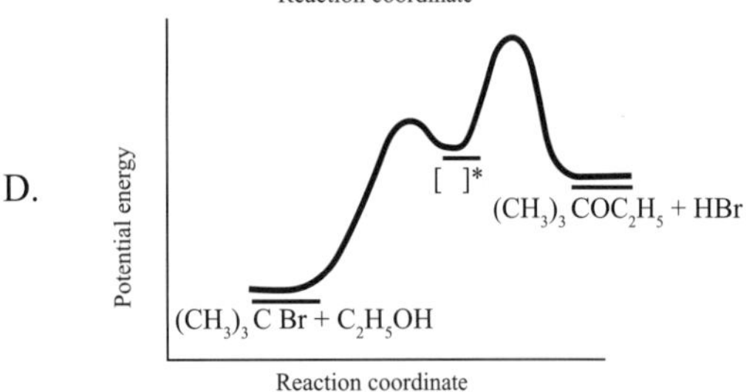

93. The free energy changes for the equilibria *cis* ⇌ *trans* of 1,2–, 1,3–, and 1,4– dimethylcyclohexane are shown below.

I. A ⇌ B

II. A ⇌ B

III. A ⇌ B

The most stable diastereomer in each case would be:

A. IA, IIB, IIIA
B. IB, IIB, IIIB
C. IA, IIA, IIIA
D. IA, IIB, IIIB
E. IB, IIA, IIIB

94. What is the hybridization of C1 in coniine?

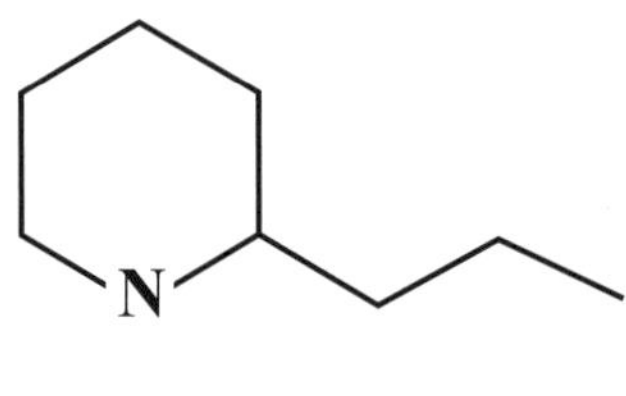

Coniine

A. sp
B. sp^2
C. sp^3
D. sd^4
E. None of the above

95. Which of the following would be the least reactive diene in a Diels-Alder reaction?

A.

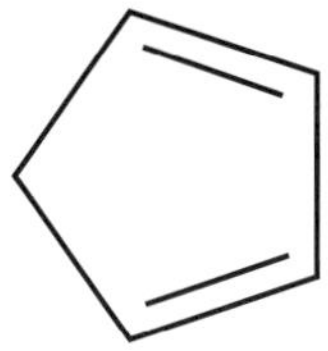

B.

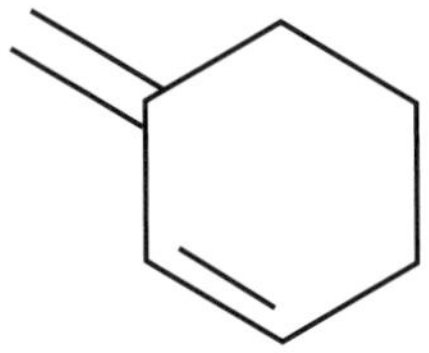

C.

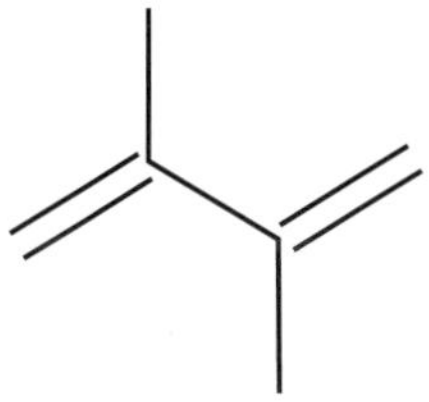

D.

E.

96. A student used a distillation apparatus to separate ethyl acetate from 1–butanol because of the difference in boiling points of these 2 compounds. This difference is most likely attributed to which of the following factors?

A. Hydrogen bonding
B. Bond hybridization
C. Temperature scanning
D. Increments of 5 degrees
E. Resonance stabilization

97. All of the following are true regarding allene (C_3H_4) EXCEPT one. Which one is the EXCEPTION?

A. The C–H bond angles are 120°.
B. The hybridization of the carbon atoms are sp and sp^2.
C. The bond angle formed by the three carbons is 180°.
D. The central carbon of allene forms two sigma bonds and two pi bonds.
E. Allene is a conjugated diene.

98. Which of the following is aromatic?

A.

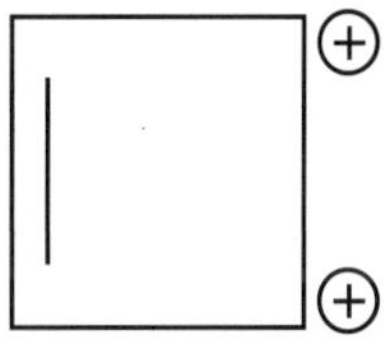

B.

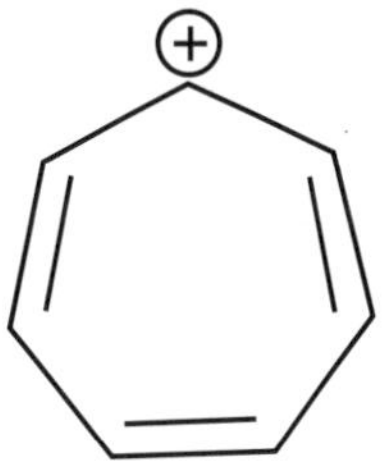

C.

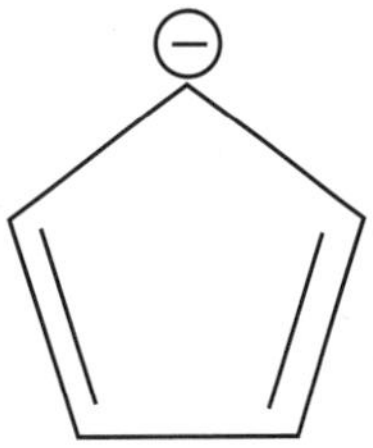

D.

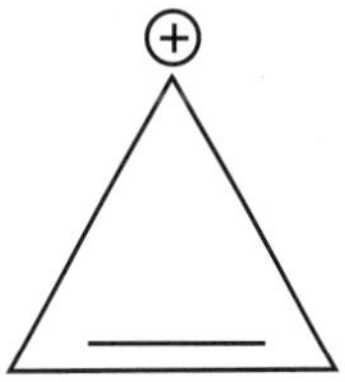

E. All of the above

99. Which of the following represents the product from the reaction shown below?

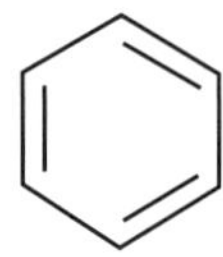

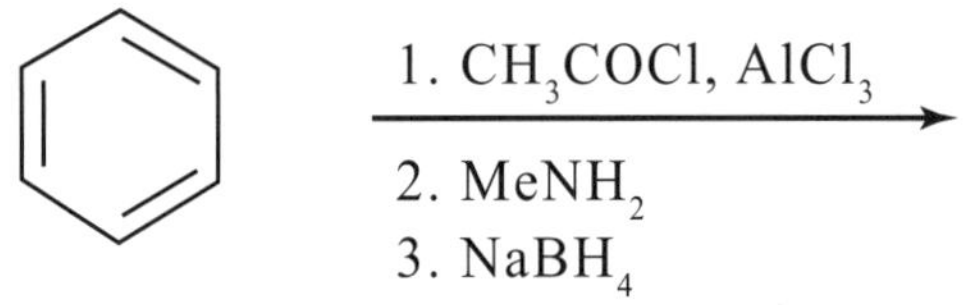

1. CH_3COCl, $AlCl_3$
2. $MeNH_2$
3. $NaBH_4$

A. 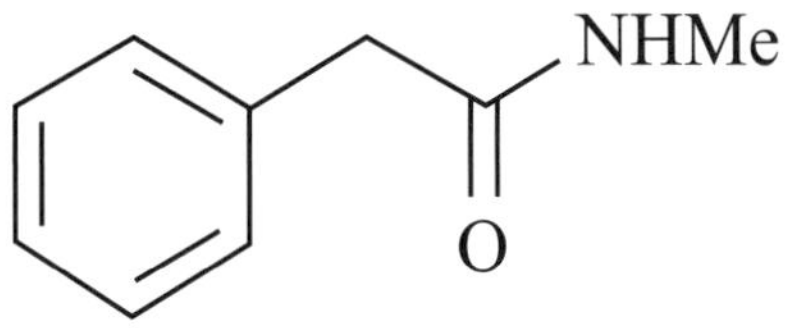 NHMe, O

B. 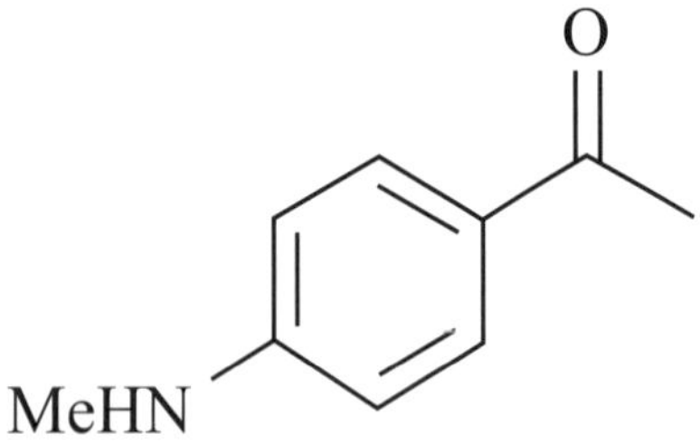 O, MeHN

C. 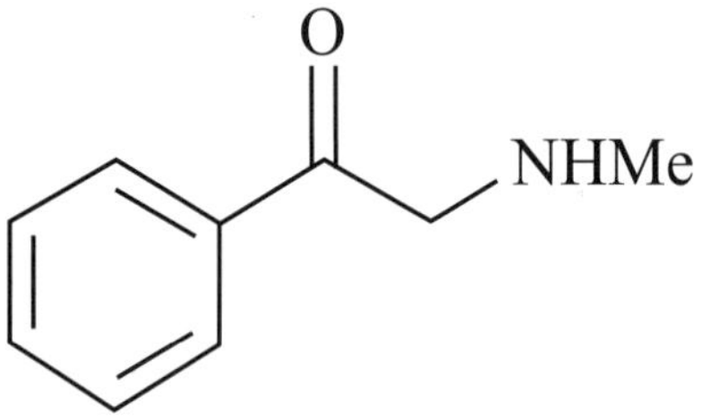 O, NHMe

D. 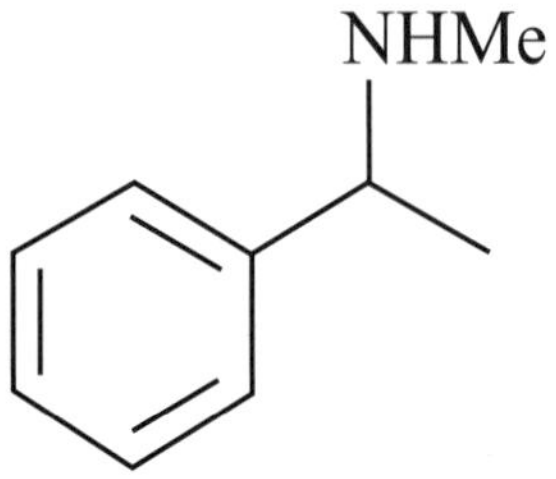 NHMe

E. 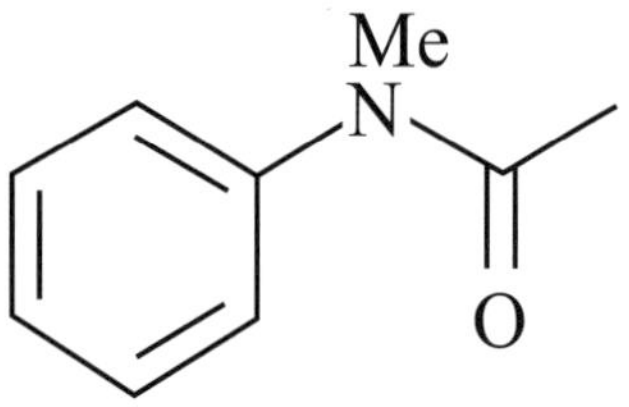 Me, N, O

100. Each of the following structures is a resonance form of the molecule shown below EXCEPT one. Which one is the EXCEPTION?

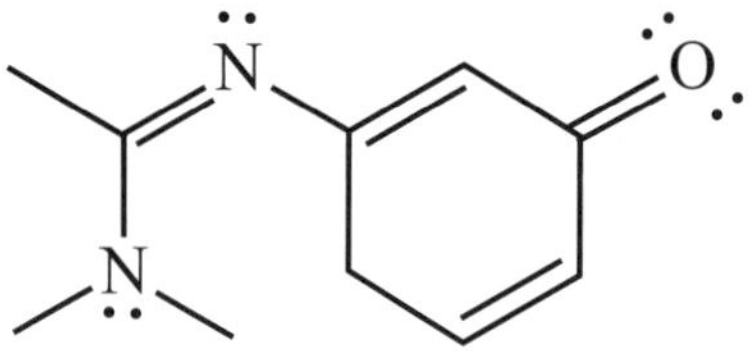

A.

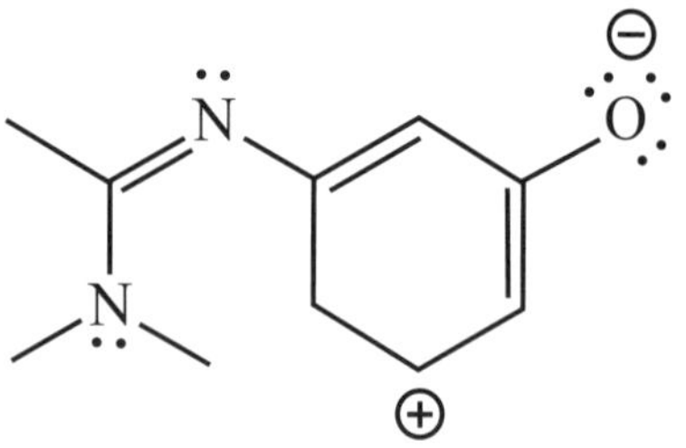

B.

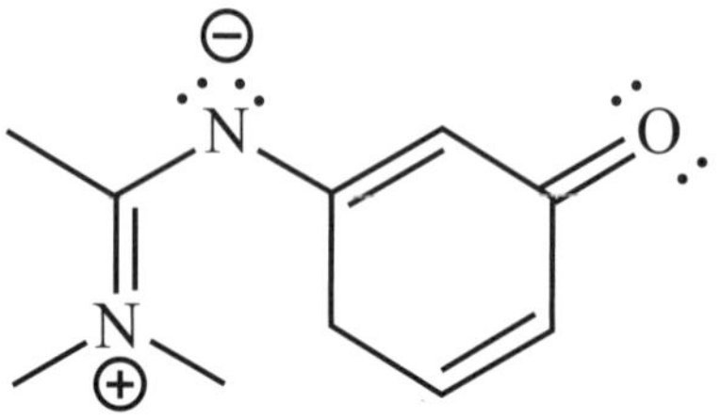

C.

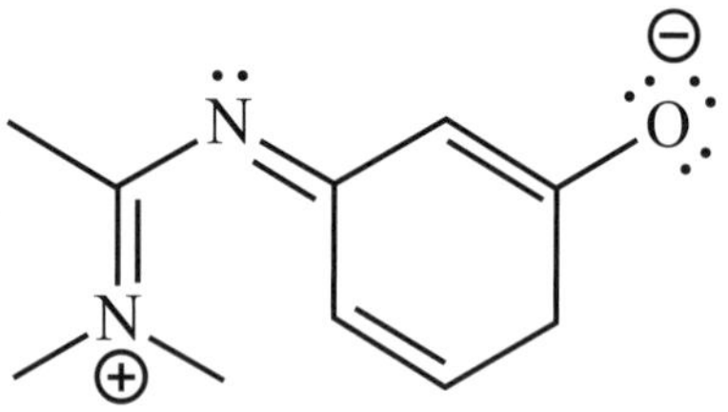

D.

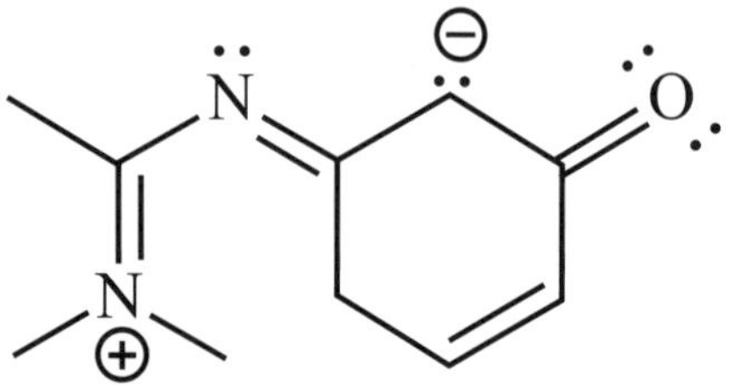

E.

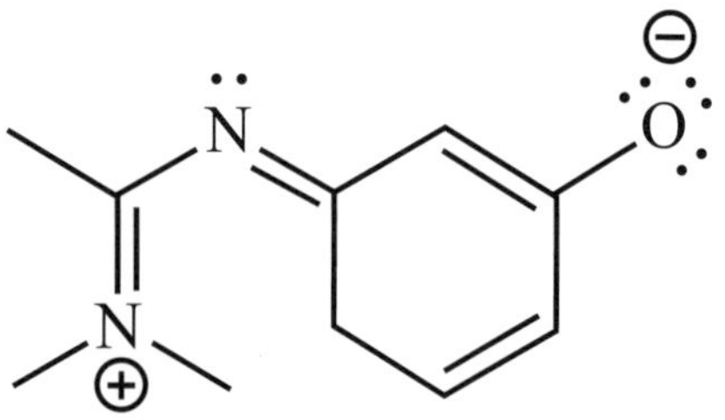

Note: We have kept the longer version of RC in this paper version of GS-1 with 50 questions in 60 minutes. If you want to do the shorter version with 40 questions in 50 minutes (which is a bit easier because of shorter passages as well), go online to oatbooks.com and you can do the shorter version for free (original book owner only).

Passage 1

Cosmic Rays

(1) The earliest telescopes were optical telescopes, allowing astronomers to view the Universe in visible light. In the 20th century, astronomers extended the range of telescopes to cover the entire electromagnetic spectrum, from radio and infrared regions, into the ultraviolet, X ray, and gamma ray bands. However, electromagnetic radiation isn't the only sort of particle that falls from the sky: ionized atomic nuclei hit the Earth's atmosphere continuously, with such "cosmic rays" providing hints on energetic processes in the Universe. Since the middle of the 20th century, astronomers have been setting up instrument systems to help determine the origin of cosmic rays.

(2) After the discovery of radioactivity at the beginning of the 20th century, scientists then discovered that there seemed to be a pervasive background radiation that was present almost everywhere. The radiation was believed to be coming from the Earth itself. In 1910, a Jesuit pries named Theodor Wulf (1868 – 1946) went up the Eiffel Tower in Paris to measure radiation levels with an "electroscope." This was a simple device consisting of a sealed gas-filled globe with a metal rod inserted in the top, connected to two thin gold leaves inside the globe. A static electric charge could be used to form the two leaves to spread apart; any radiation passing through the globe would ionize the gas, causing the charge on the leaves to discharge so that they would gradually fall back together.

(3) If the radiation was actually coming from the Earth, it would be weaker at the top of the tower – but the radiation levels were surprisingly high. Wulf suggested that this mysterious radiation might be coming from the upper atmosphere or space. He suggested that balloon flights might be conducted to confirm this notion.

(4) In 1911 – 1912 an Austrian physicist named Victor Hess (1883 – 1964) made a series of ten balloon flights with an electroscope to investigate. Hess did discover that radiation increased with altitude. There was widespread skepticism over his findings, but a German researcher named Werner Kollhoerster made five Time flights of his own and provided confirmation. Kollhoerster's last flight was on 28 June 1914; that was the day Serbian extremists assassinated the heir to the throne of the Austro-Hungarian Empire, setting off World War I, which put pure scientific research on the back burner until the end of the war in 1918.

(5) After the conflict in 1922, the American experimental physicist Robert Millikan (1868 – 1953) conducted studies of his own on the matter, launching automated balloons from Texas and performing studies from the top of tall Pike's Peak in Colorado. He reported no rise in the level of radiation; his findings were correct, but it turned out that the level of cosmic radiation in those regions was unusually low. Hess and Kollhoerster hotly contested Millikan's findings; although Millikan was not noted for being flexible in his judgments, he was very thorough, and so he conducted further studies in the mountains of California in 1925. He was forced to concede that the radiation did exist, naming it "cosmic rays."

(6) That would prove to be his only really positive contribution to the debate. Millikan insisted that cosmic rays were high-energy gamma rays, but in 1929 Kollhoerster and his colleague Walter Boethe built a "coincidence counter," using two proportional counter tubes that would go off when a single particle passed through both. After recording the passage of cosmic-ray particles through the two tubes, they placed a slab of gold between them, assuming it would block the cosmic rays. It would have if they had been photons; but it didn't, meaning they were charged particles with mass.

(7) Millikan insisted that their experiment was in error. Kollhoerster and Boethe suggested that if cosmic rays were charged particles, not photons, then they would be deflected by the Earth's magnetic field, with the cosmic-ray flux strongest at the poles and weakest at the equator. Studies by various researchers, including Millikan, were afflicted by equipment and other problems and gave ambiguous results, but in 1932 one of Millikan's ex-students, Arthur Holly Compton (1892 – 1962), announced the results of a careful series of observations to show that cosmic rays did vary with latitude as would be expected if they were charged particles. Millikan bitterly attacked Compton's results and then, confronted with new evidence that confirmed Compton's conclusions, abruptly reversed himself, claiming that he and Compton were (and had been) in complete agreement.

(8) The entire subject of cosmic rays ended up being an embarrassment to Millikan. Although he could be hidebound, he was still one of the finest experimental physicists of his generation. He was simply off his game when it came to cosmic ray studies, and he would hardly mention them in his memoirs. There was a widespread belief for a time that he had discovered cosmic rays, but Hess's work was well documented, and Hess received the Nobel Prize for physics in 1936 for the discovery.

(9) A consensus emerged that cosmic rays were generally charged atomic nuclei moving at a high velocity through space that strike the Earth's atmosphere, generating a "cascade" of a million to a billion secondary particles known as an "air shower," with the particles scattered over an ellipse hundreds of meters wide when it hits ground. The particles in the air showers proved to be a gold mine for particle physicists, since the cascades contained short-lived particles not easily found in the laboratory. In the postwar period, up to the early 1950s, cosmic rays were investigated with balloons that carried stacks of photographic emulsions to high altitude to record the traces of these particles.

(10) Cosmic rays hit the Earth at a rate of about one thousand a second per square meter, and their energies don't seem to have any upper bound, though their numbers do unsurprisingly fall off as the energy level increases. About 90% are hydrogen nuclei (protons), 9% are helium nuclei (alpha particles), and the remaining 1% are (mostly) various heavier nuclei. Since they are charged particles, their paths through space are scrambled by galactic magnetic fields, making it difficult to determine the location of their origin.

(11) There are two classes of cosmic rays, those with energies below 10^{16} electron-volts (eV) and those above that level up to 10^{20} eV or more. Astronomers believe the two classes arise from separate processes. The low energy cosmic rays are common, while the more interesting high energy cosmic rays are rare, with the entire Earth intercepting one about once every second. The low energy cosmic rays are not seen as particularly mysterious: the great Italian – American physicist Enrico Fermi suggested that ordinary charged particles could be accelerated to such energies over long periods of time by magnetic fields in our Galaxy. They are also produced by the solar wind from the Sun. Low energy cosmic rays are also not seen as particularly interesting and for the most part, users of modern cosmic ray observatories regard them as "background noise" that has to be screened out.

(12) In contrast, nobody has any clear idea of where the superpowerful cosmic rays come from. They are so powerful that they have been said to have energies comparable to a brick thrown through a plate glass window; pretty impressive performance for a submicroscopic particle. They are generally referred to as "ultra-high energy cosmic rays (UHECRs)". Galactic magnetic fields aren't strong enough to push them around, and since they hit the Earth from all directions instead of along the plane of the Milky Way in our sky, they appear to be produced by extragalactic sources, possibly by supernovas or other "cosmic catastrophes" – though some physicists have suggested they may arise from exotic processes, such as the decay of "magnetic monopoles."

(13) As earlier mentioned, about 1% of cosmic rays are "mostly" relatively heavy nuclei. However, that 1% includes a thin flux of very high-energy gamma rays, in the 10^{12} eV range, that cause air showers very similar to those created by cosmic rays, with about one gamma-ray event for every 100,000 cosmic ray events. Millikan's assertion that cosmic rays were gamma rays wasn't completely wrong – but it was very close to completely wrong. These gamma rays aren't diverted by galactic magnetic fields and so can be traced back to a source by mapping the geometry of the air shower.

(14) There are four ways to observe cosmic rays: by observing the track of faint blue "Cerenkov radiation" left by the air shower particles using something similar to a reflecting telescope; by picking up the "footprint" of the air shower using an array of particle detectors, including proportional counter tubes, scintillation detectors, and wire chambers (Somewhat confusingly, some particle detectors also observe Cerenkov light, though with the light created by passage of particles through a sealed tank of water instead of the atmosphere.); by sensing the faint fluorescence (more properly "luminescence", but the term "fluorescence" has stuck) of atmospheric nitrogen gas in the wake of the air shower; and, by picking up the radio energy generated by the air shower. This is not a popular approach, but the LOFAR low-frequency radio telescope mentioned previously has been used for this purpose.

(15) It is of course possible to build "hybrid" detector systems that use more than one of these methods. Particle detector and radio detector systems work round the clock; air Cerenkov and fluorescence detectors can only really work on clear, moonless nights.

1. Cosmic rays are considered to be:

A. footprints of the air shower.
B. random gamma rays.
C. ionized atomic nuclei.
D. short-lived particles.
E. magnetic monopoles.

2. Which of the following devices was first designed to measure radiation?

A. Balloon flights
B. Optical telescope
C. Electroscope
D. Wire chamber
E. Coincidence counter

3. Which of the following scientists is credited with beginning research on cosmic rays?

A. Victor Hess
B. Werner Kollhoerster
C. Walter Boethe
D. Arthur Holly Compton
E. Theodor Wulf

4. Which of the following represents the number of times that balloon flights were conducted manually?

A. 4
B. 7
C. 16
D. 15

5. Who of the following was awarded the Noble Prize for the discovery of cosmic rays?

A. Theodor Wulf
B. Robert Millikan
C. Arthur Holly Compton
D. Werner Kollhoerster
E. Victor Hess

6. Cosmic rays hit the Earth at which of the following rates?

A. One million a second per square meter
B. One thousand a second per square meter
C. One hundred a second per square meter
D. Varies with magnetic field
E. One billion a second per square meter

7. Which of the following statements are true about the composition of cosmic rays?

A. About 90% are hydrogen nuclei (alpha particles), 9% are helium nuclei (protons), and the remaining 1% are (mostly) various heavier nuclei.
B. About 90% are hydrogen nuclei (protons), 9% are helium nuclei (alpha particles), and the remaining 1% are (mostly) various heavier nuclei.
C. About 90% are hydrogen nuclei (protons), 9% are helium nuclei (alpha particles), and the remaining 1% are (mostly) various lighter nuclei.
D. About 90% are helium nuclei (protons), 9% are hydrogen nuclei (alpha particles), and the remaining 1% are (mostly) various heavier nuclei.
E. About 9% are hydrogen nuclei (protons), 90% are helium nuclei (alpha particles), and the remaining 1% are (mostly) various heavier nuclei.

8. How do users of modern cosmic ray observatories regard low energy cosmic rays?

A. Similar to a laminar flow
B. Background noise
C. Constituent of alpha particle dispersion
D. Proton particle dispersions

9. From where do ultra-high energy cosmic rays most possibly originate?

A. Cosmic dispersion and flow
B. Supernovas, cosmic catastrophes, or decay of magnetic poles
C. Scattering cascades that hit the ground
D. Solar wind from the sun
E. Intergalactic star and sun events

10. Of the 1% of relatively heavy nuclei found in cosmic rays, a thin flux is comprised of which of the following?

A. Alpha particles
B. Magnetic monopoles
C. Protons
D. Neurons
E. Gamma rays

11. Between approximately what years were cosmic rays investigated using balloons that carry photographic emulsions and record traces of particles in air showers?

A. 1918 – 1950
B. 1922 – 1950
C. 1910 – 1914
D. 1910 – 1915
E. 1922 – 1925

12. What does the LOFAR telescope measure?

A. Gamma rays
B. Alpha particles
C. Supernovas
D. Radio energy generated by the air shower
E. Protons

13. Which of the following declarations by Millikan was very close to being completely wrong?

A. Supernovas are one cause of cosmic rays.
B. Alpha particles account for all of cosmic rays.
C. Cosmic Rays are gamma rays.
D. There is a divided mix between protons and alpha particles within the nuclei.
E. Air showers are caused by magnetic mono poles.

14. Which of the following best typifies the two classes of cosmic rays?

A. Those with energies below 10^{13} electron-volts (eV) and those above that level up to 10^{20} eV or more
B. Those with energies below 10^{16} electron-volts (eV) and those above that level up to 10^{22} eV or more
C. Those with energies below 10^{16} electron-volts (eV) and those above that level up to 10^{20} eV or more
D. Those with energies below 10^{16} electron-volts (eV) and those above that level up to 10^{20} eV or more
E. Those with energies below 10^{14} electron-volts (eV) and those above that level up to 10^{20} eV or more

15. Particle detectors are able to pick up Cerenkov radiation and "footprints" of the air shower.

The LOFAR low-frequency radio telescope is used to detect the fluorescence of atmospheric nitrogen gas from air shower.

A. Both statements are true.
B. Both statements are false.
C. The first sentence is true while the second sentence is false.
D. The first sentence is false while the second sentence is true.

Passage 2

Artificial Neural Networks

(1) Artificial Neural Networks are a tool for computation that is based on the neuron's interconnection in the human brain's nervous system as well as that of other organisms. It is also called neural nets, artificial neural nets, or simply ANN.

(2) An artificial neural net is a non-linear type of processing system which is made to perform various kinds of tasks, especially those that do not have an exact algorithm. ANN strives to simulate the firing of synapses. Hence, artificial neural nets can be designed to solve problems based on sample data and teaching methods fed to it, which it uses as a basis for computation and output. With regards to the received training, various tasks can be operated by means of utilizing artificial neural networks that are constructed identically. Just as long as there are proper training modes, a sort of logical generalization is possible in the use and function of artificial neural networks. Generalization is the capability to recognize patterns and similarities among various inputs. Noise-corrupted patterns can also be recognized by generalization. Naturally, the equivalence of an Artificial Neural Network is BNN, which means Biological Neural Networks.

(3) One important factor of neural networks is the neural nets. Commonly, the term "neural net" pertains solely to artificial systems like artificial neural networks. However, the biological variants of neural net cannot be taken for granted because these exist apart from the artificial variant of neural net. Neural nets are not linear mathematically speaking. They cannot be described as a straight arrow, nor a simple cause-effect, stimulus-response type of relationship or model. They can be thought of as layered spatially with a linear type of effect or result of processing. Each layer has something to do with the layer it follows or is imbricated with. There is a representation of combinations of multiplicity. This makes the net a complex system.

(4) Of course, the most complex system is the biological neural system. A common neural system of a human body or that of another organism has billions of cells that interconnect with every neuron. This aspect cannot be achieved by even the latest artificial system; this multitude of complexity is why it is not likely to produce an exact reproduction of biological systems behavior.

(5) The neuron is the basic foundation from which the network systems are constructed for both Biological Neural Networks and Artificial Neural Networks. Every neuron is a system that handles signals out of inputs since it is a MIMO system (multiple-input, multiple-output). After receiving the signal, a resultant signal is produced, and then the signal is transmitted to all of the outputs. The neurons that can be found in an artificial neural network are formed into layers. The first layer is known as the input layer, which functions with interaction with the environment in order to handle input. On the other hand, the final layer is called the output layer, which handles the output in order to tender the data that has been processed. Those layers that do not have any kind of interaction with the input or the output (or the environment in general) are known as hidden layers as these lie in the layers between the output layer and the input layer. These hidden layers make the system complex due to their multiplicity and non-linear relationship, though combined in unique packets or interactions with each other.

(6) Neurons are commonly known as PE or Processing Elements as these can have different forms. The term Processing Elements is used in order to treat it differently from the biological equivalents. There is a certain network pattern into which the Processing Elements are linked. When it comes to artificial systems, PE are only electrical unlike the biological neurons that are chemical. PE may be analog, digital, or hybrid. Analog elements move in time, so to speak, while digital elements move in space, while hybrid elements simulate both temporal and spatial movements. But then again, in order to duplicate the synapse effect, there are multiplicative weights assigned to the connections. Calibration of these weights is necessary to tender the right system output. We can think of weights as the amount of information fed through multiple inputs.

(7) Two equations that define the key concept of Processing Elements represent the McCulloch-Pitts model of a neuron. The simple input and output relationship known as the McCulloch-Pitts neuron, the linear system and the step activation function are characterized by the Perceptron. However, there were some people who did not feel the early success of this work as well as the research for artificial neural networks in general. Among them were Seymore Papert and Marvin Minsky. They had a book entitled Perceptrons, published in 1969 and this was utilized for the discrediting of the artificial neural networks research. One point that Papert and Minsky highlighted was that Perceptron did not classify the non-linear patterns that can be separated from the input space.

(8) There are two main alternative uses of artificial neural nets: algorithmic solution and expert system. Algorithmic solution is raised when there is enough information regarding the data as well as the underlying theory. Unknown solutions can be directly calculated through analyzing the data as well as the data's theoretical relationship. For ease of calculation, ordinary von Neumann computer applications can be utilized. Expert system, on the other hand, is utilized when there is not enough theoretical background and data needed for the creation of any form of reliable problem model. This can be considered a stochastic model. It represents random distributions or patterns, which may bring generalizations or results that can be further tested or refined with guided assumptions or theories.

(9) Moreover, the use of artificial neural networks can be maximized in instances where there is abundant data but little amount of underlying theory, guidance or direction, if you will. When it comes to neural networks, a priori assumptions for the problem space, as well as information regarding the statistical distribution, are not required. Assumptions characterized by patterns are not needed by the neural networks. They can produce results without a distributive framework. Even so, the use of a priori information can still aid on speeding the training when used as statistical distribution of the input space.

(10) Overtraining usually becomes an issue when there are too many training examples and the system is overwhelmed to the extent of not using the useful generalizations. Overtraining can also transpire when there are so many neurons within the network, and the computation capacity exceeds its limit. Despite what sounds like high tech artificial intelligence gibberish or slang, artificial neural networks are used in many contexts. Artificial Neural Networks have been used in sales forecasting, industrial process control, customer research, and data validation, risk management and target marketing. They have also been used in medicine in diagnostics and as you might have guessed, in software games as AI. Though seemingly artificial, there are a number of scientists who believe that artificial neural networks may someday be "conscious," –resembling some of the popular media stereotypes, which we have all seen in helpful robots, cars, and "friendly" space ship computers.

(11) A historical view of ANN and BNN can be summarized as follows:

Late 1800's. There were attempts of scientific study pertaining to how the brain of human beings works. These were usually philosophical works of logic and rationalism.

1890. The first work regarding the activity pattern of the human brain was published by William James.

1943. A neuron model was developed by Warren McCulloch and Walter Pitts. This model, which is broken into a summation over weighted inputs and sum output function, is still utilized these days in the field of artificial neural networking.

1949. The Organization of Behavior was published by Donald Hebb. This work shows an outline of a law for the learning of synaptic neurons. As a commemoration of his work, this law was later renamed as Hebbian Learning.

1951. The first Artificial Neural Network was made by Marvin Minsky while he was at Princeton.

1958. It was one year after the death of John von Neumann when The Computer and the Brain was published. His work showcased propositions about several radical changes in the means, which researchers use to model the brain.

1958. Frank Rosenblatt created the Mark I Perceptron computer at Cornell University. It was an attempt to utilize the techniques of neural network for recognition of characters.

1960. Frank Rosenblatt created the book entitled Principles of Neurodynamics. This contained his ideas and researches about brain modeling.

1974. Paul John Webros discovered the backpropagation algorithm.

1986. The backpropagation algorithm was rediscovered by David Rumelhart, Geoffrey Hinton, and R. J. Williams through their book Learning Internal Representation by Error Propagation. As a gradient descent algorithm, backpropagation is utilized for the purpose of curve-fitting and finding weights that minimize errors in artificial neural networks.

1987. Slated for artificial neural networks researches, the Institute of Electrical and Electronics Engineers (IEEE) began its annual international ANN conference. The INNS or the International Neural Network Society was created.

1988. The INNS Neural Networking journal began its publication.

16. Which of the following CANNOT be performed by ANN?

A. Analyze data
B. Solve problem
C. Recognize patterns among assorted inputs
D. Replicate exact biological systems behavior
E. Calculate unknown solutions

17. Stochastic generalizations from ANN are produced from random patterns.
ANN do not require a priori information.

A. Both statements are true.
B. Both statements are false.
C. The first sentence is true while the second sentence is false.
D. The first sentence is false while the second sentence is true.

18. ANN strives to simulate:

A. systems of complexity.
B. transmission of input-output information.
C. data collation.
D. computer logic.
E. algorithms.

19. The Neural Net is:

A. linear.
B. causal.
C. effects-oriented.
D. layered.
E. cause-oriented.

20. What produces complexity within the neural net?

A. Imbrications of variance
B. Hidden layers
C. Multitudinal velocities
D. Multiple inputs
E. Complex interactions

21. MIMO stands for:

A. Multitude Inertia, Mass Organization
B. Main Inertia, Mass Organization
C. Multiple Inputs, Multiple Outputs
D. Main Inputs, Main Outputs
E. Mass Internalization, Multiple Inertia

22. ANN utilizes algorithms. ANN strives to emulate BNN.

A. Both statements are true.
B. Both statements are false.
C. The first sentence is true while the second sentence is false.
D. The first sentence is false while the second sentence is true.

23. The following network patterns in artificial systems are linked with neurons. Which one is the exeption?

A. Electrical
B. Temporal
C. Digital
D. Analog
E. Hybrid

24. Hybrid PE tend to move:

A. in time.
B. in conjunction with layers.
C. in space.
D. in time and space.
E. in a linear fashion.

25. Overtraining is the result of:

A. exceeding the maximum computation capacity.
B. too much data but not enough underlying theory.
C. too many useful generalizations.
D. expert systems using a priori assumptions.
E. algorithmic complexity.

26. ANN utilizing "Expert Systems" represent models that are:

A. guided by theory.
B. lacking in statistical data.
C. trained by a priori assumptions.
D. overtrained.
E. random and stochastic.

27. Which factor characterizes both the Artificial and the Biological Neural Networks?

A. The linear system
B. Multiplicative weights
C. The neuron as basic foundation
D. Processing Elements
E. The step activation function

28. Which of the following best describes the use of backpropagation?

A. Finding errors in a learning application
B. Minimizing error functions in neural nets
C. Limiting training to a priori assumptions
D. Introducing feedback loops
E. Propagating errors to increase learning

29. Which of the following is NOT true concerning the history of ANN?

A. Minsky created the first ANN.
B. Papert and Minsky created the Perceptron.
C. The law for the learning of synaptic neurons was renamed after Donald Hebb.
D. McCullogh and Pitts created the neuron model.
E. The book Learning Internal Representation by Error renewed interest in backpropagation algorithm.

30. The weighted functions in PE can be thought of as:

A. resultant outputs from data.
B. the quantity of data into multiple inputs.
C. hidden layers of complexity.
D. theory or a priori assumptions.
E. calibrated generalizations.

31. Based on usage in this passage, which of the following refers to "a priori"?

A. Inherent mental structures
B. Assumed theories
C. Guided training
D. Expert systems
E. Overtrained generalizations

32. The best results from ANN are produced with the use of:

A. much theory, little data.
B. much data, little theory.
C. much data and theory.
D. non-linear patterns.

33. Analog Processing Elements can be thought to work in:

A. expert systems.
B. space.
C. laycrs.
D. time.
E. generalized patterns.

34. The difference between algorithmic and expert systems basically concerns:

A. the amount of data.
B. the amount of training.
C. the amount of theory.
D. the amount of generalization.
E. the amount of neurons.

35. ANN can generalize the following EXCEPT:

A. noise.
B. similarities among assorted inputs.
C. linear computations.
D. random patterns.
E. complex distributions.

Passage 3

Music and Mathematics

(1) Many music theorists use mathematics to understand music. Indeed, musical sounds seem to display an inherent order of number properties. Although the ancient Chinese, Egyptians and Mesopotamians are known to have studied the mathematical principles of sound, the Pythagoreans of ancient Greece are the first researchers known to have investigated the expression of musical scales in terms of numerical ratios, particularly the ratios of small integers.

(2) The Greek octave had only five notes, coinciding with the principle of perfect fifths. Pythagoras discovered that differences in the ratio of the length between two strings create variations in pitch. The ratio 2:3 creates the musical fifth, 3:4 the fourth, and so on. Moreover, the ancient Greeks learned that a note with a given frequency could only be combined and played harmoniously with other notes whose frequencies were integer multiples of the first. These would eventually signify the ratio of the wavelength or frequency of a given note to another and thus, the creation of chords.

(3) In addition, Pythagoras pointed out that each note is a fraction of a string. Thus, if a musician had a string that played an A, then the next note is 4/5 the length (or 5/4 the frequency) which is approximately a C. The rest of the octave has the fractions 3/4 (approximately D), 2/3 (approximately E), and 3/5 (approximately F), before reaching 1/2 which is the octave A. With a guitar, the octave is the 12th Fret, and in terms of distance, mathematically it should be half the distance between the bridge at the lower end of the guitar and the nut where the strings cross over at the top of the guitar. Shortening the length between the two produces a higher pitch or tone – envision the strings in a piano, which range from the lower tones-longer strings to the higher tones-shorter strings.

(4) In the Western system of musical notation, the frequency ratio 1:2 is generally identified as the octave. Two different notes in this relation are often considered as fundamentally the same and only vary in pitch but not in character. Octaves of a note occur at 2n times the frequency of that note (where n is an integer), such as 2, 4, 8, 16, etc. and the reciprocal of that series. For example, 50 Hz and 400 Hz are one and two octaves away from 100 Hz because they are ½ (or 2 -1) and 4 (or 22) times the frequency, respectively. Hence, notes an octave apart are given the same note name – the name of a note an octave above A is also A. This is called octave equivalency, the assumption that pitches one or more octaves apart are musically equivalent in many ways, leading to the convention "that scales are uniquely defined by specifying the intervals within an octave."

(5) The application of mathematical concepts to music did not merely involve notes and harmony. The attempt to structure and communicate new ways of composing and hearing music has led some composers to incorporate the golden ratio and Fibonacci numbers into their work.

(6) In mathematics and the arts, two quantities are in the golden ratio if the ratio of the sum of the quantities to the larger quantity is equal to the ratio of the larger quantity to the smaller one. The Fibonacci numbers are the numbers in the following integer sequence: 0,1,1,2,3,5,8, 13,21,34,55,89,144. By definition, the first two Fibonacci numbers are 0 and 1, and each subsequent number is the sum of the previous two. The most important feature in the sequence of Fibonacci ratios – the ratio of a Fibonacci number with its bigger adjacent – is that it converges to a constant limit known as the golden ratio of 0.61803398...

(7) The golden section is employed by musicians to generate rhythmic changes or to develop a melody line. James Tenney reconceived his piece For Ann (rising), which consists of up to twelve computer-generated upwardly glissandoing tones , having each tone start with the golden ratio (in between an equal tempered minor and major sixth) below the previous tone, so that the combination tones produced by all consecutive tones are a lower or higher pitch already, or soon to be, produced.

(8) In Béla Bartok's Music for Strings, Percussion and Celesta, the xylophone progression occurs at the intervals 1:2:3:5:8:5:3:2:1 – a sort of bell curve of a golden ratio. French composer Erik Satie used the golden ratio in several of his pieces, including Sonneries de la Rose+Croix. The golden ratio is also apparent in the organization of the sections in the music of Debussy's Reflets dans l'eau (Reflections in Water), from Images (1st series, 1905), in which "the sequence of keys is marked out by the intervals 34, 21, 13 and 8, and the main climax sits at the phi position."

(9) Also, many works of Chopin, mainly Etudes (studies) and Nocturnes are formally based on the golden ratio. This results in the biggest climax of both musical expression and technical difficulty after about 2/3 of the piece. The mathematician Michael Schneider analyzed the waveform of the Amen break and found that the peaks are spaced at intervals in the golden ratio.

(10) An emerging and modern connection between music and mathematics is being made from the relationship of fractals and the generation of melodic form. Fractals are visual representations of certain mathematical functions, which show increasing detail upon magnification. A very important phenomenon of fractals is that they manifest self-similarity at all scales. Benoit Mandelbrot, one of the fathers of fractal geometry (and the man who coined the term fractal), loosely defines fractals as "shapes that are equally complex in their details as in their overall form. That is, if a piece of a fractal is suitably magnified to become of the same size as the whole, it should look like the whole, either exactly, or perhaps only slightly deformed." Today, we see fractal imagery all over the net in graphic design. Its self-replicating form is also found in nature: imagine broccoli, or even the circulatory system as fractal. Composers are also taking this idea to music.

(11) One would expect that the construction of such complex shapes would require complex rules, but in reality, the algorithms (equations) that generate fractals are typically extraordinarily simple. Their visual results, however, show great richness. The seeming paradox is easily demystified: these algorithms involve "loops."

(12) The key to the richness of detail that fractals exhibit is something that mathematicians call iteration. Most equations that we learned in school are linear – that is, the input is proportional to the output. For example, the equation x2 - 1 = 0 is a linear equation. The equations that generate fractals, however, are nonlinear. Nonlinear equations involve iteration, which means that the solution of the equation is repeatedly fed back into itself. It is an arresting thought that something produced from a purely mathematical procedure can be so aesthetically pleasing.

(13) Algorithms (or, at the very least, formal sets of rules) have been used to compose music for centuries; the procedures used to plot voice-leading in Western counterpoint, for example, can often be reduced to algorithmic determinacy. The term is usually reserved, however, for the use of formal procedures to make music without human intervention, either through the introduction of chance procedures or the use of computers.

(14) Many algorithms that have no immediate musical relevance are used by composers as creative inspiration for their music. Algorithms such as fractals, L-systems, statistical models, and even arbitrary data (e.g. census figures, GIS coordinates, or magnetic field measurements) are fair game for musical interpretation. The success or failure of these procedures as sources of "good" music largely depends on the mapping system employed by the composer to translate the non-musical information into a musical data stream.

(15) There is no universal method to sort different compositional algorithms into categories. One way to do this is to look at the way an algorithm takes part in the compositional process. The results of the process can then be divided into music composed by computer and music composed with the aid of computer. Music may be considered composed by computer when the algorithm is able to make choices of its own during the creation process.

(16). Another way to sort compositional algorithms is to examine the results of their compositional processes. Algorithms can either provide notational information (sheet music) for other instruments or provide an independent way of sound synthesis (playing the composition by itself). There are also algorithms creating both notational data and sound synthesis.

(17). Algorithmic techniques have also been employed in a number of systems intended for direct musical performance, with many using algorithmic techniques to generate infinitely variable improvisations on a predetermined theme. An early example was the 1982 computer game Ballblazer of Lucasfilm Games, where the computer improvised on a basic jazz theme composed by the game's musical director Peter Langston; later in the life of that company, now rechristened LucasArts, an algorithmic iMUSE engine was developed for their flagship game, Dark Forces. Similar generative music systems have caught the attention of noted composers. Brian Eno has produced a number of works for the Koan generative music system, which produces ambient variations for web-pages, mobile devices, and for standalone performance.

36. In a musical scale, 13 notes separate each octave of 8 notes. The 5th note and 3rd note comprise the basic foundation of the chords. These are based on the whole tone, which is two steps from the 1st note of the scale. The pattern represents:

A. The Greek octave.
B. The Fibonacci sequence.
C. Fractals.
D. An algorithmic technique.
E. The golden section.

37. Which of the following phenomena in Nature would NOT resemble the self-replicating form of a fractal?

A. Snow flakes
B. Lightning
C. Circulatory system
D. Wind
E. Broccoli

38. In terms of tone, the middle point on a string in a guitar is known as:

A. a half-tone.
B. the middle 5th.
C. C Major.
D. an octave.

39. Which of the following statements is the best interpretation of the principle of the golden ratio?

A. Each two measures add up to make the next one sequentially proportionate to the lower measure.
B. The length of a whole relates to its large part in the same way that the large part relates to the small part.
C. The proportion of the smaller parts is exponentially derivative to the larger parts.
D. The whole is an expanding sequence of the smaller parts.

40. The key to the richness of details exhibited by fractals are what mathematicians call:

A. non-linear equations.
B. iteration.
C. loops.
D. regeneration.
E. magnified details.

41. The paradox of fractals is stated to be that:

A. its algorithms involve loops.
B. the richness of fractals is self-replicating.
C. the construction of complex shapes requires extraordinarily simple equations.
D. something produced from a purely mathematical procedure can be so aesthetically pleasing.
E. their visual results show great richness.

42. In Béla Bartók's Music for Strings, Percussion and Celesta, the xylophone progression demonstrates:

A. the Fibonacci numbers inverted.
B. a bell curve of a golden ratio.
C. he harmonic ratios of the Pythagoreans.
D. the golden ratio starting at phi and going downwards.
E. a combination of the golden ratio and the Fibonacci numbers.

43. The ancient Greeks measured notes and harmony using frequency ratios. Modern musicians use the golden section to generate rhythmic changes or to develop a melody line.

A. Both statements are true.
B. Both statements are false.
C. The first statement is true, the second statement is false.
D. The first statement is false, the second statement is true.

44. Based on statements in the passage, if one note has a frequency of 400 Hz, the note an octave below it, would be which of the following frequencies?

A. 200 Hz
B. 400 Hz
C. 600 Hz
D. 800 Hz
E. All of the above

45. What makes fractals an important phenomenon in musicology?

A. Their algorithms are very simple.
B. They can produce pleasant music from a purely mathematical procedure.
C. Composers use them as creative inspiration for their music.
D. They manifest self-similarity at all scales.

46. What is the main idea of the passage?

A. Math can be found in all music.
B. Music can be defined using mathematical techniques.
C. Either the golden ratio or the Fibonacci numbers occur in all music.
D. There is an intricate yet measurable relationship between music and math.
E. The form and content of music and mathematics are essentially the same.

47. Algorithms in music usually refer to:

A. formal procedures to make music without human intervention.
B. formal sets of rules that produce fractals.
C. equations.
D. the mapping system of a composer.
E. notational data and sound synthesis.

48. The name of a note an octave above A is also A because a note with a given frequency could only be combined with another note whose frequency is an integer multiple of the first.

A. Both the statement and reason are correct and related.
B. Both the statement and the reason are correct but NOT related.
C. The statement is correct but the reason is NOT.
D. The statement is NOT correct, but the reason is correct.
E. NEITHER the statement NOR the reason is correct.

49. Which of the following would be the best conclusion for the closing paragraph?

A. Indeed, such developments serve to prove that mathematics is as much an art as it is a science.
B. Still, whatever connects music with mathematics, both of them remain two different disciplines.
C. Over the years, mathematics and music do not form such strong opposites as they are commonly considered to do; after all, certain connections and similarities between them explain why some musicians like mathematics and why mathematicians generally love music.
D. Although a less popular notion, mathematical applications have indeed greatly contributed to the world's reservoir of beautiful musical creations.

50. The Pythagoreans investigated musical scales in terms of:

A. mathematical iterations.
B. ratios of small integers.
C. harmonic proportions.
D. rough trigonometry.
E. basic fractions.

GS-1 Physics Practice Test Time limit: 50 minutes

No calculator permitted.

You may use the following values for physical constants:

- **acceleration due to gravity on the surface of the earth: $g = 10\ m/s^2$**
- **speed of light in a vacuum: $c = 3.0 \times 10^8\ m/s$**
- **charge of an electron: $Qe = 1.6 \times 10^{-19}$ coulomb**

Please do not begin until your timer is ready.

1. Which of the following is conserved in an elastic collision?
I. Momentum
II. Kinetic energy
III. Entropy of the universe

A. I only
B. I and II only
C. I and III only
D. I, II and III
E. None of the above

2. A body is in translational equilibrium if it is:

A. moving with constant velocity only.
B. moving with constant acceleration only.
C. either at rest or moving with constant velocity.
D. at rest only.
E. decelerating.

3. A ball is tossed up into the air in the +y direction. Neglecting air resistance, just before the ball hits the ground, the velocity of the ball is:

A. zero and the acceleration is negative.
B. positive and the acceleration is negative.
C. positive and the acceleration is positive.
D. negative and the acceleration is positive.
E. negative and the acceleration is negative.

4. A point charge q at point a was moved to point b with a force F. Points a and b are a distance r from charge Q. What is the work done in moving q from point a to point b?

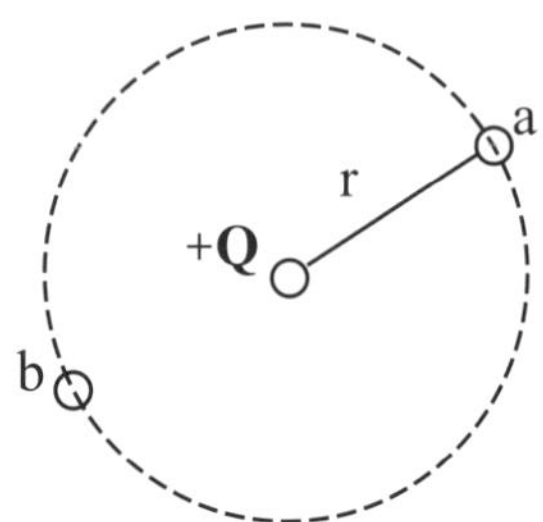

A. $2Fr^2$
B. $2Fr$
C. Fr
D. 0
E. Cannot be determined from the information provided

5. Two mechanical waves of the same frequency pass through the same medium. The range of amplitudes possible when the two waves pass through the medium is between four and eight. Which of the following describes the possible amplitudes of the two waves?

A. 6 units and 2 units
B. 8 units and 4 units
C. 12 units and 4 units
D. 10 units and 2 units
E. 24 units and 18 units

6. A 10 kg block is accelerated at 2 m/s^2 up a frictionless plane inclined at 30 degrees to the horizontal. The force acting parallel to the plane pushing the block upwards is:

A. 100 N.
B. 25 N.
C. 50 N.
D. 70 N.
E. 10 N.

7. A charged rod is placed between two insulated conducting spheres as shown in the diagram. The two spheres have no net charge. Region II has the same polarity as which of the following Regions?

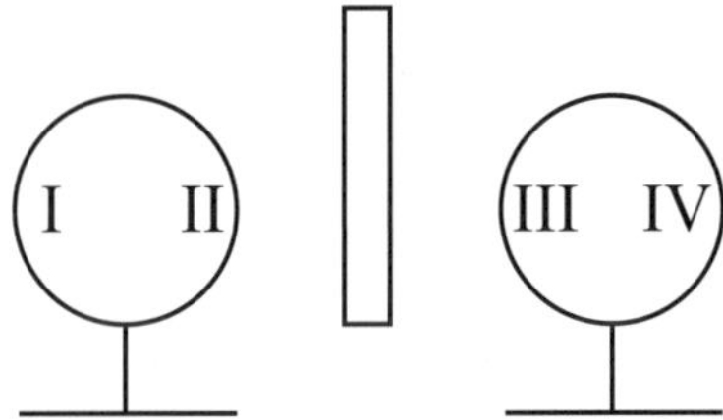

A. I and III only
B. I and IV only
C. I only
D. III only
E. IV only

8. A man travels to a planet that has twice the radius of the Earth and twice the mass. His weight on that planet compared to his weight on Earth is:

A. doubled.
B. tripled.
C. halved.
D. quadrupled.
E. quartered.

9. A 7 kg mass was attached to an elastic string of length 5 m with elastic constant k. The string was then attached to a horizontal support such that the mass hung downward. The string was stretched by 0.20 m in the downwards direction and then released. The time x required for one complete cycle of oscillation was calculated for the 7 kg mass. The value x represents the:

A. amplitude.
B. frequency.
C. period.
D. displacement.
E. resonance.

10. Which of the following physical quantities would be the result of multiplying megawatts by the amount of time?

A. Charge
B. Energy
C. Power
D. Current
E. Capacitance

11. Without the presence of air resistance, the horizontal speed of a projectile at any point in its flight is equal to which of the following?

A. Total speed
B. Vertical speed
C. Final vertical speed
D. Initial vertical speed
E. Initial horizontal speed

12. If an object is made to resonate, all of the following properties of the system would be at its maximum EXCEPT one. Which one is the EXCEPTION?

A. Power
B. Energy
C. Amplitude
D. Speed
E. None of the above

13. A 0.2 kg ball accelerates from rest at 5 m s^{-2} for five seconds. It then collides with a 0.5 kg ball which is initially at rest. The smaller ball stops moving while the larger ball begins its motion. After the collision, how fast is the larger ball initially moving?

A. 2.0 m s^{-1}
B. 10 m s^{-1}
C. 2.5 m s^{-1}
D. 5.0 m s^{-1}
E. 20 m s^{-1}

14. The diagram below is a schematic for a typical light microscope which is composed of two convex lenses which act independently. The objective or lens for the object O creates a real image which is magnified by the eyepiece.

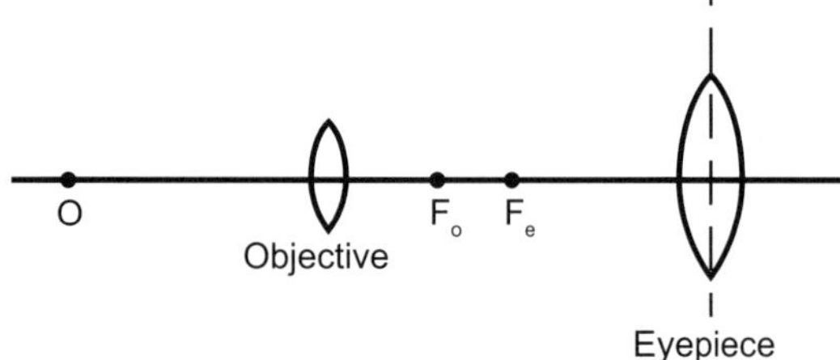

F_o = focal point of objective
F_e = focal point of eyepiece

The real image created by the objective will be:

A. enlarged and erect.
B. enlarged and inverted.
C. the same size and erect.
D. diminished and erect.
E. diminished and inverted.

15. In the Young slit experiment, light appears to bend around the corners of the slits. This property of light is called:

A. refraction.
B. reflection.
C. diffraction.
D. selection.
E. forced vibrations.

16. The following is a graph of velocity as a function of time for a moving vehicle. Which of the graphs below is most consistent with the same event, during the same time frame, but graphed as acceleration as a function of time?

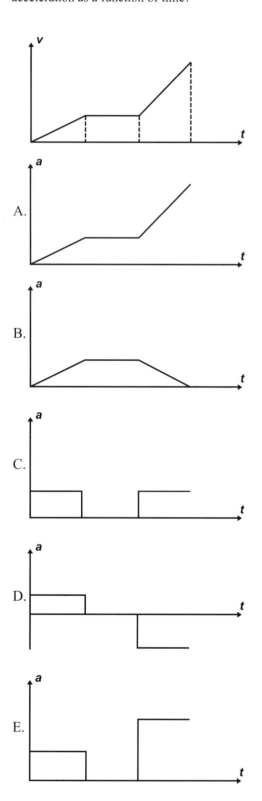

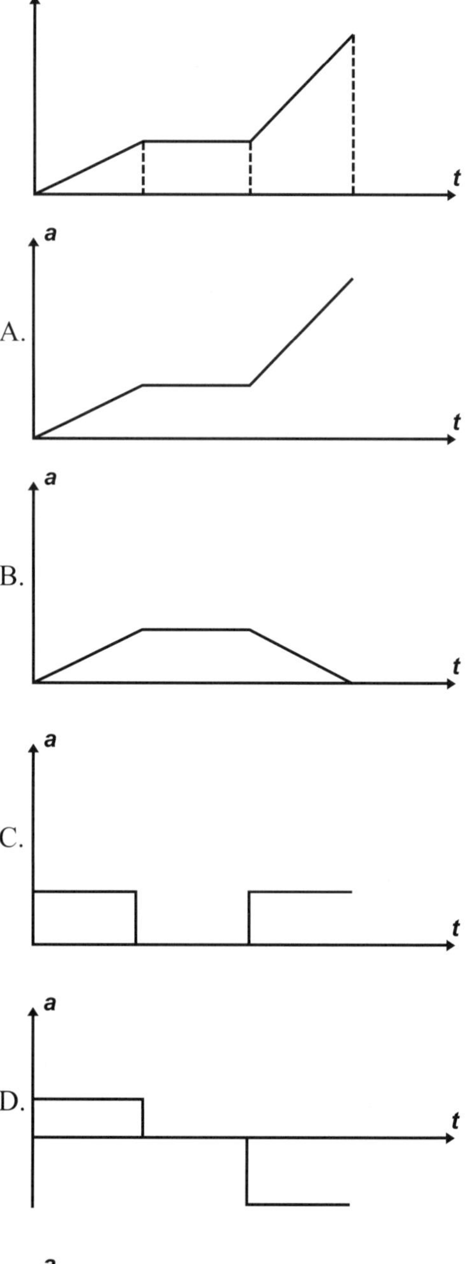

17. Sound travels at about 343 m s^{-1} in air, and markedly faster in liquids and solids. Sonar is one of the applications of sound used extensively in undersea mapping. A transmitter emits a pulse of sound and the time it takes to return is used to determine the depth. If the sound wave takes 20 seconds to return, and sound travels four times as quickly in water as in air, how deep is that region?

A. 3 430 m
B. 6 860 m
C. 13 720 m
D. 27 440 m
E. 33 430 m

18. A vertically oriented spring is stretched by 0.50 m when a mass of 1 kg is suspended from it. What is the work done on the spring?

A. 5.0 J
B. 2.5 J
C. 0.5 J
D. 20.0 J
E. 10 J

19. The following system includes a frictionless pulley and a cord of negligible mass. Since the system is at rest, what can be said about the force of friction between the platform and the large weight?

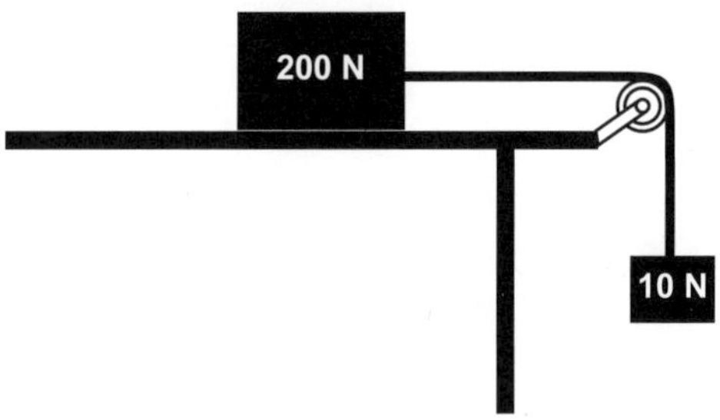

A. It is 200 N.
B. It is 10 N.
C. It is 190 N.
D. It is 210 N.
E. In this case, the force of friction is not necessarily present.

20. Two charged particles are a distance x apart. If the charges on the two particles remains the same while the distance between them is doubled, how does the force between the particles change?

A. It stays the same.
B. It decreases by a factor of 4.
C. It decreases by a factor of 2.
D. It decreases by a factor of $\sqrt{2}$.
E. It decreases by a factor of $\sqrt{3}$.

21. For an object moving in uniform circular motion, the direction of the instantaneous acceleration vector is:

A. tangent to the path of motion.
B. equal to zero.
C. opposite to the direction of motion.
D. directed radially outward.
E. directed radially inward.

22. A mass of 100 kg is placed on a uniform bar at a point 0.5 m to the left of a fulcrum. Where must a 75 kg mass be placed relative to the fulcrum in order to establish a state of equilibrium given that the bar was in equilibrium before any weights were applied?

A. 0.67 m to the right of the fulcrum
B. 0.67 m to the left of the fulcrum
C. 0.38 m to the right of the fulcrum
D. 0.38 m to the left of the fulcrum
E. Exactly at the fulcrum

23. A water heater has pipes to supply water to the collector that heats the water which then leaves the container via draining pipes. It was found that 1 L of water from the supplying pipes to the collector weighed more than 1 L of water from the draining pipes from the collector when an accurate weighing apparatus was used. Why is this?

A. The density of the water in the supplying pipes is less than that of the water in the draining pipes.
B. The density of the water in the supplying pipes is greater than that of the water in the draining pipes.
C. The pressure of the water in the supplying pipes is less than that of the water in the draining pipes.
D. The pressure of the water in the supplying pipes is greater than that of the water in the draining pipes.
E. None of the above.

24. An airplane is encircling an airport with DECREASING speed. When the airplane reaches point P, what is the general direction of its acceleration?

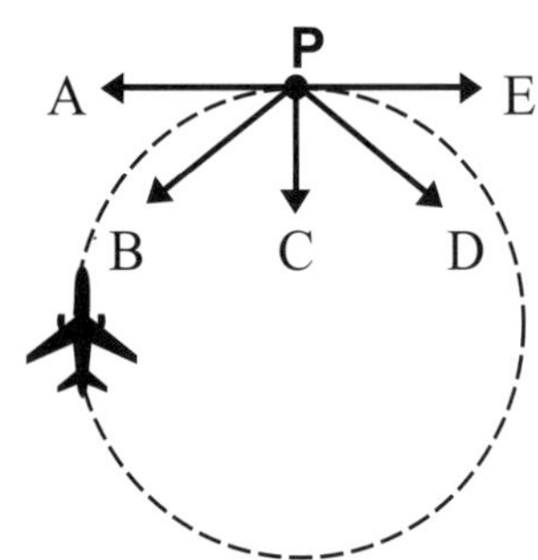

25. The level of water in each arm of a manometer gives the pressure difference between the reaction vessel and the atmosphere. If the water level in the right side is higher, then the reaction vessel is at a higher pressure than the atmosphere and vice-versa. Given that at the start of the reaction, the water levels in both arms of the manometer were equal, all the gases are insoluble, negligible temperature change, and the liquid in the reaction vessel evolves gaseous products, what did the apparatus look like after the reaction?

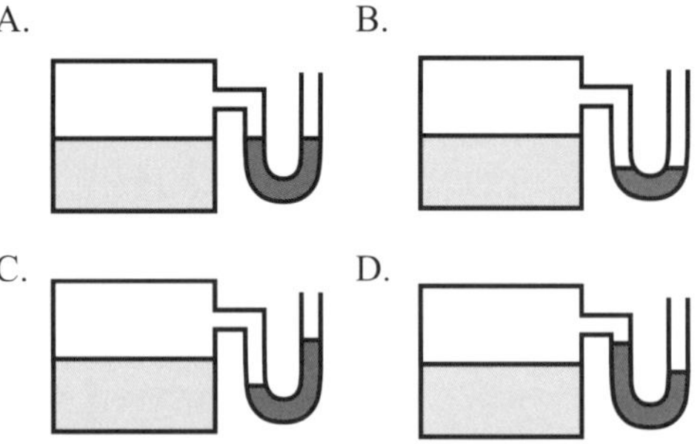

26. A stone is dropped into a well. Ten seconds later a splash is heard. How deep is the water level below the well opening (ignoring the time taken for sound to travel)?

A. 1000 m
B. 500 m
C. 50 m
D. 200 m
E. 750 m

27. Consider the diagram of the compound circuit. The three bulbs 1, 2, and 3 – represented as resistors R in the diagram – are identical. Which of the following statements are true?

I. Bulb 3 is brighter than bulb 1 or 2.
II. Bulb 3 has more current passing through it than bulb 1 or 2.
III. Bulb 3 has a greater voltage drop across it than bulb 1 or 2.

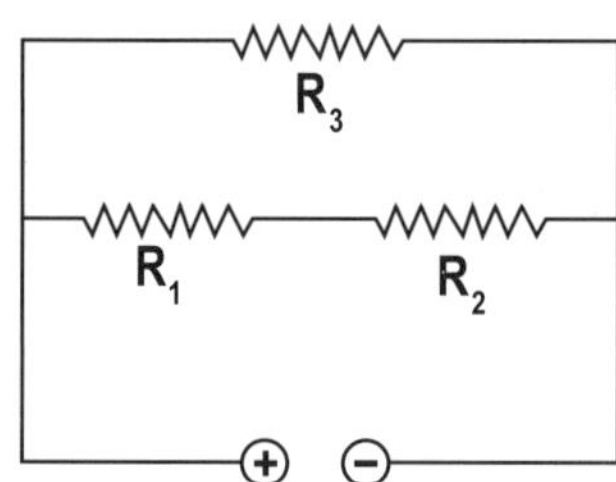

A. I only
B. I and II only
C. I and III only
D. I, II and III
E. None of the above

28. Why would a neutron be preferred to a proton for bombarding atomic nuclei?

A. It is smaller than a proton.
B. It weighs less than a proton.
C. It has no charge.
D. It can be obtained from a nucleus.
E. It is faster than a proton.

29. What is the refractive power of an objective lens with a focal length of 0.50 cm?

A. 0.2 diopters
B. 2.0 diopters
C. 20 diopters
D. 100 diopters
E. 200 diopters

30. The disk *B* is rotating freely with an angular velocity ω on frictionless bearings, as shown in the diagram below. A second identical disk *A*, initially not rotating, is placed on top of *B* so that both disks rotate together without slipping. When the two disks are rotating together, which of the following is half of what it was before?

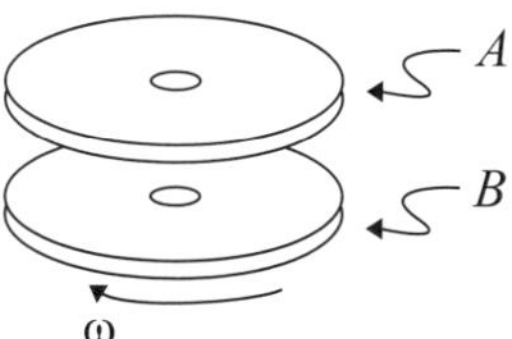

A. Angular velocity of *A*
B. Angular velocity of *B*
C. Moment of inertia of *A*
D. Moment of inertia of *B*
E. Angular momentum of both disks

31. After leaving a flat horizontal surface, the driver of a car follows a road that eventually goes up a hill where the car stops at a traffic light. How does the frictional force on the car now on an incline compare to the value when the car was on level ground?

A. No change
B. It increased.
C. It decreased.
D. The direction of change depends on the angle of elevation.
E. The direction of change depends on the tires of the car.

32. A ball is placed in water and floats such that ½ of the height of the ball can be seen above the surface of the water. The density of water is 1 g/cm^3. The same ball was placed in fluid X where one quarter of the height of the ball was found to project over the surface. What is the density of fluid X?

A. 0.67 g/cm^3
B. 0.25 g/cm^3
C. 0.75 g/cm^3
D. 0.38 g/cm^3
E. 1 g/cm^3

33. A mechanical wave has the following measured values.

amplitude = 0.50 N m^{-2}
speed = 7.5 x 10^3 m s^{-1}
intensity = 4.5 x 10^{-3} W m^{-2}
phase angle = $\pi/6$ radians
wavelength = 1.5 m

What is the frequency of this wave?

A. 1.1 x 10^4 Hz
B. 5.0 x 10^3 Hz
C. 3.7 x 10^3 Hz
D. 12.0 Hz
E. 1.5 Hz

34. Which of the following would you expect to remain constant when light travels from one medium to another and the media differ in their refractive indices?

A. Velocity
B. Frequency
C. Wavelength
D. Intensity
E. None of the above

35. A sound wave emanating from a stationary observer bounces off an object approaching with velocity v. The original wave, relative to the reflected wave, has:

A. a higher wavelength but a lower velocity.
B. a lower wavelength and the same velocity.
C. a higher wavelength and the same velocity.
D. a lower wavelength but a higher velocity.
E. same wavelength with higher velocity.

36. Given the directions and magnitudes of current in the copper wires below, what is the magnitude of current in wire R?

Q = 7 A
T = 8 A
S = 4 A
U = 11 A

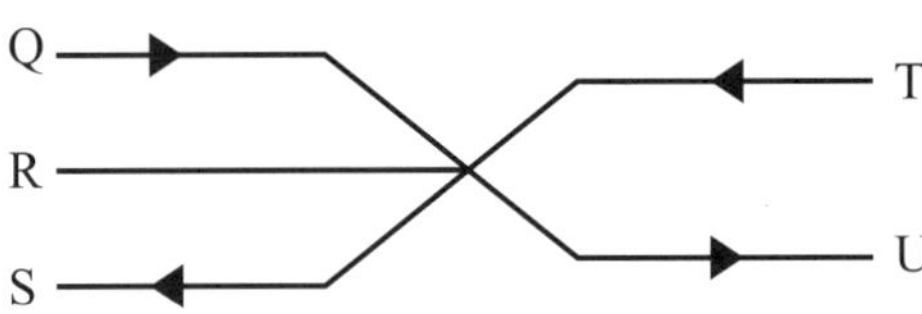

A. 0 A
B. 7 A
C. 15 A
D. 18 A
E. 30 A

37. The following represents the movement of charges in a wire. Which of the following best describes the direction of the magnetic field at point P?

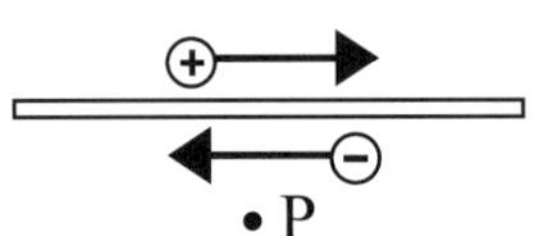

A. To the left of the diagram
B. To the right of the diagram
C. Out of the plane of the screen or page
D. Into the plane of the screen or page
E. Based on the information in the diagram, there should be no magnetic field.

38. All of the following are vector quantities EXCEPT one. Choose the one EXCEPTION.

A. Force
B. Electric field
C. Acceleration
D. Velocity
E. Energy

39. The newton (symbol: N) is the SI derived unit of force. Which of the following represents a newton in SI base units?

A. $kg{\cdot}m{\cdot}s^2$
B. $kg{\cdot}m/s^2$
C. $kg/m{\cdot}s^2$
D. $kg{\cdot}\ s^2/m$
E. $m{\cdot}\ s^2/kg$

40. Which of the following types of radioactive emissions involves the emission of a helium nucleus?

A. Alpha decay
B. Beta decay
C. Gamma ray
D. Only 2 and 3
E. None of the above

1. Stephen is 4ft tall, and he is growing ½ in. every two months. John is 3ft 10in and is growing 1in. every three months. If these rates remain constant, how tall will Stephen and John be when they are the same height?

A. 4ft 6in
B. 4ft 10in
C. 5ft
D. 5ft 6in
E. 6ft

2. Which of the following are possible values of x if $x^2 - 7x + 5 = -7$?

A. -3
B. 3
C. 4
D. A and C
E. B and C

3. What is the mean value of the set {7 , 7 , 8 , 10 , 13}?

A. 7
B. 8
C. 9
D. 10
E. 11

4. If an equilateral triangle has a base of length 3, what is the measure of the angle between the base and the left side?

A. 60°
B. 45°
C. 30°
D. 90°
E. Insufficient information to draw a conclusion

5. If a six-sided die is rolled three times, what is the probability that every roll will turn up an even number?

A. 3/2
B. 1/2
C. 1/6
D. 1/8
E. 1/16

6. If f is a function that satisfies $f(x) = 2f(x)$ for all real numbers x, which of the following must be true of $f(1)$?

A. $f(1) = 2$
B. $f(1) = 1$
C. $f(1) = 0$
D. Either $f(1) = 1$ or $f(1) = 0$
E. Insufficient information to draw a conclusion

7. A certain blueberry bush can produce a maximum of 400 berries in a season. If one year it produces only 30% of its maximum yield and the next year it produces 85%, how many berries does it produce over the two-year period?

A. 200
B. 340
C. 400
D. 460
E. 600

8. If 2 km is equal to 1.2 miles, then 3.5 miles is approximately equal to how many km?

A. 2.7
B. 4.75
C. 5.4
D. 5.8
E. 12

9. Which of the following is the value of $\cot\left(\frac{7\pi}{6}\right)$?

A. -1
B. -1/2
C. $\sqrt{2}$
D. $\sqrt{3}$
E. $\frac{(\sqrt{3})}{2}$

10. Consider the point p with coordinates (5 , 1) in the Cartesian plane. What is sin θ where θ is the angle between the x-axis and the line from the origin to p?

A. 1/50

B. $\dfrac{1}{\sqrt{26}}$

C. 1/5

D. 1/2

E. $\dfrac{\sqrt{3}}{2}$

11. If a cup of sand has a mass of 360 g, about how many cups are in 20 kg of sand?

A. .06
B. 18
C. 55.6
D. 100
E. 720

12. Which of the following is the best approximation for $\dfrac{\left[\left(7.2\times10^{3}\right)\left(4.61\times10^{8}\right)\right]}{\left(2.23\times10^{7}\right)}$?

A. 1.5×10^{-4}
B. 1.5×10^{-2}
C. 1.5×10^{3}
D. 1.5×10^{4}
E. 1.5×10^{5}

13. What is the length of a diagonal of a rectangle with sides length 3 and 5?

A. 4
B. $\sqrt{15}$
C. $\sqrt{34}$
D. 8
E. 15

14. Three days, 14 hours, and 26 minutes is equal to how many minutes?

A. 3266
B. 4026
C. 4826
D. 5126
E. 5186

15. Which of the following is the length of each side of a square inscribed in a circle with a radius of 3?

A. 3
B. $3\sqrt{2}$
C. 5.2
D. 6
E. 9

16. 3x is to 6y as 5xy is to:

A. 10x
B. 10y
C. 10x/y
D. $10x^2$
E. $10y^2$

17. Which of the following is the value of x if $(3x + 2)^2 - x = 6$?

A. 1/5
B. 2/5
C. 1
D. 2/3
E. 2/7

18. Which of the following is the length of the side labeled S in the right triangle below?

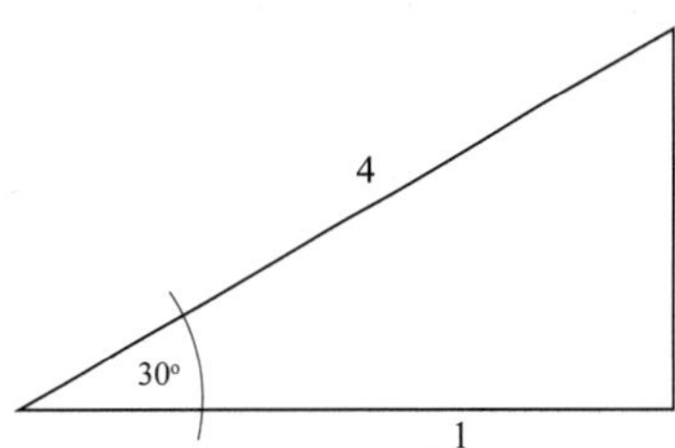

A. 1/2

B. $\dfrac{\sqrt{3}}{2}$

C. $\sqrt{2}$

D. 2

E. $2\sqrt{3}$

19. Which of the following is equal to sin x if csc $x = \frac{2}{\sqrt{3}}$ and if $\frac{3\pi}{2} < x < 2\pi$?

A. $-\frac{\sqrt{3}}{2}$
B. -1/2
C. 1/2
D. $\frac{\sqrt{3}}{2}$
E. $\frac{1}{\sqrt{2}}$

20. If $(2/x) + 3 > 5 - (1/x)$, then which must be true?

A. $(1/x) > (2/3)$
B. $(1/x) < (2/3)$
C. $(3/2) > x$
D. $(3/2) < x$
E. A and C

21. A cylinder has a height of 10 cm and a base diameter of 6 cm. Which of the following is the best approximation of the total surface area, in cm^2?

A. 245
B. 220
C. 180
D. 120
E. 60

22. A car is travelling at 65 mph. What fraction of an hour will it take for the car to travel 25 miles?

A. 1/4
B. 5/13
C. 1/2
D. 2/3
E. 23/30

23. While shopping for clothing John purchases three pairs of pants at $39.99 each, four shirts at $15.75 each, and a dozen socks at $3.00 a pair. Which of the following best approximates John's total purchase?

A. $60
B. $200
C. $220
D. $240
E. $300

24. Which of the following is 75% of 7/2?

A. 11/6
B. 21/8
C. 5/2
D. 3
E. 13/4

25. If the planet Earth has a mass of 5.97×10^{24} kg, and the planet Jupiter has a mass of 1.90×10^{27} kg, approximately how many times more massive is Jupiter than Earth?

A. 3.2×10^{-3}
B. 3.2×10^{1}
C. 3.2×10^{2}
D. 3.2×10^{3}
E. 3.2×10^{51}

26. How many pounds does 4.5 kg equal if 1 kg is equal to 2.2 pounds?

A. 2
B. 4.5
C. 7.2
D. 9
E. 9.9

27. Which of the following represents the distance between the points (-2 , 1) and (10 , 6) in the Cartesian plane?

A. $2\sqrt{3}$
B. $2\sqrt{11}$
C. 13
D. 17
E. $12\sqrt{5}$

28. Taylor has a container with 12 blue marbles and 8 yellow marbles. If she draws two marbles in a row without replacement, what is the probability that both marbles are yellow?

A. 14/95
B. 14/57
C. 4/19
D. 5/19
E. 1/3

29. Which of the following equations describe a line passing through points (-1 , 3) , (1 , 0) and (5 , -6) in the Cartesian plane?

A. $y = -(3/2)x + 1$
B. $y = (3/2)x + 3/2$
C. $3y + 3x = 5$
D. $y + 2x = 2/3$
E. $2y + 3x = 3$

30. Which of the following is equivalent to the fraction $\dfrac{\left[2-\left(\frac{6}{5}\right)\right]}{\left[1+\left(\frac{2}{5}\right)\right]}$?

A. 1
B. 1/2
C. 4/7
D. 11/5
E. 2

31. In a college classroom of 143 students the ratio of women to men was 4 to 7. How many of the students were male?

A. 13
B. 36
C. 52
D. 81
E. 91

32. Which of the following is smallest?

A. $\dfrac{1}{\sqrt{3}}$
B. 11/23
C. 2/3
D. 3/5
E. 7/13

33. Which of the following is equal to x if $\left(\frac{.06}{2.7}\right)\left(\frac{81}{x}\right) = 5.4$?

A. 1/3
B. 1
C. 2
D. 9/5
E. 20/3

34. A tree that is 4 meters tall will grow in height by a maximum of 40% for every subsequent year. Which of the following represents the best approximation of the maximum increase in height the tree can have over the next 3 years?

A. 1.6
B. 4.8
C. 6.4
D. 7.0
E. 11.0

35. Which of the following is the value of x if $x \neq -2,\ x \neq 3$, and $\dfrac{2}{[3(x+2)]} + \dfrac{3}{(x-3)} = \dfrac{(5x-1)}{(x^2-x-6)}$?

A. 3/4
B. 15/4
C. 15
D. -2
E. -6

36. To the nearest multiple of 10, which of the following best approximates 17.4×9.7?

A. 100
B. 160
C. 170
D. 180
E. 200

37. On a trip to and from the grocery store Sid travelled at an average speed of 28 mph. If it took him 18 minutes to get to the store and 12 minutes to get back home, what was his average speed on the way home?

A. 20 mph
B. 24 mph
C. 28 mph
D. 30 mph
E. 35 mph

38. A jar contains 3 green balls and 6 red balls. If 3 balls are drawn without replacement, what is the probability that the first 2 will be green and the third will be red?

A. 1/11
B. 1/12
C. 1/13
D. 1/14
E. 1/15

39. If 2 cups of water, 1 cup of 90% apple juice and 3 cups of 60% apple juice are mixed, what is the percentage of apple juice in the mixture?

A. 45%
B. 50%
C. 60%
D. 75%
E. 90%

40. On a math quiz, 1/3 of the 36 students in the class scored a 10, 1/12 scored a 9, ¼ scored an 8, and the rest scored a 7. What was the median quiz score?

A. 10
B. 9.5
C. 9
D. 8
E. 7

 END OF THIS TEST SECTION.

Answer Keys & Solutions

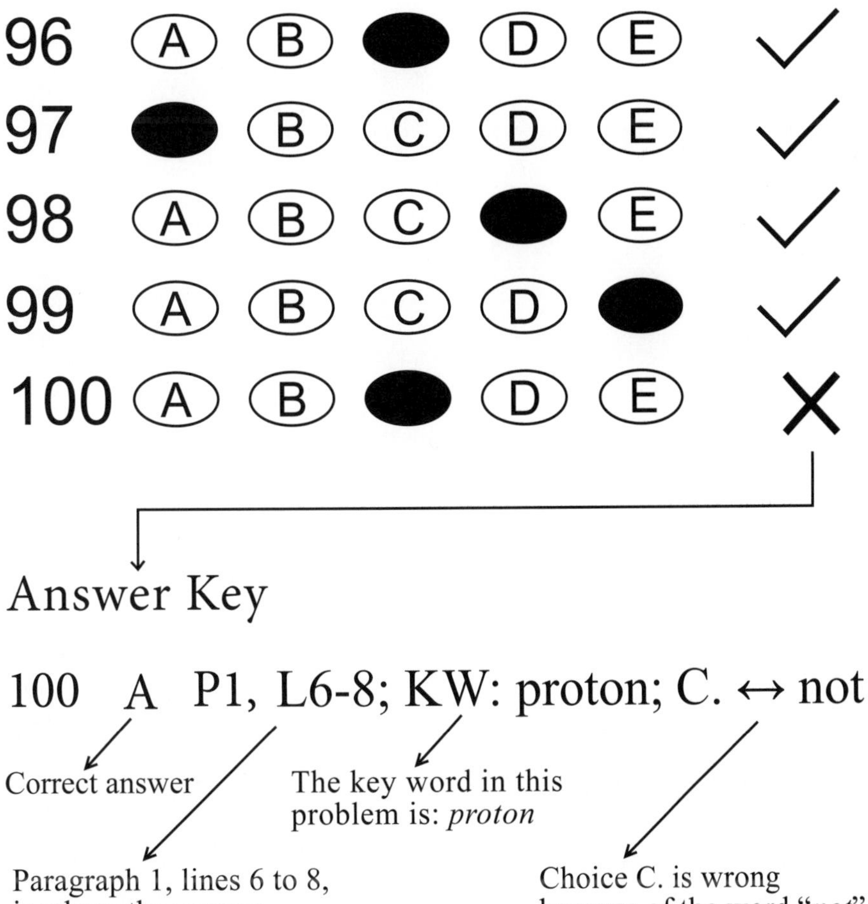

Answer Document
96 A B D E
97 B C D E
98 A B C E
99 A B C D
100 A B D E
Answer Key
100 A P1, L6-8; KW: proton; C. ↔ not
Correct answer
The key word in this problem is: *proton*
Paragraph 1, lines 6 to 8, is where the answer can be found
Choice C. is wrong because of the word "*not*"

GOLD STANDARD OAT ANSWER KEY

GS-1: Natural Sciences Test

		Cross-reference
1.	C	BIO 15.5
2.	A	BIO 7.5, 8.3
3.	E	BIO 12.4
4.	B	BIO 15.1, 15.3
5.	E	BIO 17.1, 17.2 , 17.2.3
6.	C	BIO 17.1, 17.2
7.	B	BIO 14.5.1
8.	E	BIO 2.2, BIO 16.6.4
9.	A	BIO 6.3.3, 5.4.4
10.	A	BIO 4.1, CHM 9.7; CHM 9.7
11.	C	BIO 14.5
12.	E	BIO 19.7
13.	E	BIO 7.2, 7.3, 7.5.1
14.	B	BIO 7.5.2, 10.3
15.	C	BIO 4.3, 2.5, 2.5.1
16.	B	BIO 4.1, 15.7, Chapter 15 Appendix
17.	B	BIO 1.2.2, BIO 3, BIO 20.5
18.	E	BIO 15.2
19.	C	BIO 6.2.3
20.	E	BIO 1.4.1, 17.6.4
21.	C	BIO 1.1.3
22.	D	BIO 1.1.1, 4.1
23.	D	BIO 2.2, BIO 16.6.4
24.	D	BIO 19.2
25.	E	BIO 1.1, 5.1.1, 5.1.3
26.	D	BIO 14.2
27.	C	BIO 4.4
28.	E	BIO 14.3
29.	B	BIO 4.2
30.	C	BIO 14.2
31.	E	BIO 1.2.2, 3.0
32.	D	BIO 2.2
33.	A	BIO 9.4.1
34.	D	BIO 17.6.3, 17.6.6
35.	E	BIO 4.1, 4.7; CHM 8.2, 10.1, 10.2

		Cross-reference
36.	E	BIO 20.2.2
37.	E	BIO 7 Appendix
38.	B	BIO 16.3, 19.2-19.4 and Appendix
39.	E	BIO 16.4.2, 17
40.	A	BIO 11.3, 11.3.3
41.	A	CHM 8.3, 1.4
42.	E	CHM 3.4, 6.1
43.	D	CHM 1.4
44.	E	CHM 5.3.1
45.	A	CHM 6.6, 6.5
46.	A	CHM 1.3, 1.5
47.	B	CHM 10.1
48.	C	CHM 2.3
49.	A	CHM 4.2, 4.3.2
50.	C	CHM 4.2, ORG 10.1
51.	B	CHM 4.1.7
52.	E	CHM 11.4
53.	D	CHM 11
54.	B	CHM 10.1, 10.2
55.	D	CHM 5.3.2
56.	D	CHM 3.5
57.	E	CHM 2.4, 2.4.1
58.	C	CHM 1.1-1.5
59.	B	CHM 2.3
60.	D	CHM 10.4
61.	E	CHM 6.9
62.	E	CHM 1.5.1, 5.2, 6.2, 6.9.1
63.	C	CHM 2.1, 2.2, 2.3
64.	B	CHM 6.1
65.	D	E; CHM 8.10
66.	E	CHM 8.7
67.	A	CHM 5.1.1, 5.1.2
68.	A	CHM 4.1.2, 4.1.8
69.	C	CHM 9.3
70.	A	CHM 12.3.1
71.	A	ORG 2.1, 2.2, 2.3
72.	E	ORG 1.6, 7.1, 8.1, 9.4

		Cross-reference
73.	A	CHM 6.3, ORG 1.6, 4.2.1, 6.2.4, 11.1.1
74.	D	ORG 4.2, 7.1, 8.1, 14.1
75.	D	ORG 1.1, 8.1
76.	B	CHM 6.3, ORG 5.2.2, 10.2
77.	C	ORG 7.2.2
78.	D	ORG 13.3, CHM 12
79.	B	CHM 3.5, ORG 3.3, 10.1
80.	C	ORG 7.1
81.	A	ORG 13.2.1
82.	A	ORG 12.1.2
83.	C	ORG 14.2
84.	E	ORG 3.1, 4.1
85.	C	ORG 13
86.	C	ORG 2.1, 2.2, 2.3
87.	E	ORG 6.2.4
88.	E	ORG 7.2.3
89.	A	ORG 2.3.1, 2.3.2, 2.3.3
90.	B	ORG 4.2.1
91.	C	CHM 9.5, 9.7, 9.8, 9.10, ORG 6.2.1
92.	C	CHM 8.2, 8.10, 9.5
93.	E	ORG 3.3, 12.3.2 F
94.	C	CHM 3.5; ORG 1.2, 1.3
95.	B	ORG 4.2.4
96.	A	ORG 4.2.2, 6.1, 9.4, 13.1; CHM 12
97.	E	CHM 3.5; ORG 1.2, 1.3, 4.1, 4.2
98.	E	ORG 5.1.1
99.	D	ORG 1.6, 5.2, 5.2.1, 5.2.2, 6.2.2, 7.2.3
100.	C	CHM 3.5; ORG 1.2, 1.3

To estimate your standard score, sign in to oatbooks.com then click Tests in the top Menu. Cross-references above refer to subsections from chapters in the Gold Standard Book Set.

GS-1: Reading Comprehension Test

1.	C	18.	B	35.	C
2.	C	19.	D	36.	B
3.	E	20.	B	37.	D
4.	D	21.	C	38.	D
5.	E	22.	A	39.	B
6.	B	23.	B	40.	B
7.	B	24.	D	41.	C
8.	B	25.	A	42.	B
9.	B	26.	E	43.	A
10.	E	27.	C	44.	A
11.	B	28.	B	45.	D
12.	D	29.	B	46.	D
13.	C	30.	B	47.	A
14.	D	31.	B	48.	C
15.	C	32.	B	49.	D
16.	D	33.	D	50.	B
17.	A	34.	C		

GS-1: Physics Test

		Cross-reference			Cross-reference
1.	B	PHY 4.4; CHM 8.8, 8.9	20.	B	PHY 9.1.2
2.	C	PHY 4.1, 4.1.1	21.	E	PHY 3.3
3.	E	PHY 2.5, 2.6	22.	A	PHY 4.1, 4.1.1
4.	D	PHY 9.1.4, 9.1.5	23.	B	PHY 6.1.1
5.	A	PHY 7.1.3	24.	B	PHY 3.3
6.	D	PHY 2.1, 2.2	25.	C	PHY 6.1.2
7.	D	PHY 9.1.1	26.	B	PHY 1.5, 2.6.1
8.	C	PHY 2.4	27.	D	PHY 10.1, 10.2, 10.3
9.	C	PHY 7.1.2	28.	C	PHY 12.1
10.	B	PHY 5.1, 5.7	29.	E	PHY 11.5
11.	E	PHY 2.4, 2.6	30.	B	PHY 4.1, 4.2, 4.5
12.	D	PHY 7.1.2, 7.1.4	31.	C	PHY 3.2, 3.2.1
13.	B	PHY 1.6, 2.6, 4.3, 4.4	32.	A	PHY 6.1.1, 6.1.2
14.	E	PHY 11.5	33.	B	PHY 7.1.2
15.	C	PHY 7.1.3, 11.1, 11.3, 11.4	34.	B	PHY 11.4
16.	E	PHY 1.3, 1.4, 1.4.1	35.	C	PHY 8.5, 8.2
17.	C	PHY 1.3	36.	A	PHY 10.3.1
18.	B	PHY 7.2.1	37.	D	PHY 9.2.3
19.	B	PHY 3.2, 3.2.1, 3.4	38.	E	PHY 1.1, 5.2
			39.	B	PHY 2.2
			40.	A	PHY 12.3

GS-1: Quantitative Reasoning Test

		Cross-reference			Cross-reference			Cross-reference
1.	A	QR 3.2, 3.2.1, 8.2, 8.2.1	14.	E	QR 3.1, 3.1.1	28.	A	QR 7.1, 7.1.2
2.	E	QR 4.6, 4.6.1	15.	B	QR 5.2, 5.2.3, 6.3, 6.3.3	29.	E	QR 4.5, 4.5.4
3.	C	QR 7.2, 7.2.2	16.	E	QR 2.4, 2.4.2	30.	C	QR 2.4, 2.4.2
4.	A	QR 5.2, 5.2.2	17.	B	QR 4.1, 4.1.1, 4.3, 4.3.1	31.	E	QR 2.6
5.	D	QR 7.1	18.	E	QR 6.1, 6.1.2	32.	B	QR 2.4, 2.4.1
6.	C	QR 4.1, 4.1.4	19.	B	QR 6.1, 6.1.4, 6.2, 6.2.1	33.	A	QR 2.4, 2.41, 2.4.2
7.	D	QR 2.4.3, 8.3	20.	E	QR 4.2, 4.2.2	34.	D	QR 8.2, 8.2.3
8.	D	QR 2.6	21.	A	QR 5.3, 5.3.3	35.	B	QR 4.3, 4.3.1, 4.3.3
9.	D	QR 6.1, 6.1.4, 6.2, 6.2.1	22.	B	QR 2.6	36.	C	QR 2.2, 2.2.1
10.	B	QR 5.1, 5.1.1, 5.2, 5.2.2, 6.1, 6.1.1	23.	B	QR 2.2, 2.2.3	37.	E	QR 3.1, 3.1.1, 8.2, 8.2.2
11.	C	QR 2.6, 3.2, 3.2.1	24.	B	QR 2.4, 4.2	38.	D	QR 7.1, 7.1.2
12.	E	QR 2.5, 2.5.2	25.	C	QR 2.5, 2.5.2	39.	A	QR 2.4.3, 8.3, 8.3.3
13.	C	QR 5.2, 5.2.2, 6.3, 6.3.3	26.	E	QR 2.6	40.	D	QR 7.2, 7.2.2
			27.	C	QR 4.5, 4.5.2, 5.1, 5.1.1			

To estimate your standard score, sign in to oatbooks.com then click Tests in the top Menu. Cross-references above refer to subsections from chapters in the Gold Standard Book Set.

GS-1 SOLUTIONS

Question 1 C

See: BIO 15.5

Mutations are rare, inheritable, random changes in the genetic material (DNA) of a cell. Mutations are much more likely to be either neutral (esp. silent mutations) or negative (i.e. cancer) than positive for an organism's survival. Nonetheless, such a change in the genome increases genetic variability. Only mutations of gametes, and not somatic cells, are passed on to offspring. The following are some forms of mutations:

- Point mutation is a change affecting a single base pair in a gene
- Deletion is the removal of a sequence of DNA, the regions on either side being joined together
- Inversion is the reversal of a segment of DNA
- Translocation is when one chromosome breaks and attaches to another
- Duplication is when a sequence of DNA is repeated.
- Frame shift mutations occur when bases are added or deleted in numbers other than multiples of three. Such deletions or additions cause the rest of the sequence to be shifted such that each triplet reading frame is altered.

Question 2 A

See: BIO 7.5, 8.3

The spleen contains white pulp and red pulp. While the white pulp contains leukocytes (including antigen presenting cells) which filter red blood cells as well as foreign particles, the red pulp stores erythrocytes. It does not, however, produce platelets which are formed from fragments of large bone marrow cells or megakaryocytes.

Question 3 E

See: BIO 12.4

Inspiration is active and requires the contraction of the diaphragm by the phrenic nerve. The diaphragm will thus move downward, while the thoracic cage is pushed outwards increasing the volume of the chest cavity. This will thus cause a negative internal pressure which will allow air to enter the lungs. Hence, only answer choice **E.** is correct.

Question 4 B

See: BIO 15.1, 15.3

The reaction indicates that the allele for the normal and abnormal gene exists in the mother (Aa) and 2 abnormal alleles exist in the father (aa). As such, a Punnett square can be produced for this couple.

A = chromosome with normal gene

a = chromosome with abnormal gene

	a	**a**
A	Aa	Aa
a	aa	aa

Hence, 50% of boys will manifest the disease: boys (actually either sex since this is not sex-linked) could be either Aa or aa.

Question 5 E

See: BIO 17.1, 17.2 , 17.2.3

The vascular bundle is scattered in monocots. In dicot stems, it is common that the xylem and phloem tissues are present on the same radius and just opposed to each other in conjoint vascular bundles (ring patterned). Depending on the number and position of phloem group, conjoint vascular bundles can be of two types: collateral type and bi-collateral type.

Collateral vascular bundles are very common and seen in stems of dicotyledons (with some exceptions). Cambium may be present or absent in between xylem and phloem patches making the vascular bundle open or closed, respectively.

Bi-collateral vascular bundles contain two (= bi) patches of phloem on either sides of the xylem on the same radius. The outer phloem or external phloem remains towards the periphery of the central cylinder and the inner or internal phloem remains towards the center.

Question 6 C

See: BIO 17.1, 17.2

The cuticle is a continuous layer of waxy substances covering the outer surfaces of the epidermis of plants, it contains cutin and protects against water loss (or gain) and other damage. The term is also used for the hard outer covering or case of certain organisms such as arthropods and turtles.

The epidermis is a single-layered group of cells that covers plants' leaves, flowers, roots and stems.

Stomata, the plural of stoma, refers to the minute pores in the epidermis of the leaf or stem of a plant that allows movement of gases in and out of the intercellular spaces.

Even if you had never heard of bulliform cells, you should have gotten the answer correct by knowing the preceding plant structures.

Bulliform cells are large, bubble-shaped, empty-looking, colorless epidermal cells that occur in groups on the upper surface of the leaves of many grasses. During drought, the loss of moisture through vacuoles leads the leaves of many grass species to close as the two edges of the grass blade fold up toward each other. Once adequate water is available, these bulliform cells enlarge and the leaves open again.

Question 7 B

See: BIO 14.5.1

First off, it is important to know that a blastomere represents the first week of cell replication. The point at which a blastomere is committed to becoming a germ cell is different from the point at which the germ cell actually starts to function as a germ cell (i.e. producing cell-specific proteins). Determination is the point at which a cell is committed to becoming a particular type of cell, although it may not display any specific characteristics that would yet identify it as a specific type of cell. After determination, a cell will differentiate into a particular type of cell, and the fully differentiated cell is called *specialized.* Determination is the crucial point at which the fate of the blastomere is decided.

Question 8 E

See: BIO 2.2, BIO 16.6.4

Protists are a diverse group of eukaryotic microorganisms thus they have nuclei. The protists do not have much in common besides a relatively simple organization - either they are unicellular, or they are multicellular without specialized tissues. This simple cellular organization distinguishes the protists from other eukaryotes, such as fungi, plants and animals.

Question 9 A

See: BIO 6.3.3, 5.4.4

Osteoclasts are responsible for the release of calcium to the blood.

Question 10 A

See: BIO 6.3.3, 5.4.4; CHM 9.7

The equilibrium of a catalyzed reaction remains constant (constant amount of reactants and products); the rate at which equilibrium occurs increases.

Question 11 C

See: BIO 14.5

Implantation of the developing embryo into the uterine lining occurs during blastulation whereby the embryo has developed into a blastocyst.

Question 12 E

See: BIO 19.7

The tree line is the ecological boundary between forest and tundra and thus does not divide the tundra. Tundra can be further subdivided into alpine, arctic or Antarctic (frozen). Tundra is known for permafrost and short growing seasons but "frozen" or "antarctic" tundra is incapable of supporting vegetation because it is too cold and dry. Most of Antarctica (the continent) is covered by ice fields.

Question 13 E

See: BIO 7.2, 7.3, 7.5.1

Oxygen from lungs → pulmonary vein → heart → aorta → arteries to body tissues → body tissues (capillaries) → veins from body tissues (includes renal) → vena cava → heart → pulmonary arteries → lungs. Note that a portal system or portal vein shuttles blood from one capillary bed to another.

Question 14 B

See: BIO 7.5.2, 10.3

Blood (or hydrostatic) pressure is proportional to the filtration rate.

Question 15 C

See: BIO 4.3, 2.5, 2.5.1

There are two main differences between Trials 1 and 2 in Table 1: (1) the [inhibitin] is increased by a relatively small amount (approx. 10^{-6} mmol/L); (2) the [trypsin] is increased by a relatively large amount (by a factor of 10). Answer choices **B.** and **D.** cannot account for the constant rate observed for the two reactions since a significant increase in inhibitor, or decrease in enzyme should cause a decrease in the reaction rate. However, a significant increase in [trypsin] (difference #2) with a concomitant minor increase in [inhibitin] could allow the enzyme to overcome the effects of the inhibitor, resulting in a constant rate of reaction.

Question 16 B

See: BIO 4.1, 15.7, Chapter 15 Appendix

This question requires knowledge of the definition of anabolism and catabolism. A catabolic reaction involves the breakdown of macromolecules, whereas an anabolic reaction involves the synthesis of macromolecules from individual building blocks (BIO 4.1). PCR entails the synthesis (amplification) of a new DNA strand using a DNA template and free nucleotides, therefore, it is an anabolic reaction that synthesizes new DNA strands.

Background: The polymerase chain reaction (PCR) is a powerful biological tool that allows the rapid amplification of any fragment of DNA without purification. In PCR, RNA primers are made to flank the specific DNA sequence to be amplified. These RNA primers are then extended to the end of the DNA molecule with the use of a heat-resistant DNA polymerase. The newly synthesized DNA strand is then used as the template to undergo another round of replication.

Question 17 B

See: BIO 1.2.2, BIO 3, BIO 20.5

The question states that AZT is an analog of thymidine and differs from thymidine in that it lacks the 3'–OH group. This OH group is crucial in the synthesis of DNA strands because it is required to form the 5'–3' phosphodiester linkage which holds the DNA backbone together (BIO 1.2.2). Consequently, since there is a 3'–N_3

rather than a 3'–OH, once this nucleotide analog is incorporated into the DNA, synthesis of the DNA strand will be blocked as no subsequent nucleotide will be able to form a bond with the 3' carbon atom. Moreover, the retroviral RNA must be converted to DNA in a process known as reverse transcription. In this case, the RNA strand will serve as a template to generate a single strand of DNA. Hence, it is reverse transcription of the viral RNA that will be disrupted by AZT. Recall that conventional transcription uses uridine instead of thymidine, and so AZT would not affect the conversion of DNA to RNA (BIO 3).

Question 18 E

See: BIO 1.2.2, BIO 3

An antibody-antigen interaction involving serum and red blood cells leads to clumping or agglutination. Type O blood is the "universal donor" because the red blood cells have no antigens. However, type O serum contains anti-A and anti-B antigens. I, II and III contain red blood cells with either some A or B or both antigens, thus resulting in antibody-antigen interaction with type O serum.

Question 19 C

See: BIO 6.2.3

The semicircular canals, which are found in the inner ear, are responsible for maintaining a sense of equilibrium.

Question 20 E

See: BIO 1.4.1, 17.6.4

In multicellular plants, the structural functions of cell junctions are provided for by cell walls. The analogues of communicating cell junctions in plants are called plasmodesmata (BIO 17.6.4). 1. Communicating junctions, like gap junctions in animal cells, are narrow tunnels which allow the free passage of small molecules and ions. One gap junction channel is composed of two connexons (or hemichannels) which connect across the intercellular space (BIO 1.4.1).

Question 21 C

See: BIO 1.1.3

Receptor-mediated endocytosis is mediated by clathrin-coated vesicles (CCVs). Exocytotic vesicles are usually not clathrin coated, most of them have no coat at all.

In exocytosis, the transient vesicle fusion with the cell membrane forms a structure shaped like a pore (= *porosome*). Porosomes contain many different types of protein including chloride and calcium channels, actin, and SNARE proteins that mediate the docking and fusion of vesicles with the cell membrane. The primary role of SNARE proteins is to mediate vesicle fusion through full fusion exocytosis or open and close (= "kiss-and-run fusion") exocytosis.

Question 22 D

See: BIO 1.1.1, 4.1

Answer choices **A** and **C** are consistent with simple diffusion. Answer choice **C** is equivocal. Answer choice **D** suggests the presence of a transporter (carrier mediated transport) because there must be a limited number of carriers, if the concentration of dopamine gets too high, the carriers would be saturated thus the rate of crossing the membrane would level off (plateau).

Question 23 D

See: BIO 2.2, BIO 16.6.4

The Archaea (AKA archeabacteria) are a domain of single-celled microorganisms. These microbes have no cell nucleus or any other membrane-bound organelles. Initially, archaea were termed "extremophiles" because of their ability to live in harsh or extreme environments, but they have since been found to also live in a broad range of habitats.

Protobionts are systems that are considered to have possibly been the precursors to prokaryotic cells.

Question 24 D

See: BIO 19.2

J-shaped curves are a classic representation of exponential growth. The J-shaped curve is characteristic of populations that are introduced into a new or unfilled environment, or alternatively, whose numbers have been drastically reduced by a catastrophic event and are rebounding.

Question 25 E

See: BIO 1.1, 5.1.1, 5.1.3

The question essentially provides the following information: (i) the concentration of potassium (the only cation) on both sides of the membrane is equal; (ii) the concentration of the anions on side X (Cl^- and $Prot^-$) must be equal to side Y (Cl^- alone). Therefore:

$$Cl^-_x + Prot^-_x = Cl^-_y$$

Thus:

$$Cl^-_x < Cl^-_y$$

Since $[Cl^-]_y > [Cl^-]_x$, there exists a chemical gradient for diffusion (BIO 1.1.1) from Y to X (i.e. answer choice **A.** is incorrect). The electrical gradient depends on the membrane potential (BIO 5.1.3). The electrical and chemical gradients balance at an equilibrium which is dynamic (answer choice **E.**; other answer choices do not take into account the dynamic equilibrium).

Note: The Gibbs–Donnan effect (also known as the Donnan effect or Gibbs–Donnan equilibrium) is the name for the behavior of charged particles near a semi-permeable membrane to sometimes fail to distribute evenly across the two sides of the membrane.

Question 26 D

See: BIO 14.2

Spermatogonia (diploid) are male germ cells which can produce primary spermatocytes.

Each primary spermatocyte duplicates its DNA and eventually undergoes meiosis I to produce two haploid secondary spermatocytes. Each of the two secondary spermatocytes further undergo meiosis II to produce two spermatids (haploid). Thus 1 primary spermatocyte produces 4 spermatids. The spermatids then undergo spermiogenesis to produce spermatozoa.

Question 27 C

See: BIO 4.4

Glucose (from glycogen) is the first and most common source to produce ATP. Amino acids, which requires the breakdown of protein in muscle which would be fed into the Krebs cycle, would only be used when all else fails.

Question 28 E

See: BIO 14.3

You must be familiar with the graph of the menstrual cycle in order to know which curve is referring to which hormone. There are four hormones involved: luteinizing hormone (LH), follicle stimulating hormone (FSH), estrogen and progesterone. If the menstrual cycle is understood well, you should immediately know that both estrogen and progesterone are secreted by the corpus luteum which came from the ovary. Alternatively, if the pituitary hormones are known, it is easy to eliminate LH and FSH because they are secreted by the anterior pituitary. Notice the LH surge before ovulation (III) which remains low in the 2nd part of the menstrual cycle.

Question 29 B

See: BIO 4.2

In this case, the inhibitor (I) binds the active site of the enzyme (E) reversibly and thus, it can be displaced by the substrate (S). Therefore, if [S] is gradually increased for a given [I], the inhibitor will be displaced from the active site of the enzyme and the effect of the inhibitor will be overcome as the enzyme reaches its normal maximal velocity (V_{max}). On the other hand, the K_m of the enzyme, which represents the [S] at half V_{max} should increase. In our example, the same V_{max} for the enzyme will be reached if enough S is added, however, this increase in [S] needed to overcome the effect of the inhibitor will raise the K_m accordingly. You should be aware that the larger the K_m, the less efficient the enzyme because a higher [S] is required to reach a given velocity of the reaction.

Question 30 C

See: BIO 14.2

Down's syndrome, or trisomy 21, is caused by the presence of triplicate copies of chromosome 21 in the afflicted individual. Since a normal genotype consists of two chromosome 21s, the overall number of chromosomes in a Down's syndrome patient is increased by one (46 + 1 = 47N). In both meiosis and mitosis, the separation of chromosomes (in meiosis I) or sister chromatids (in mitosis and meiosis II) occurs during anaphase, thereby eliminating answer choices **A.** and **B.** Recall that meiosis is divided into two steps. During the reduction division, the homologous chromosomes pair at the equatorial plate and separate to form two daughter cells consisting of a haploid (N) number of chromosomes. During the second meiotic division, the chromosomes line up at the center of the cell (just as they would in mitosis) and the sister chromatids separate to form two daughter cells of a haploid number of chromosomes. Since the homologous chromosomes pair up only in meiosis 1, we expect that the failure of chromosomes 21 to separate will occur, with a greater likelihood, in Anaphase I.

Question 31 E

See: BIO 1.2.2, 3.0

You must know that A pairs with T and C pairs with G. However, the question is asking about RNA, not DNA. In RNA, T is replaced by U. Therefore, the complementary sequence of CAG is GUC.

Question 32 D

See: BIO 2.2

The question is asking for a feature that *eukaryotes* have that *prokaryotes* (i.e. bacteria) do not have. A cell wall is listed, however, a cell wall is a feature that the *prokaryote* has that some eukaryotes have (i.e. plants and fungi).

One of the major differences between *prokaryotes* and *eukaryotes* is that *prokaryotes* contain no membrane bound organelles. Therefore, a *eukaryote* would have lysosomes, while a *prokaryote* would not.

Question 33 A

See: BIO 9.4.1

This is very simple question. You should know that the liver produces bile and the gallbladder stores it.

Question 34 D

See: BIO 17.6.3, 17.6.6

During dark phase (= dark stage/reaction = light independent stage/reaction), the reduced $NADPH_2$ transfers its hydrogens to CO_2 which is reduced to carbohydrate. The dark stage takes place in the stroma of the chloroplast. Unlike the light stage, the dark stage is controlled by enzymes and therefore affected by temperature. The enzyme is ribulose bisphosphate carboxylase oxygenase (RUBISCO).

Question 35 E

See: BIO 4.1, 4.7; CHM 8.2, 10.1, 10.2

Endergonic is defined as "absorbing energy in the form of work." In metabolism, an endergonic process is anabolic (energy is stored) which is usually coupled with ATP. Reduction is defined as a gain in electrons (GERC: Gain Electrons Reduction Cathode). Anabolic reactions refers to the set of metabolic pathways that construct molecules from smaller units using energy. Activation energy can be defined as the minimum energy required to start a chemical reaction. It's relationship to entropy is nowhere as clear as the other answer choices.

Question 36 E

See: BIO 20.2.2

The primary structure refers to the amino acid linear sequence of the protein held together by covalent peptide bonds. Keep in mind that the primary structure is the order of the amino acids in the protein. For this reason, even post-translational modifications such as disulfide formation, phosphorylations and glycosylations are considered a part of the primary structure (these are all types of covalent bonding).

The dipeptide cystine is composed of two cysteine amino acids joined by a disulfide bond (= bridge) and can help to stabilize the tertiary structure and to some degree, the quaternary structure of proteins (and rarely involved in secondary structure). H-bonding, which is non-covalent, is prominent in secondary and tertiary protein structures.

Question 37 E

See: BIO 7 Appendix

Even if you had forgotten the equation, because EF is a fraction (often given as a %), it has no units, so the numerator and denominator must have the same unit.

EF = stroke volume / end diastolic volume

Cardiac output = stroke volume × heart rate

Question 38 B

See: BIO 16.3, 19.2-19.4 and Appendix

The question discusses evolution within two different species. Within a species, the passage distinguishes between "local" populations and "other" populations which suggests that the populations live apart (= *allopatric*; BIO 16.3). Since the local population evolves differently (i.e. "*more capable of attacking the host . . .*"), genetic drift may be implicated. Recall that genetic mutations are usually either negative or neutral with regard to the organism's survival (BIO 15.5). Note: interspecific means 'between different species' whereas intraspecific means 'within the same species'.

Question 39 E

See: BIO 16.4.2, 17

Answer choice **E** is both irrelevant and untrue since plant cells have both chloroplasts and mitochondria.

Question 40 A

See: BIO 11.3, 11.3.3

Some common relations in brackets: carpals (wrist), metacarpals (palm), phalanges (fingers), tarsals (ankle), metatarsals (foot), phalanges (toes).

Question 41 A

See: CHM 8.3, 1.4

From Table I we are not given ΔH formation; rather, we are provided with a different parameter which the table describes as the enthalpy of combustion ΔHc of carbon. The end product of combustion (the oxide) of carbon is carbon dioxide. Now we can use Hess's Law knowing that the ΔHc for $C_{graphite} = -393.3$ kJ mol^{-1} and for $C_{diamond} = -395.1$ kJ mol^{-1}. We can summarize the process as follows:

$C_{graphite} \rightarrow CO_2$ ΔHc = −393.3 kJ mol^{-1}

$CO_2 \rightarrow C_{diamond}$ ΔHc = 395.1 kJ mol^{-1}

$C_{graphite} \rightarrow C_{diamond}$ ΔHc = 1.8 kJ mol^{-1}

{Notice the change in direction of the equation for $C_{diamond}$ was necessary in order to cancel the CO_2; thus the sign for ΔHc was changed from negative to positive}

Question 42 E

See: CHM 3.4, 6.1

By definition, a Lewis acid is a chemical species which accepts an electron pair (CHM 3.4). Answer choice **A**. is the Bronsted-Lowry definition of an acid (CHM 6.1).

Question 43 D

See: CHM 1.4

The relative atomic mass of O is ≈ 16; that of H is 1.0; and that of S is ≈ 32. Thus the relative molecular mass of H_2SO_3 is (2 × 1.0) + 32 + (16 × 3) = 82. The mass of the molecular oxygen (16 × 3 = 48) is more than half of 82. There is only one answer choice (**D.**) which is greater than 0.5! Alternatively, you can do it the old fashioned way: 48/82 + calculate!

Question 44 E

See: CHM 5.3.1

On the Surface:

x = molarity of $Mg_3(PO_4)_2 \rightarrow$ Solve for x

$(.005M\ Mg^{2+})(.005\ L) + (3x)(.015\ L) = (.05M\ Mg^{2+})(.02\ L)$

Note the 3 in front of x because there are 3 potential Mg^{2+} generated from each $Mg_3(PO_4)_2$ in aqueous solution. Solve for x:

$(3x)(.015\ L) = (.05M\ Mg^{2+})(.02\ L) - (.005M\ Mg^{2+})(.005\ L)$

$x = [(.05)(.02) - (.005)(.005)] / (0.045)$

Thus x = 0.022 M.

Going Deeper: a detailed calculation follows . . .

Let's begin with the total number of moles of Mg^{2+} present in the final solution: 0.05 moles/L × 0.02 L = 0.001 moles of Mg^{2+}. Next, let's look at the number of moles of Mg^{2+} obtained from $MgCl_2$: 0.005 moles/L × 0.005 L = 0.000025 moles of Mg^{2+}. Now we know the number of moles of Mg^{2+} we need supplied from $Mg_3(PO_4)_2$: (0.001 – 0.000025) moles = 0.000975 moles. Thus from the 15 mL of $Mg_3(PO_4)_2$ we need 0.000975 moles of Mg^{2+}. But each mole of $Mg_3(PO_4)_2$ contains 3 moles of Mg^{2+} Therefore, the concentration of $Mg_3(PO_4)_2$ = [(0.000975 moles)/(0.015 L)] × 1/3 = 0.022 mol L^{-1} = 2.2×10^{-2} M.

Sometimes on the real OAT, they will not calculate the answer; they will just confirm that you know how to set up the solution such as the answer choices in this question.

Question 45 A

See: CHM 6.6, 6.5

Using $K_b = ([X^+][OH^-]) / [XOH]$; X is most probably a Group I metal since it is monovalent (= univalent = a valence of one).

Assuming that $[X^+] = [OH^-]$ approximately

$K_b = [OH^-]^2 / [XOH]$, where XOH approximates 1.0 M at equilibrium, thus:

$1.0 \times 10^{-6} = [OH^-]^2 / 1$

$[OH^-]^2 = 1.0 \times 10^{-6}$

$[OH^-] = 1.0 \times 10^{-3}\ mol\ dm^{-3}$

$pOH = -log[OH^-] = -log(1.0 \times 10^{-3}) = -(-3) = 3$

Using pH + pOH = 14, we get:

pH = 14 – pOH = 14 – 3 = 11

Question 46 A

See: CHM 1.3, 1.5

Using Number of moles = (Mass)/(Relative molecular mass)

For PCl_3: Number of moles = (68.75 g)/[(31.0 + 35.5 × 3) g mol^{-1}] = 68.75/137.5 = 1/2

Equation: $P_4\ (s) + 6Cl_2 \rightarrow 4PCl_3$

Thus, Number of moles of P_4 = 1/4 × Number of moles PCl_3 = 1/4 × 1/2 mole = 1/8 mole

Using 1 mole of particles = 6.0×10^{23} particles (Avogadro's # = 6.023×10^{23} particles/mole)

1/8 mole P_4 = 1/8 × 6.0×10^{23} = 3/4 × 10^{23} = 0.75×10^{23} P_4 molecules

Question 47 B

See: CHM 10.1

The reduced species of the electrochemical equilibrium with the most negative E° value is the strongest reducing agent (CHM 10.1). Memory aside (!), it is of value to note that a reducing agent reduces the other substance, thus a reducing agent is oxidized. Note that only answer choices **B.** and **C.** are oxidized (= *lose electrons*). When you write the two relevant equations as oxidations, instead of reductions like the table provided, you will note that only answer choice **B.** has a positive E° value indicating the spontaneous nature of the reaction. The table provided demonstrates half-reactions written as reduction potentials. In order to write the oxidation, simply reverse the reaction and change the sign of E°:

Oxidation: $Cr^{2+} \rightarrow Cr^{3+} + e^-$ E° = 0.410

Question 48 C

See: CHM 2.3

As one moves across the periodic table, the atomic radius decreases as a result of the increasing effective nuclear charge (*without an increase in the number of atomic orbitals*). In other words, the nucleus becomes more and more positive from left to right on the periodic table resulting in the drawing of negatively charged orbital electrons nearer and nearer to the nucleus. As a result, atoms will accept electrons more readily as we go across the periodic table and the electron affinity (EA) becomes more negative (*less positive*). For example, halogens have very negative EA values because of their strong tendencies to form anions. Alkaline earths have positive EA values.

Question 49 A

See: CHM 4.2, 4.3.2

Any dipole-dipole interaction (ie, due to the separation of charges or difference in electronegativities between H and Cl) present requires energy to be broken before the HCl can enter the gaseous phase, thereby making HCl more difficult to boil (*i.e. the boiling point is elevated*). Neither Cl_2 nor H_2 have a separation in charge. Note that for the molecule HF, the boiling point is even greater due to H-bonding which is an even stronger intermolecular force than simple dipole-dipole interactions.

Question 50 C

See: CHM 4.2, ORG 10.1

Ethers possess a highly electronegative atom (*oxygen*), but no hydrogen atom is directly bonded to an oxygen or any other electronegative atom. As a result, another molecule with an electropositive hydrogen (i.e. water) can form hydrogen bonds with the oxygen atom of an ether, but the ether's hydrogen atoms will not be involved in hydrogen bonding.

Question 51 B

See: CHM 4.1.7

Keep in mind that: Partial pressure = Mole fraction × Total pressure

Since the total pressure is 100 atm, the mole fraction of 0.40 for HCl represents 40 atm; we are given 35 atm for Cl_2, thus 100 – (40 + 35) = 25 atm.

Question 52 E

See: CHM 11.4

Using Fraction of activity remaining = (Final activity)/(Initial activity)

Fraction of activity remaining = (10.8 dpm g^{-1})/(43.0 dpm g^{-1}) = 1/4, approximately

Using Fraction of activity remaining = $(1/2)^{\text{number of half-lives}}$

$1/4 = (1/2)^x$, thus x = 2

Question 53 D

See: CHM 11

Recall that an alpha particle is a helium nucleus (^4_2He) and a beta particle is an electron ($^0_{-1}e^-$).

Equation I: $^{238}_{92}U \rightarrow {}^x_yZ + 3\,^4_2He + 2\,^0_{-1}e^- + 3$ (gamma rays)

Since the sum of the atomic numbers and mass numbers on either side of the equation must be equal:

$238 = x + (3 \times 4) + (2 \times 0) + (3 \times 0)$

$x = 226$

$92 = y + (3 \times 2) + (2 \times -1) + (3 \times 0)$

$y = 88$

Thus, from the answer choices, Z = Ra; note that gamma rays are a form of electromagnetic radiation (CHM 11) and thus have no charge and no mass.

Question 54 B

See: CHM 10.1, 10.2

Written as standard reduction potentials, we get:

$O_2 + 2H_2O + 4e^- \leftrightarrow 4OH^-$ $E^o = +0.401$ V Cathode (gain of electrons)

$2Fe^{2+} + 4e^- \leftrightarrow 2Fe$ $E^o = -0.440$ V Anode (loss of electrons)

$E^o_{reaction} = E^o_{reduction} - E^o_{oxidation}$

$E^o_{reaction} = +0.401 - (-0.440) = +0.841$ V

Question 55 D

See: CHM 5.3.2

Equation: $FeX_2 \leftrightarrow Fe^{2+} + 2X^-$

Solubility s can be calculated using the above equation and $K_{sp} = [Fe^{2+}][X^-]^2$:

$K_{sp} = (s)(2s)^2 = 4s^3$

Thus $s^3 = (K_{sp}/4) = (5.0 \times 10^{-16})/4 = (1.25 \times 10^{-16})$
$= 0.125 \times 10^{-15} = 1/8 \times 10^{-15}$

$s = [\text{cube root}(1/8)] \times [\text{cube root}(10^{-15})] = 1/2 \times 10^{-5}$
$= 5.0 \times 10^{-6}$ mol L^{-1}

The calculation can be done in under a minute without a calculator.

Question 56 D

See: CHM 3.5

P: 3 bonds

Phosphorus is in Group V. It can therefore either have a valency of 3 or 5 (*you can memorize this or determine it through VSEPR modeling*). Answer choice **D**., which has three bonds to each phosphorous, is the only answer which fulfils this requirement.

Question 57 E

See: CHM 2.4, 2.4.1

Metals have high melting points and densities. They are excellent conductors of heat and electricity due to their valence electrons being able to move freely. This fact also accounts for the major characteristic properties of metals: large atomic radius, low ionization energy, high electron affinities and low electronegativity. Groups IA and IIA are the most reactive of all metal species. Of course, metals tend to be shiny and solid (with the exception of mercury, Hg, a liquid at STP). They are also ductile (they can be drawn into thin wires) and malleable (they can be easily hammered into very thin sheets). Metals form positive ions by losing electrons.

Metalloids (or semimetals) conduct better than nonmetals but not as well as metals.

Question 58 C

See: CHM 1.1-1.5

Let us use the process of elimination. Answer choice **A.** is false because it would support a lighted splint (*translation: fire burns in the presence of oxygen!*). Answer choice **B.** (molecular weight or MW = 28 g/mol) is somewhat lighter that air which is mostly nitrogen (78%, MW = 28 g/mol) with oxygen (21%, MW = 32 g/mol). Answer choice **D.** is really an anion (*carbonate*) not a gas (P2) and answer choice **E.** is a solid. Thus we are left with carbon dioxide (MW = 44 g/mol) which is heavier than air and does not support a lighted splint.

Question 59 B

See: CHM 2.3

Lithium only has one valent electron (Group I, PT; CHM 2.3). Therefore, one would expect only one covalent bond per lithium atom with no extra valent electrons on the lithium (that is, no lone pairs nor single electrons).

Question 60 D

See: CHM 10.4

A is the positively charged electrode i.e. anode in the diagram so the electrolyte used is irrelevant.

Question 61 E

See: CHM 6.9

Since the pH is less than the pK_a of the indicator, the undissociated form predominates.

$pH = 2;\ pK_a = -\log K_a = -\log(4 \times 10^{-4}) = 4 - \log(4) > 2$

{for the math see CHM 6.5.1, and the end of CHM 6.6.1}

Since the pH of the solution is less than the pK_a of the indicator, reduced pH means increased $[H^+]$, looking at Reaction I and remembering Le Chatelier's Principle, if the stress is on the right side of the equilibrium (i.e. increased $[H^+]$), the reaction shifts to the left which gives the red color (i.e. increased [HMe]).

Going Deeper: Note that from the math described, we know that the pK_a of methyl orange must be between 3 and 4 which suggests that if the pH of the solution is 2, it must be red, if it a pH of 5 (for example), it must be yellow. However, if the pH is between 3 and 4, the color would be a combination of yellow and red which would mean orange. Normally, indicators switch between their 2 colors (i.e. red and yellow in this example) over a pH range of about 2.

Question 62 E

See: CHM 1.5.1, 5.2, 6.2, 6.9.1

Answer choice **A.** can be eliminated since the oxidation numbers of the atoms in the reactants and products remain constant (CHM 1.6). A neutralization (answer choice **B.**) would involve an acid/base reaction, however, only acid is present in the equation. The precipitation of sulfur involves the replacement of the chlorine atoms with sulfur (CHM 1.5.1; cf. CHM 5.2, 6.2, 6.9.1) to form FeS(s), and, the replacement of sulfur atoms with chlorine to form HCl (= double replacement; CHM 1.5.1, also called *metathesis*).

Question 63 C

See: CHM 2.1, 2.2, 2.3

The roman numerals of the Group A atoms (which include the metals; see CHM 2.3F) indicate the number of electrons in the outer shell of the atom. In this case, both answer choices **B.** and **C.** have 2 valence electrons; however, answer choice **B.** represents the structure of He, a nonmetal. Answer choice **E.** has a d orbital. Keep in mind that in general, a transition metal is one which forms one or more stable ions which have incompletely filled d orbitals. Thus answer choice **E.** is Cr (not a Group II metal) but the more stable state would have the d orbital half filled thus $3d^5$, $4s^1$.

Question 64 B

See: CHM 6.1

K_{a2} is the expression describing the further dissociation of the conjugate base from the K_{a1} expression; in other words, the dissociation of the second proton. For the reaction:

$HS^- \rightarrow H^+ + S^{2-}$

$K_{a2} = [products] / [reactants] = [H^+][S^{2-}] / [HS^-]$.

Question 65 D

See: E; CHM 8.10

$\Delta G = \Delta H - T\Delta S$

"The sublimation of carbon dioxide occurs quickly at room temperature" means that it is spontaneous and so ΔG must be negative (by definition). Sublimation means:

Solid CO_2 + heat $\rightarrow$ vapor

Entropy (randomness) is clearly increasing (thus positive ΔS) because we are moving from a structured, ordered solid to randomly moving gas particles. Heat is required so it is endothermic meaning ΔH is positive. The question is asking about the reverse reaction so all 3 signs are reversed: ΔG is now positive; ΔH is now negative; ΔS is now negative.

Going deeper: Notice that a negative ΔS multiplied by a $-T$ (see the Gibbs free energy equation) creates a positive term which overshadows the effect of the negative ΔH and thus ΔG is still positive. Also, please keep in mind that sometimes the real OAT will provide the Gibbs free energy equation but sometimes they won't.

Question 66 E

See: CHM 8.7

The easiest way to objectively answer the question is to round the figures which can be done because the values of the specific heats are so far apart thus: 4 J/g•°C for water and 1 J/g•°C for glass. Using dimensional analysis (paying attention to the units):

Water: (40 J)/(4 J/g•°C) = 10 °C for 1 gram.

Glass: (40 J)/(1 J/g•°C) = 40 °C for 1 gram.

Question 67 A

See: CHM 5.1.1, 5.1.2

This question tests your understanding of *colligative properties*. From the equation

$T_b = K_B m$, where K_B is constant, or the molality is the factor to be considered. Recall that m = (Number of moles solute)/(1000 g solvent) and number of moles = (Mass of substance present)/(Relative molecular mass). Since glucose has a smaller relative molecular mass than sucrose, there will be a greater number of moles of glucose present when equal masses of the two substances are used. Therefore, the molality of glucose is greater and hence the boiling point elevation is greater.

Question 68 A

See: CHM 4.1.2, 4.1.8

A gas most closely approaches ideality at very low pressures (*thus making the relative volume that the gas particles occupy and the attractive forces between them negligible*) and at high temperatures (*so that the energy loss in inelastic collisions is negligible*). {*Plow and Thigh !*}

Question 69 C

See: CHM 9.3

By looking at Table 1, we can see that when the concentration of X is quadrupled (factor of 4^1) while [Y] is unchanged (Exp. 1 and 3), the rate is increased by a factor of $4 = 4^1$. Thus the order of the reaction with respect to X is 1. When the concentration of Y is doubled (factor of 2^1) while [X] remains the same (Exp. 1 and 2), the rate of reaction is quadrupled (factor of $4 = 2^2$). Thus, the order of reaction with respect to Y is 2. The rate equation is Rate = $[X][Y]^2$. {*Notice that the stoichiometric coefficients are not relevant*}

Question 70 A

See: CHM 12.3.1

A buret would be better but a graduated cylinder is by far the best on the list.

Question 71 A

See: ORG 2.1, 2.2, 2.3

A chiral carbon or stereogenic carbon center (or stereocenter) must be bonded to 4 different substituents. For this reason, ignore all carbons with double bonds (notice double bonds in the rings labeled A and C) and ignore all carbons bonded to hydrogen twice (some in rings B and E). We are left with 5 centers of chirality which are all in rings B and C (C5, C6, C9, C13 and C14; note that 13 is not labeled in the diagram but it is clearly in ring B between 12 and 14).

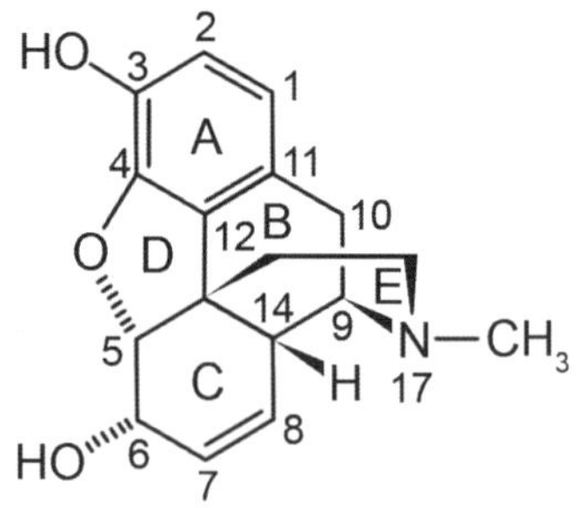

Question 72 E

See: D; ORG 1.6, 7.1, 8.1, 9.4

Keep in mind that alkyl lithiums and Grignard reagents (i.e. RMgBr) general partially negative carbons which will be attracted to partially positive carbons thus creating carbon-carbon bonds.

First identify the compound as 4-propyl-4-octanol and consider quickly sketching it in a way that resembles the tertiary alcohol in the mechanism provided so that you can more easily compare the various R groups. Doing so reveals 2 propyl groups attached to the central carbon meaning that there is either a propyl lithium or propyl MgBr (Grignard) being used. The 4-propyl-4-octanol also has a butyl group (R') which must originate from the ester thus it must be pentanoate. The nature of R" is irrelevant since it is part of the leaving group and thus is not found in the product.

The General Reaction Mechanism:

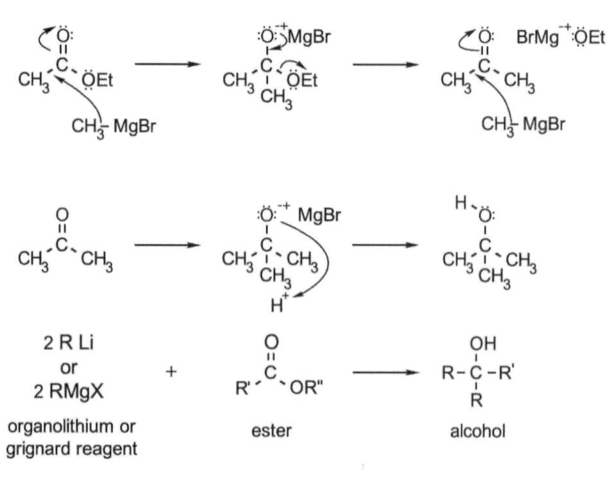

In case you were tripped up by nomenclature, here is hexyl pentanoate:

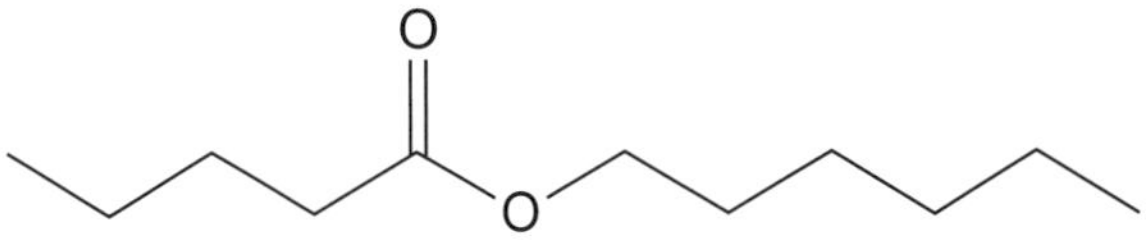

Question 73 A

See: CHM 6.3, ORG 1.6, 4.2.1, 6.2.4, 11.1.1

A base can be defined as a proton (H^+) acceptor. The strongest base would more likely carry a negative charge (opposites attract) and would create the most stable product. Alkanes are very stable and it is extremely difficult to remove a proton. Furthermore, primary anions (I) are extremely unstable thus it strongly wants a proton. This is followed by an ethoxide group (II) and then a compound that does not even have a negative charge (III; it has an electronegative N which would not be as attractive for a proton as a negatively charged O or C).

Question 74 D

See: ORG 4.2, 7.1, 8.1, 14.1

This question tests your memory of a couple of the IR absorption peaks. The absolute minimum to memorize are the bands for an alcohol (OH, 3200 – 3650) and that for the carbonyl group (C = O, 1630 – 1780) because these are the two most encountered functional groups in OAT organic chemistry.

Bottle II has a peak at 1710 (carbonyl) 3333 - 3500 (hydroxyl) = carboxylic acid (i.e. benzoic acid). Bottle IV has a peak at 3333 so it must be the alcohol. Without doing anything else, there is only one possible answer, **D**.

{*For fun, draw the structures of the four compounds*; allyl, ORG 4.2, add -OH to make it an alcohol; benzoic acid - ORG 8.1; the four carbon ketone 2-butanone (= *methyl ethyl ketone*) and the four carbon aldehyde butyraldehyde (= *butanal*) - ORG 7.1}

Question 75 D

See: ORG 1.1, 8.1

Formic acid (HCOOH) is a carboxylic acid whose structure is shown by answer choice **D**. Note that answer choices **A**., **B**. and **E**. can be quickly discounted because carbon needs to form 4 bonds to be neutral (ORG 1.1). Similarly, oxygen needs 2 bonds to be neutral, eliminating answer choice **B**.

Question 76 B

See: CHM 6.3, ORG 5.2.2, 10.2

When a compound becomes more acidic, Ka increases (CHM 6.3) thus pKa decreases because pKa = – log Ka. That's all!

The following information is for the curious minded (!) but was certainly not needed in order to answer the question: (i) substituents affect the acidity of phenols (ORG 10.2); (ii) halides (i.e. Br) are weakly deactivating groups but they are O-P Directors (ORG 5.2.2); (iii) activating groups (O-P Directors except halides) decrease the acidity of the phenol (ORG 10.2); (iv) in summary, where EDG = electron donating group and EWG = electron withdrawing group, we get:

EDG	EWG	EWG: Halogens
activates the ring	deactivates the ring	weakly deactivating
O/P Directing	Meta Directing	O/P Directing
i.e. alkyl groups	i.e. nitro ($-NO_2$)	i.e. bromine
acid weakening	acid strengthening	acid strengthening
increase pKa	decrease pKa	decrease pKa

The Reasoning: Electron withdrawing groups can stabilize the negative charge on oxygen which encourages oxygen to lose a proton (i.e. become more acidic). One more time for fun! When a compound becomes more acidic, Ka increases (CHM 6.3) thus pKa decreases because pKa = – log Ka. That's all!

Question 77 C

See: ORG 7.2.2

This question provides us with only one answer which could possibly have the correct geometry! Nonetheless, let's work through the mechanism.

The story goes something like this: The catalyst (H^+), being the most charged substance is implicated first. Thus the electrons from the electronegative oxygen (O in the carbonyl, C = O) are attracted to the proton (H^+) and bonds. To remain neutral oxygen loses its pi bond with carbon, leaving only a single bond and secondary carbocation. The $\delta-$ charge on the oxygen from the *diol* (= a compound with 2 alcohol – OH – groups) attacks the positively charged carbocation. The extra hydrogen on the oxygen which now attaches to carbon is kicked out as a proton (regenerating our catalyst). Now we have our "*hemi-ketal*": the ketone has been converted into a hydroxyl group and the diol (*minus one hydrogen*).

Next, the proton strikes again! It can be attracted to the hydroxyl group which falls off as water (*a great leaving group*), thus we have a secondary carbocation, again. Now we have a partial negative charge (the oxygen of the free arm of the diol) and a positive charge (the carbocation) in close proximity in the same molecule! In a very fast *intra*molecular reaction, the nucleophile meets the carbon nucleus and regenerates the proton catalyst. The product is answer choice **C**., a ketal.

Question 78 D

See: ORG 13.3, CHM 12

Overheating may destroy the pure compounds or increase the percent impurities. Some of the methods which are classically used to prevent overheating include boiling slowly, the use of boiling chips (= ebulliator, which makes bubbles) and the use of a vacuum which decreases the vapor pressure and thus the boiling point. A nucleophile could only create unwanted products and thus prevent the isolation of a pure product from the original mixture.

Going Deeper: Boiling chips, or boiling stones, are small chunks of inert material. A few are added to a liquid before it is heated and they tend to promote steady, even boiling. In theory, a liquid should boil when it is heated at its boiling point. The temperature should remain constant because the excess heat is dissipated in overcoming the heat of vaporization required to move liquid molecules into the gas phase. In practice, spontaneous formation of gas bubbles within the liquid can be slow which could lead to super-heating and ultimately, large violent bubbles. Boiling chips produce small gas bubbles where the liquid molecules can evaporate and initiate boiling at a steady even rate.

Question 79 B

See: CHM 3.5, ORG 3.3, 10.1

Since epoxides are by definition 3-membered rings, they will have the same geometry as cyclopropane. Hence, their bond angles should be 60° (ORG 3.3).

Question 80 C

See: ORG 7.1

The α carbon is the carbon adjacent to the carbon of the carbonyl group of the molecule and it has increased acidity because of the resonance stabilization of the anion.

Note that the carboxylic acid hydrogen is the most acidic hydrogen of this molecule but that hydrogen is not directly bonded to a carbon.

Question 81 A

See: ORG 13.2.1

If the material in the GLC absorbs each compound equally well, then they cannot be separated by this method.

Note that GLC is similar to fractional distillation - both processes separate the components of a mixture primarily based on boiling point (or vapor pressure) differences. Fractional distillation is usually used to separate components of a mixture on a large scale, whereas GLC can be used on a much smaller scale. Neither is directly dependent on the melting point.

Question 82 A

See: ORG 12.1.2

This is a common type of OAT question. You should be familiar with the concept of isoelectric point from the organic chemistry review.

The isoelectric point is defined as the pH at which an amino acid is immobile in an electric field due to the neutrality of the molecule (note that the negative charge on the carboxyl group cancels out the positive charge on the amino group). If we are in a medium which is more acidic (= lower pH) than the isoelectric point, the carboxyl group will become protonated to give a molecule with an overall positive charge. At a pH greater than the isoelectric point, the amino group will lose its proton and give a negatively charged methionine.

Note that the acidic component (–COOH) of the amino acid acted like an acid by donating a proton (and becoming $-COO^-$). The basic component of the amino acid ($-NH_2$) acted like a base and received a proton ($-NH_3^+$). But overall, being the isoelectric point, the molecule is neutral.

Question 83 C

See: ORG 14.2

Observe that the ^1H NMR spectrum has 3 groups of lines or peaks; thus there are 3 groups of chemically equivalent protons. Additionally, since the relative areas of the peaks is 3:2:3, the number of protons in the groups is in the ratio 3:2:3.

Next, there is spin-spin splitting in two of the peaks. One peak is a triplet, indicating the presence of 2 adjacent non-equivalent protons. The other peak is a quadruplet, indicating the presence of 3 adjacent non-equivalent protons. Since the 3rd peak is not split, the protons that caused it must not be adjacent to any non-equivalent protons. The only choice consistent with these requirements is $CH_3CH_2COOCH_3$.

Question 84 E

See: ORG 3.1, 4.1

$CH_3CH_2CH(CH_3)CH(CH(CH_3)_2)CH_2CH{=}C(CH_3)_2$

- Eliminate **D** by noticing at the right end of the molecule there is a double bond followed by a **C** with 2 methyl groups attached. The location of the double bond also helps to orient the direction of the molecule and avoid potential traps.
- In the middle of the molecule, there are 2 methyl groups attached to a CH which is in turn attached to a CH so this eliminates answer **C**: $CH(CH(CH_3)_2)$
- And finally, to the far left, **A** and **B** start as though the molecule has 2 methyl groups attached to a CH which is incorrect since the molecule begins with 1 methyl: CH_3CH_2
- Of course, you can come to the solution any way you are

comfortable but this is one systematic way to avoid traps.

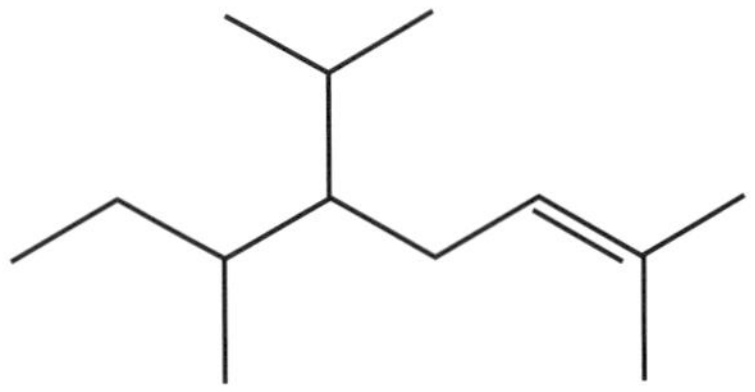

Question 85 C

See: ORG 13

All of the answer choices are useful to help an extraction to occur except answer choice **C**. Ideally, a solvent dissolves the solute (for example, when you add salt in water) but you do not expect nor would the objective be to create a molecule between the water and the solute because that would change the nature of the solute (i.e. salt or caffeine, etc).

Aside: it is important to note that it is more efficient to perform several small extractions using a small amount of solvent each time rather than one extraction using a large amount of solvent.

Question 86 C

See: ORG 2.1, 2.2, 2.3

Two of the structures below are (Z)–2–butene and (E)–2–butene which are stereoisomers of each other, not structural isomers. They have the same molecular formula, same connectivity, but different spatial arrangement. These would constitute stereoisomers thus there would be only 5 structural isomers in all. See isomers below:

1. (E) and (Z) 2–butene;
2. 1–butene;
3. 2–methyl–propene;
4. cyclobutane; and,
5. methyl–cyclopropane (not illustrated)

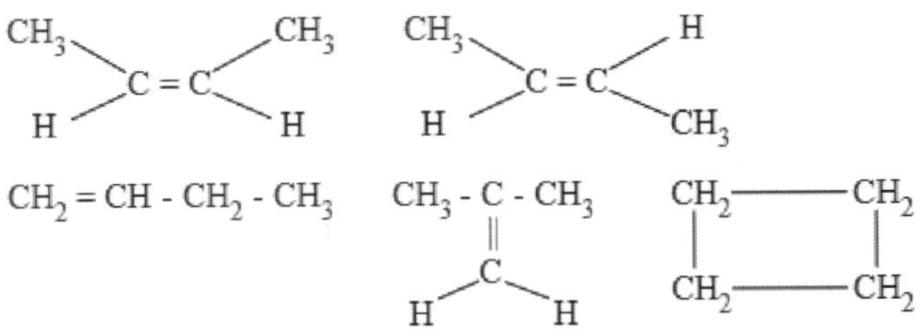

$CH_3(H)C=C(H)CH_3$ (cis) $CH_3(H)C=C(H)CH_3$ (trans)

$CH_2=CH-CH_2-CH_3$ $CH_3-C(=CH_2)-CH_3$ $CH_2-CH_2-CH_2-CH_2$ (cyclic)

Question 87 E

See: ORG 6.2.4

This is Elimination 1st order, E1, meaning that: (a) 2 atoms will be eliminated from the original molecule (turning a single bond into a double bond); and (b) the "1" means that the rate determining step depends on the concentration of 1 molecule. The rate determining step (RDS) is the slowest step in a reaction mechanism.

1. FAST: the proton is attracted to the partial negative charge on oxygen in –OH forming a great leaving group (water). Answer **B**.
2. SLOWEST: the oxygen in the water substituent pulls electrons away from the central carbon to get rid of its formal positive charge and now neutral water leaves the tertiary carbocation. Answers **A** and **D**.
3. FAST: electrons in a neighboring C–H bond are attracted to the carbocation forming a C = C bond and kicking out the proton which is regenerated (= catalyst).

Question 88 E

See: ORG 7.2.3

This is a typical imine formation, which involves the nucleophilic attack of the amino hydrogen on the central carbonyl carbon of the reactant on the left, followed by a dehydration. Since H_2O is being removed, this reaction is considered a dehydration, not a decarboxylation (= loss of CO_2). In addition, answer choice **C**. is incorrect because cleavage would consist of the reverse reaction (i.e. the formation of two molecules from one, through the breaking of bonds). The N and C in the imine are sp^2 hybridized, eliminating answer choice **D**. An enamine is formed when a secondary amine is used but the reaction in this problem uses a primary amine.

Question 89 A

See: ORG 2.3.1, 2.3.2, 2.3.3

A stereogenic or chiral carbon is a carbon atom which is asymmetric which means that it is attached to four different atoms or groups. Having a chiral carbon is usually a prerequisite for a molecule to have chirality, though the presence of a chiral carbon does not necessarily make a molecule chiral (i.e. a meso compound). A meso compound has an internal plane of symmetry which bisects the molecule and thus it displays no optical activity.

The 1st and 4th molecules happen to be named pentane-2,3,4-triol or 2,3,4-pentanetriol. Notice the position of the chiral carbons (asterix *) as well as the absence of an internal plane of symmetry. Notice that if the molecule was folded along the dotted line, the top part would not match the bottom part: no symmetry within the molecule.

Going Deeper: the following information would not affect your answer but it will help to train your eyes. Keep in mind that a Fisher projection is a 2D way to represent 3D molecules in which all horizontal lines are actually pointing towards the viewer. Notice the perspective of the viewer we placed above the 3D image of the molecule. Notice that the first OH group is to the left of the viewer which you can see in the Fisher projection also. It is also easy to see why the 3rd OH group is to the right of the viewer. But notice the 2nd OH group (on carbon–3) in the 3D representation of the molecule is pointing away from the viewer. But in order to do a Fisher projection, the horizontal groups must point towards the viewer. The only way to do this is to rotate the bond 180 degrees so that they point towards the viewer but, of course, the 2nd OH now ends up on the right side.

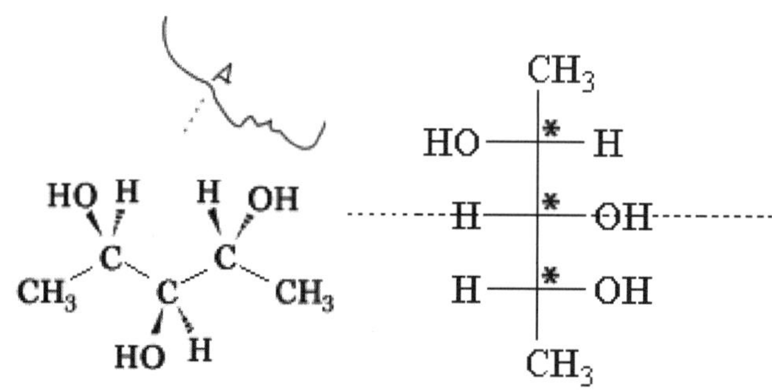

The second molecule happens to be named 1,3–difluorocyclohexane. Notice the position of the chiral carbons (asterix *) as well as the internal plane of symmetry (meso compound). Notice that each chiral carbon is attached to: (1) **H**; (2) **F**; (3) a carbon attached to a carbon attached to **F**; (4) a carbon attached to a carbon that is not attached to **F**.

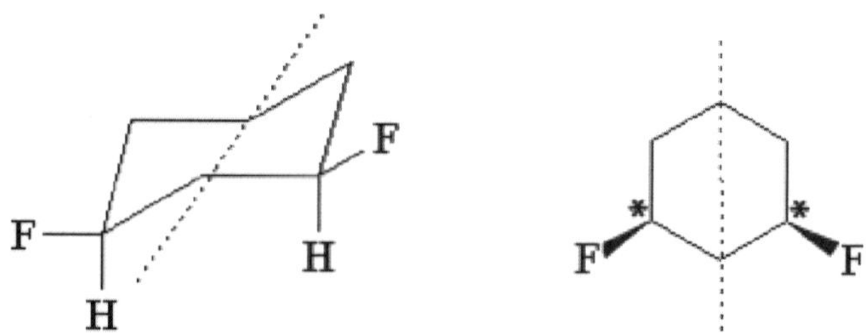

The 3rd molecule has 2 chiral carbons * but has an internal plane of symmetry (meso). Notice that the ring has a double bond on the right side but none on the left: this fact is important to understand how the 2 carbons became chiral.

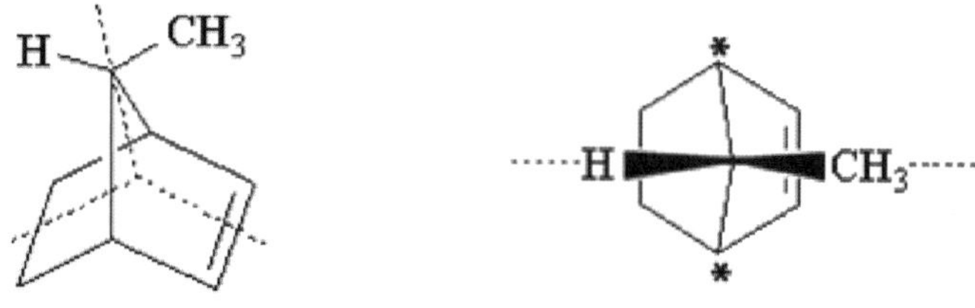

The fourth molecule (pentane-2,3,4-triol) shows an internal plane of symmetry with chiral carbons noted *.

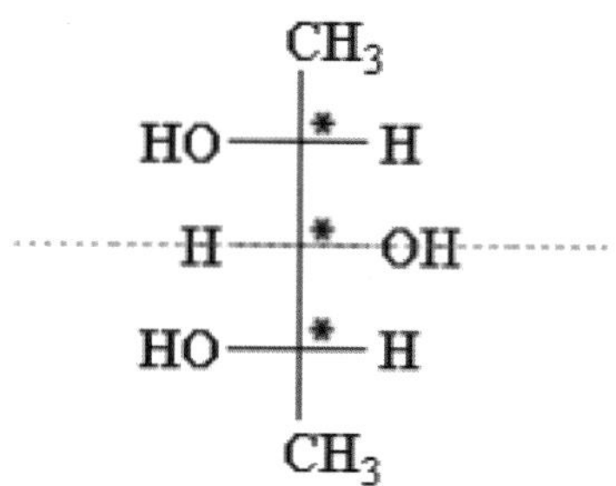

Question 90 B

See: ORG 4.2.1

This question asks us to remember 'Mark's rule': alkene + acid → under ionic conditions (i.e. no: uv, hf, increased energy/heat), hydrogen adds preferentially to where its buddies are (= *the greatest number of other H's at the double bond* = a simplification of Markovnikoff's rule. Thus answer choice **B**. is the major product and **A**. is the minor product.

Question 91 C

See: CHM 9.5, 9.7, 9.8, 9.10, ORG 6.2.1

This question tests your understanding of a catalyst: they speed up the rate of a reaction (kinetics), they decrease the activation energy, they do not affect K_{eq}, they are not used up in a reaction, and finally, they do not affect thermodynamics, $\Delta G°$ (CHM 9.5, 9.7, 9.8, 8.10). If you're interested in dehydration of alcohols (!) see ORG 6.2.1.

Question 92 C

See: CHM 8.2, 8.10, 9.5

When a compound reacts with the solvent, the process is referred to as a *solvolysis* reaction.

Because of the stability of tertiary compounds, one compound is in rate-determining step: t–butyl bromide in solution can simply dissociate into Br^- and the stable t–butyl .

Now a nucleophile would be happy to *quickly* mate with the positive carbocation (*nucleophilic substitution, first*** order* = S_N1). If the nucleophile is hydroxide, or water, then the product would be the tertiary alcohol tert–butanol $(CH_3)_3C$-OH {*note –OH substituted –Br*}. If the nucleophile is ethoxide, or ethanol, then the product would be the ether $(CH_3)_3C$-OCH_2CH_3. {*The preceding product can be named t–butyl ethyl ether, or, ethoxy t–butane*; see ORG 10.1}

The solvolysis reaction occurs spontaneously, which means $\Delta G < 0$, which also means that the great likelihood is that $\Delta H < 0$. The latter is called an *exothermic* reaction. Since energy is released, the reactants must have a higher energy and the products must have a lower energy. The only possible answers are **A**. and **C**. However, the intermediate in **A**. has a low energy which indicates stability implying that any further reaction is not likely to be spontaneous (from the mechanism just described we know this to be false, untrue and unpleasant to hear!). Answer choice **C**. suggests a higher energy intermediate which would be happy to engage in a further reaction to create a low energy, very stable final product.

Question 93 E

See: ORG 3.3, 12.3.2 F

This question tests two concepts.

1. Just like atoms or molecules, groups attached to a ring have electrons in their outermost shells. Like charges repel. Thus *electron shell repulsion* means substituents want to be maximally apart.

2. There are two positions for substituents of a ring: *axial* and *equatorial*. Equatorial substituents are maximally apart.

Question 94 C

See: CHM 3.5; ORG 1.2, 1.3

C1 is the first carbon in cyclic coniine which is the carbon in the ring attached to the propyl substituent (or ligand). It has 4 bonds: 1 to propyl, one to N, one to the carbon in the ring 'above' and one bond to H which is not shown in the structure but assumed to be there in this neutral molecule. Thus 4 bonds to carbon (1s + 3p) must be $4sp^3$ hybridized bonds.

For your interest: notice that C1 is the only chiral carbon in coniine.

Question 95 B

See: ORG 4.2.4

The Diels–Alder reaction is a cycloaddition reaction between a conjugated diene and a substituted alkene (= the dienophile) to form a substituted cyclohexene system.

Diene + dienophile = cyclohexene

All Diels-Alder reactions have four common features: (1) the reaction is initiated by heat; (2) the reaction forms new six-membered rings; (3) three π bonds break and two new C–C σ bonds and one new C–C π bond are formed; (4) all bonds break and form in a single step.

The Diels Alder diene must have the two double bonds on the same side of the single bond in one of the structures, which is called the s-cis conformation (s–cis: cis with respect to the single bond). If double bonds are on the opposite sides of the single bond in the Lewis structure, this is called the s-trans conformation (s-trans: trans with respect to the single bond).

Answer choices **C** and **D** can gain the correct s–cis conformation by rotation about a C–C bond. Here is an example:

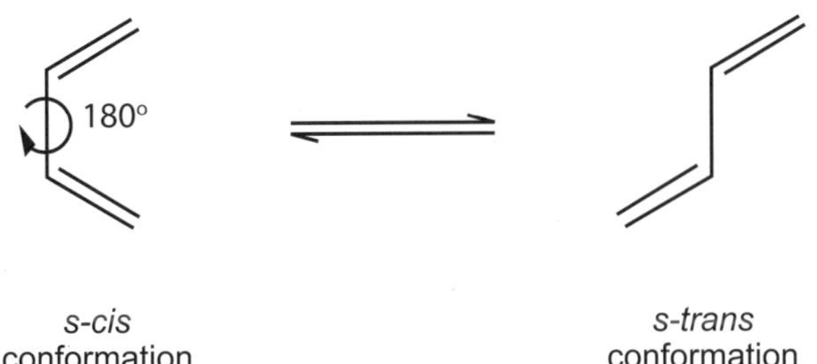

{Side Note: in the preceding equilibrium, 98% would be in the more stable s-trans conformation of 1,3–butadiene (answer choice **D**) in order to minimize electron shell repulsion. Nonetheless, both conformations are possible.}

Notice that the diene in answer choice **B** can never gain the correct conformation because the C–C bond between the alkenes is constrained within the ring. In fact, answer choice **B** is unreactive in a Diels-Alder reaction because 3 methylenecycloxenene is 100% s-trans:

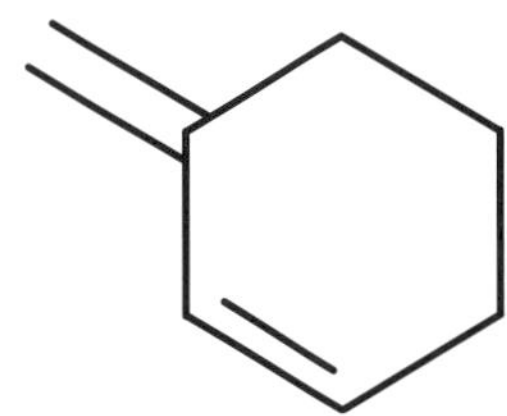

On the other hand, notice that answer choice A, cyclopentadiene, is constrained by the ring and is thus 100% s–cis (i.e. both double bonds are 'permanently' on the same side of the single bond between them):

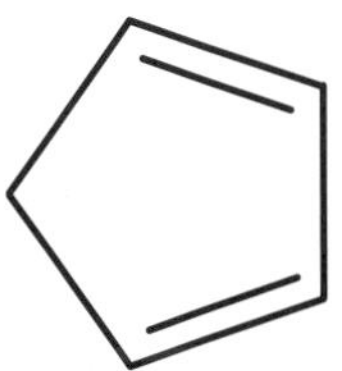

Question 96 A

See: ORG 4.2.2, 6.1, 9.4, 13.1; CHM 12

Distillation is the process by which compounds are separated based on differences in boiling points. Alcohols (1–butanol) have a partially negatively charged oxygen and a partially positively charged hydrogen which can engage in hydrogen bonding which increases the boiling point. Esters (ethyl acetate) have a partially negative oxygen but no partially positive hydrogen so no hydrogen bonding with itself. For this same reason, esters are more volatile than carboxylic acids of similar molecular weight.

Question 97 E

See: CHM 3.5; ORG 1.2, 1.3, 4.1, 4.2

Consider the structure of allene and review the answer choices.

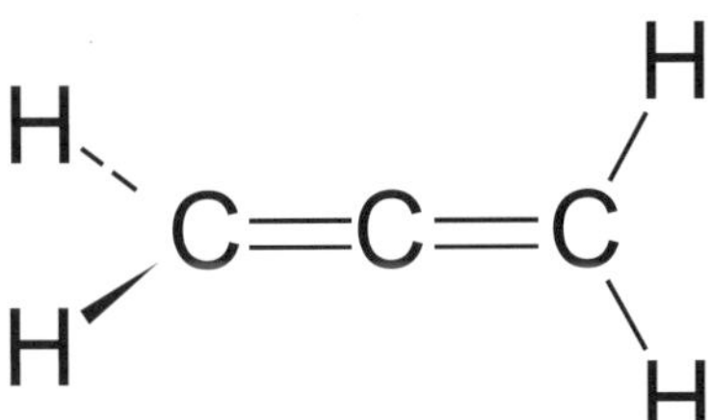

Notice that the 2 carbons at the end of the molecule are in the center of a triangle: trigonal planar 120° sp^2 hybridization with neighboring atoms (ORG 1.2,1.3; CHM 3.5). Notice that the C in the center of allene is in the middle of a line: linear 180° sp hybridization.

Note that dienes can be divided into 3 classes, depending on the relative location of the double bonds:

1. Cumulated dienes, like allene, have the double bonds sharing a common atom.
2. Conjugated dienes, like 1,3–butadiene, have conjugated double bonds separated by one single bond.
3. Unconjugated dienes (= isolated dienes) have the double bonds separated by two or more single bonds. They are usually less stable than isomeric conjugated dienes.

Question 98 E

See: ORG 5.1.1

If a compound does not meet all the following criteria, it is likely not aromatic.

1. The molecule is cyclic.
2. The molecule is planar.
3. The molecule is fully conjugated (p orbitals at every atom in the ring).
4. The molecule has 4n + 2 π electrons.

Notice that the number of π delocalized electrons must be even but NOT a multiple of 4. So 4n + 2 number of π electrons, where n = 0, 1, 2, 3, and so on, is known as Hückel's Rule.

Thus the number of pi electrons can be 2, 6, 10, etc.

Of course, benzene is aromatic (6 electrons, from 3 double bonds), but cyclobutadiene is not, since the number of π delocalized electrons is 4. However, the cyclobutadienide (2−) ion is aromatic (6 electrons).

A, **B**, **C** and **D** are all cyclic and planar. **A**, **B** and **D** have positive charges that will attract the negative pi electrons from neighboring carbons creating resonance forms delocalizing the pi electrons over all carbons in the ring. Answer choice **C** has an extra pair of p orbital electrons and thus, again, all carbons would be involved in the delocalization of pi electrons. In terms of the total number of electrons for each molecule, **A** has 2 π electrons (i.e. 1 double bond), **B** has 6 π electrons, **C** also has 6 π electrons (2 double bonds and 1 lone pair) and **D** has 2 π electrons (i.e. 1 double bond).

Question 99 D

See: ORG 1.6, 5.2, 5.2.1, 5.2.2, 6.2.2, 7.2.3

Note that Me = methyl = CH_3.

Step 1: Friedel Crafts acylation using aluminium chloride produces acetophenone (other names: phenyl methyl ketone, phenylethanone). It is the simplest aromatic ketone.

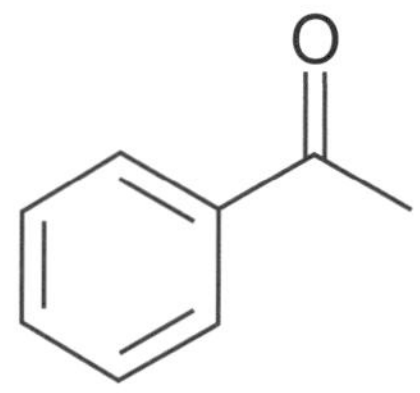

O

Step 2. When an aldehyde or a ketone reacts with a primary amine, an imine (Schiff base) is formed. Thus the primary amine $MeNH_2$ condenses with acetophenone to form an N-methylimine [Ph(Me)C=NMe] and water as the inorganic by-product.

Step 3. Sodium borohydride, a mild reducing agent compared to lithium aluminium borohydride, reduces the imine turning the double bond into a single bond to give the secondary amine.

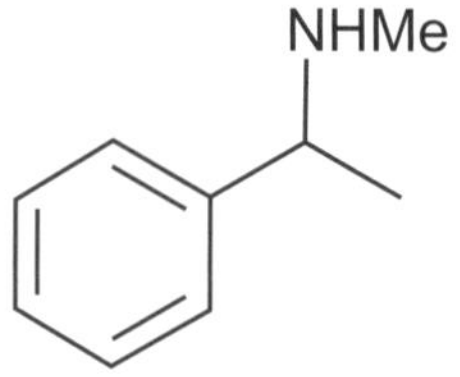

NHMe

Question 100 C

See: CHM 3.5; ORG 1.2, 1.3

First, let's number the carbons in the ring. Oxygen is attached to C1 and so N is attached to C3. So in the original molecule, we see that there are double bonds in the ring between C2 = C3 and C5 = C6. All of the answer choices follow the rules of drawing resonance structures except answer choice **C**. Let's carefully follow the electrons for answer choice **C** and thus we can understand what went wrong.

Our starting material:

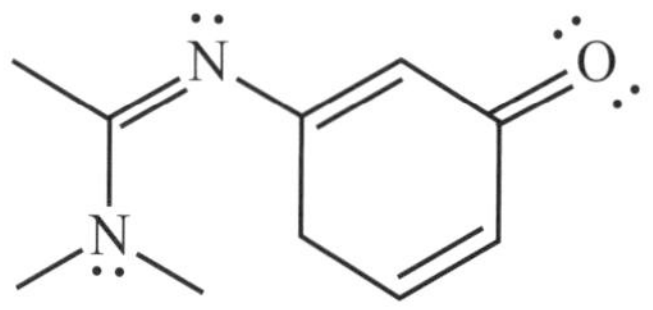

N O N

Keep in mind that oxygen is the most electronegative atom in the molecule and thus 'wishes' to withdraw electrons to itself.

1. The nitrogen is positively charged because it contributed its lone pair of electrons to carbon.
2. Carbon's double bond with the 2nd nitrogen breaks and thus nitrogen has a negative charge and an extra lone pair (note: this describes answer choice **B**.).

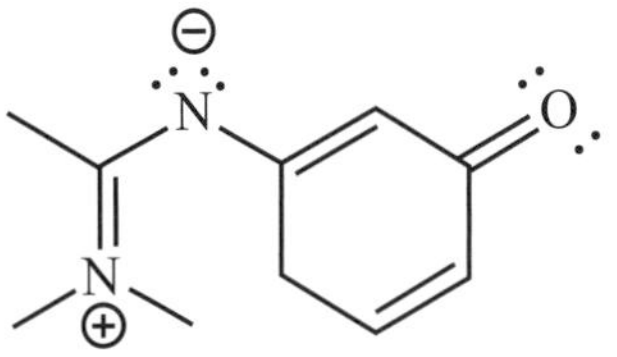

3. Nitrogen's lone pair bonds with C3 which breaks C3 = C2 so now C2 has a lone pair and a formal negative charge (C2 is secondary carbanion and this describes answer choice **D**).

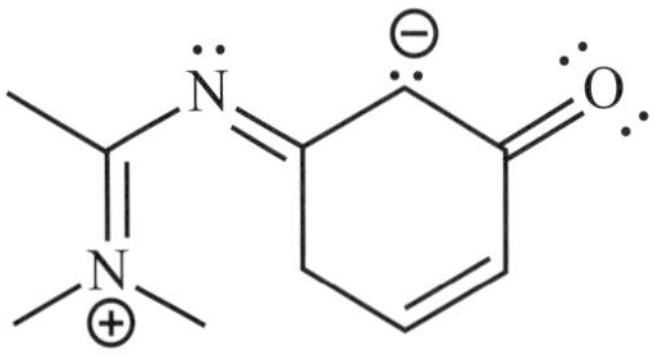

4. Remember that oxygen wants the electrons more than any other atom in this molecule. C2's lone pair bonds with C1 as C = O breaks so now oxygen has the lone pair and the formal negative charge (this describes answer choice **E**).

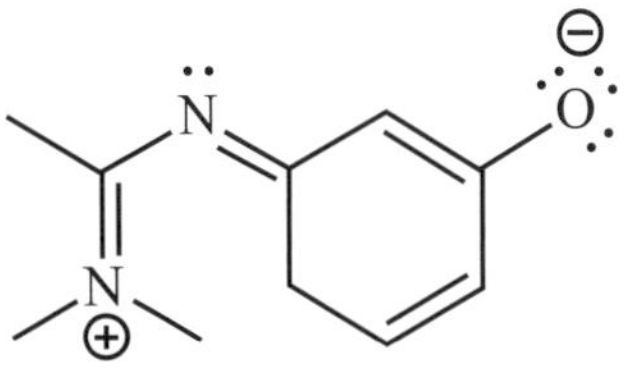

5) We just worked out why answer choice **E** is correct. Well, the only difference between **E** and **C** is that **E** correctly has the double bond C5 = C6 like the starting material but answer choice C incorrectly places the double bond at C4 = C5. That would only be possible if C6 had a + charge and C4 had a – charge.

6) And finally, answer choice **A** is like the starting material except, instead of oxygen pulling electrons from nitrogen along 'the top' (!!) of the molecule, oxygen pulls electrons from the C5 = C6 double bond creating a C6 = C1 double bond, a lone pair on oxygen and a secondary carbocation at C5 (because it lost its bond).

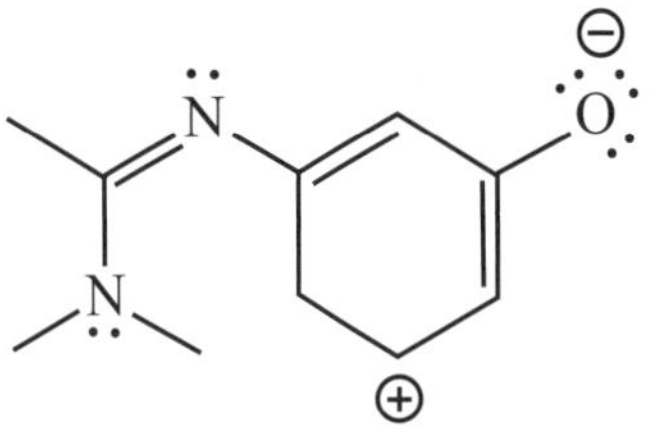

Question 1. C

Question Type: Recall

Strategy: SI; prior knowledge; P1 S3

This question can be somewhat tricky to a non-science candidate. The term "cosmic ray" is slightly mentioned in Paragraph 1 without any explicit reference to its meaning or scientific label. However, in Sentence 3, we can infer from the following line that "cosmic rays" pertain to the ionized atomic nuclei hitting the Earth's atmosphere: "ionized atomic nuclei hit the Earth's atmosphere continuously, with such 'cosmic rays' providing hints on energetic processes . . ."

The other answers are merely distractions. Option **A** is a typical decoy in the OAT RC, wherein one of the options is mentioned in one of the last two paragraphs. Indeed, the idea of "footprints of the air shower" is indicated in Paragraph 14. However, such elements are only one of the means to track cosmic rays. Paragraph 9 denotes the same idea pertaining to "short-lived particles." This makes **D** also incorrect.

The hypothesis that cosmic rays are gamma rays was put forward by Robert Millikan, but it is conclusively eliminated in Paragraph 13. **B** is thus incorrect. Finally, in Paragraph 12, some physicists suggested "the decay of magnetic monopoles" to generate cosmic rays – they are not cosmic rays themselves. This eliminates **E**.

Question 1. C

Question Type: Recall
Strategy: SI; prior knowledge; P1 S3
This question can be somewhat tricky to a non-science candidate. The term "cosmic ray" is slightly mentioned in Paragraph 1 without any explicit reference to its meaning or scientific label. However, in Sentence 3, we can infer from the following line that "cosmic rays" pertain to the ionized atomic nuclei hitting the Earth's atmosphere: "ionized atomic nuclei hit the Earth's atmosphere continuously, with such 'cosmic rays' providing hints on energetic processes . . ."

The other answers are merely distractions. Option **A** is a typical decoy in the OAT RC, wherein one of the options is mentioned in one of the last two paragraphs. Indeed, the idea of "footprints of the air shower" is indicated in Paragraph 14. However, such elements are only one of the means to track cosmic rays. Paragraph 9 denotes the same idea pertaining to "short-lived particles." This makes **D** also incorrect.

The hypothesis that cosmic rays are gamma rays was put forward by Robert Millikan, but it is conclusively eliminated in Paragraph 13. **B** is thus incorrect. Finally, in Paragraph 12, some physicists suggested "the decay of magnetic monopoles" to generate cosmic rays – they are not cosmic rays themselves. This eliminates **E**.

Question 2 C

Question Type: Recall
Strategies: SaL, PoE; P2 S3 and S4

Question 3 E

Question Type: Recall
Strategies: SaL, attention to details; P2 S2 to S3
This question can be confusing because several names of scientists are mentioned within the passage. The main strategy here is to locate either the very first scientist who was named in the passage or the scientist whose work was associated to the earliest date. Fortunately, you only have to look for the one who was first mentioned in Paragraph 2:

"In 1910, a Jesuit priest named Theodor Wulf (1868 – 1946) went up the Eiffel Tower in Paris to measure radiation levels with an 'electroscope'."

The work of the other scientists came at later dates. Paragraph 4 identifies (A) Victor Hess as the physicist who made a series of ten balloon flights with an electroscope to investigate the phenomenon in 1911 to 1912. (B) Werner Kollhoerster is the German researcher who confirmed Hess' findings by conducting his own flights sometime in 1914. (C) Walter Boethe entered the picture only in 1929 when, together with Kollhoerster, he built a "coincidence counter" to study the real nature of cosmic rays (P6). Paragraph 7 would prove that (D) Arthur Holly Compton conducted his own studies in 1932.

E is the best answer.

Question 4 D

Question Types: Recall; Math-related
Strategies: SaL, attention to details; P4 S1 to S3
In 1911-1912, Victor Hess made a series of 10 balloon flights with an electroscope to investigate Wulf's suggestion that the radiation might be coming from the upper atmosphere or space. On the other hand, the German researcher named Werner Kollhoerster made 5 flights of his own, the last of which was on June 28, 1914 Thus, a total of 15 balloon flights were conducted manually.

Question 5 E

Question Type: Recall
Strategy: SI; P8, S4
Hess received the Nobel Prize for Physics in 1936 for discovering cosmic rays; although there was a widespread belief for a period of time that Robert Millikan discovered cosmic rays.

Question 6 B

Question Type: Recall
Strategy: SaL; P10, S1

Question 7 B

Question Type: Recall
Strategies: SaL, attention to details; P10, S2

Question 8 B

Question Type: Recall
Strategies: SaL or SI, attention to details in P11
This is a very easy question, although you need to make a careful reading of Paragraph 11 in order to weed out the other keywords and confirm "background noise" as the correct answer.

Question 9 B

Question Type: Recall
Strategies: SaL and SI
This question can only be confusing because of the other valid-sounding keywords. Also, option **B** is verbatim of the elements mentioned in Paragraph 12, which seems too easy and can make you suspicious if this is indeed the correct answer. Nevertheless, **B** is the best choice.

Question 10 E

Question Type: Recall
Strategies: SaL, PoE; P13, S1

Question 11 B

Question Type: Recall
Strategies: SI, attention to details; P5 S1, P9 S1 and last sentence
This question looks as though you would need to do a careful reading and then take note of specific dates from Paragraph 4 to Paragraph 7. However, the correct answer can be simply inferred from the last sentence of Paragraph 9:

"In the postwar period, up to the early 1950s, cosmic rays were investigated with balloons that carried stacks of photographic emulsions to high altitude to record the traces of these particles."

The postwar period is indicated in the passage to have begun in 1922 when Robert Millikan started conducting studies by launching automated balloons. This is stated in Sentence 1 of Paragraph 5. This confirms B (the period between 1922 and 1950) to be the best answer.

Question 12 D

Question Type: Evaluation Question (Implication)
Strategies: SI, PoE; P14, last sentence.
This question requires you to carefully understand and infer the relevance of the LOFAR telescope to the information discussed in Paragraph 14.

In the last sentence of Paragraph 14, it is mentioned that "the LOFAR low frequency radio telescope has been used for this purpose." As to the exact purpose, we can refer to the last part of Sentence 1 in the same paragraph where the detection of radio energy generated by the air shower is mentioned as the purpose for using LOFAR low-frequency radio telescope.

You may also opt to eliminate the other options by checking if any mention of the LOFAR telescope in relation to gamma rays, alpha particles, supernovas, or protons is mentioned.

Question 13 C

Question Type: Recall
Strategy: SaL; P13, S3

Question 14 D

Question Type: Recall
Strategy: Sal; P11, S1

Question 15 C

Question Type: True False Statements (Two Statements)
Strategies: SI; P14, S1
The first two measures of observing cosmic rays mentioned in Sentence 1 of Paragraph 14 prove the first statement to be true. On the other hand, the last sentence of the same paragraph indicates that the LOFAR low-frequency radio telescope is used to pick-up the radio energy generated by the air shower.

Question 16 D

Question Type:Exception/Negative Question; Evaluation Question
Strategies: SI, attention to details; P2, P4, P8

While this question asks you to select what is NOT a quality of ANN, the terms used in the different options are not verbatim of the descriptions used in the passage. Hence, identifying the best answer requires inferring from the relevant paragraph.

First, you need to locate the part of the passage that discusses the various functions of ANN, which is Paragraph 2. Next, evaluate the statements within the paragraph. Sentence 3 pertains to the functions specified in **A**, **B**, **E**. Sentence 5 pertains to **C**.

Alternatively, you can look at Paragraph 8 to infer that (A) analyzing data, (B) solving problems, (C) recognizing patterns, and (E) calculating unknown solutions can be performed by the ANN. This leaves **D** as the only option, which is not mentioned.

Paragraph 4 does denote that ANN cannot replicate exact biological systems behavior. Therefore, **D** is the correct answer.

Question 17 A

Question Type: True False Statements (Two Statements)
Strategy: SI; P8 last sentence, P9 S2
In the last sentence of Paragraph 8, the first statement is found to be true while the latter is supported by Sentence 2 in Paragraph 9.

Question 18 B

Question Type: Evaluation Question (Implication)
Strategies: SI, attention to details; P5, S1 to S2
This question tests your interpretation of the first two sentences of Paragraph 5:

"The neuron is the basic foundation from which the network systems are constructed for both Biological Neural Networks and Artificial Neural Networks. Every neuron is a system that handles signals out of inputs since it is a MIMO system (multiple-input, multiple-output)."

Question 19 D

Question Type: Recall
Strategies: SI, PoE; P3, P5
This is another question that requires you to recall and infer information at the same time on particular parts of the passage. You may combine the process of elimination and careful understanding of information to narrow down the best choice.

In Paragraph 3 Sentences 4 and 5, the passage is clear in eliminating the neural net as (A) linear, (B) causal or (E) cause-oriented, and (C) effects-oriented. To further confirm your answer, going over the discussions in Paragraph 3 Sentence 6 and Paragraph 5 Sentence 4 would support the idea that the neural net is layered. The correct answer is **D**.

Question 20 B

Question Type: Recall
Strategy: SaL; P5 last sentence

Question 21 C

Question Type: Recall
Strategy:SaL; P5, S2

Question 22 A

Question Type: True False Statements (Two Statements); Evaluation Question (Implication)
Strategies: SaL, SI; P8 S1
This question combines an assessment of your recall and inference skills. The first statement can be easily confirmed with Paragraph 8 Sentence 1.

On the other hand, the second statement is generally implied in the passage. Some clues can be found in Paragraph 1 (". . . is based on the neuron's interconnection in the human brain's nervous system"), in Paragraph 2 ("ANN strives to simulate the firing of synapses."), and in Paragraph 11("The first work regarding the activity pattern of the human brain was published by William James." and "The Computer and the Brain . . . showcased propositions about several radical changes in the means, which researchers use to model the brain.")

Question 23 B

Question Type: Exception/Negative Question
Strategies: SaL, never lose sight of the question; P6 S4 to S5
(A) Electrical is stated in Paragraph 6 Sentence 4 while (C) digital, (D) analog and (E) hybrid are stated in Sentence 5 of the same paragraph. Although (B) temporal is also stated, this time in Sentence 6, it refers to the simulation of hybrid elements and not by the neurons. Therefore, the correct answer is **B**.

Question 24 D

Question Type: Recall
Strategies: SI, never lose sight of the question; P6 S6
Although this is a recall question, it also requires simple inference since the correct option does not use the exact same terms used in the passage. Moreover, the other choices tend to trick you with qualities that are associated with either the neurons or the ANN. Take note that the question asks for a characteristic of the hybrid PE (Processing Element).

From Paragraph 6 Sentence 6, "hybrid elements simulate both temporal and spatial movements." Temporal means time while spatial means space. **D** is thus the best option.

Question 25 A

Question Type: Recall
Strategy: SaL; P10 S2

Question 26 E

Question Type: Recall
Strategies: SI; P8 S5 to S7
This is another type of recall question that also compels you to do a little inference because of the way the question stem and the choices are reworded from the passage. The answer is a paraphrase from Paragraph 8 Sentences 5 to 7.

Question 27 C

Question Type: Evaluation Question (Main Idea)
Strategy: SI; P5 S1
This question measures your overall comprehension of the similarities and differences discussed between ANN and BNN. The best support for this question can be found in Sentence 1 of Paragraph 5. The best answer is **C**.

Question 28 B

Question Type: Recall
Strategy: SI; P11 (1986) S2
This question needs you to be quick in locating the required information within the passage. At the same time, you need to carefully understand the brief description in order to match the paraphrased options.

Paragraph 11 is the summarization of the historical view of ANN and BNN. Under the 1986 data in Sentence 2, the purpose of backpropagation is stated as minimizing error functions in neural nets.

Question 29 B

Question Type: Exception/Negative Question
Strategies: SaL, PoE, attention to details; P7 S4 to S5, P11 (1958)
This question mixes up two significant points in the development of the ANN research:

1. The 1958 data denotes that "Frank Rosenblatt created the Mark I Perceptron computer at Cornell University."
2. Reviewing Paragraph 7, Sentences 4 and 5 tell us that Papert and Minsky wrote a book entitled Perceptrons discrediting the ANN research.

This means that the statement in B, which says "Papert and Minsky created the Perceptron," is incorrect. They wrote and published Perceptrons, not the Perceptron. It was Frank Rosenblatt who created the Perceptron.

Indeed, you need to pay close attention to the subtle differences in the information as you eliminate each option in order to determine the best answer.

A is supported by Paragraph 11 in the 1951 history of the ANN: "The first Artificial Neural Network was made by Marvin Minsky while he was at Princeton."

C and **D** are also explicitly stated in Paragraph 11 in the 1949 and the 1943 data of the ANN history, respectively.

For option **E**, you can infer from the 1986 overview in Paragraph 11 that this statement is also correct.

The best answer to this question is, therefore, **B**.

Question 30 B

Question Type: Recall
Strategies: SaL, attention to details; P6 last sentence

Question 31 B

Question Type: Evaluation Question (Implication)
Strategies: SI, attention to details; P9, P10
In this question, you will need to use contextual clues in order to determine the best option. Paragraph 9 repeatedly emphasizes a priori as unnecessary in the processing of data with artificial neural networks. This idea is expressed using different terms such as "little amount of underlying theory" and "assumptions characterized by patterns are not needed by the neural networks." The closest answer is **B**.

(A) "Inherent mental structures" is not really mentioned in Paragraph 9. (C) "Guided training and (D) "expert systems" are mentioned in Paragraph 8, but they are not associated with a priori assumptions. (E) "Overtraining" and "generalizations" are also mentioned in the immediately following paragraph, but they are two separate albeit contextually associated concepts.

Question 32 B

Question Type: Recall
Strategy: SI; P9 S1
The answer to this question is a paraphrase of the first sentence in Paragraph 9.

Question 33 D

Question Type: Recall
Strategy: SaL; P6 S6

Question 34 C

Question Type: Evaluation Question (Implication)
Strategies: SI, PoE; P8
This question requires your understanding of the concepts discussed in Paragraph 8 and distinguish them from the succeeding information presented in the succeeding paragraphs. While algorithmic solutions are used when there is enough information and underlying theory, expert systems are useful when there is not enough theoretical background and data. The difference in the use of the two systems clearly relies on the amount of available data that they have to process.

(A) Analysis, (B) training, and (D) generalization are tasks that can be performed by the ANN, based on the amount of data fed to the network. (E) Neurons form as the basic framework of the ANN. This confirms C as the correct answer.

Question 35 C

Question Type: Exception/Negative Question
Strategy: SI; P2 S1, S6 and S7, P8 last sentence
Sentence 1 of Paragraph 2 states that ANN is a non-linear type of system. The last sentence cites the capacity of neural networks to generalize and recognize (A) noise-corrupted patterns and (B) similarities among assorted inputs. In the last sentence of Paragraph 8, artificial neural networks are also known to generalize (D) random patterns and (E) complex distributions. These narrow down our option to C as the exception to ANN's generalization capabilities.

Question 36. Answer: B

Question Type: Application Question
Strategies: SI, attention to details; P6 S2
By just looking at the pattern of the musical scale given in this question, you will find the numbers 1, 2, 3, 5, 8, and 13 coinciding with the Fibonacci sequence of 0, 1, 1, 2, 3, 5, 8, 13 discussed in Paragraph 2. This makes **B** as the best answer.

A is wrong because, as Sentence 1 of Paragraph 2 indicates, the Greek octave has only 5 notes while the question specifies an octave of 8 notes. **C** is too general to be the best match for this question. Fractals, according to Paragraph 10, are visual patterns that show a replicating sequence, which could be based on the Fibonacci numbers or ANY OTHER system.

D sounds off: the question describes a musical scale, which does not equate a technique. On the other hand, **E** sounds like a probable option. However, you must remember that determining whether the golden section is observed or not in a musical composition requires looking at the ratio of the various rhythmic scales or melodic lines. You would not be able to tell if a golden section is present or not by taking just a single musical scale into account.

Question 37 D

Question Type: Exception/Negative Question
Strategies: SaL, prior knowledge, attention to details; P10 S7
The quickest way to answer this question is to consider which of the options would not have visible traits and patterns. Only the (D) wind has a gaseous property and therefore, difficult to visually observe any pattern. Moreover, it can exhibit erratic traits such as direction and speed to create any regular, self-replicating form.

In the second to the last sentence of Paragraph 7, the passage names the (C) circulatory system and (E) broccoli as examples of fractals in nature. From common knowledge, (A) snowflakes are known examples of fractals while (B) lightning does exhibit some sort of a repeating pattern.

Question 38 D

Question Type: Evaluation Question (Implication)
Strategies: SI, paraphrasing, attention to details; P3 S4
This question requires your ability to interpret the information given in Paragraph 3. Sentence 4 of this paragraph specifically states that the octave in a guitar "should be half the distance between the bridge at the lower end of the guitar and the nut where the strings cross over at the top of the guitar." This essentially implies the octave to be the middle point on a string in a guitar. The best answer is **D**.

The other answers are meant to mislead you to either draw from or assume that you need prior knowledge in music in order to answer this question.

Question 39 B

Question Type: Evaluation Question (Main Idea)
Strategies: SI, PoE; P6 S1
In Paragraph 6, the golden ratio is defined as two quantities having a ratio of the sum of to the larger quantity equaling the ratio of the larger quantity to the smaller one. This clearly eliminates **C**: no mention is made about the quantities being raised to an exponent.

A is a probable paraphrase except that it uses the term "sequentially" while the passage's definition implies equality. The same is the case in **D**: the golden section does not necessarily require an "expanding sequence" although this is usually a resulting pattern. The closest choice is **B** as the phrase "in the same way that" connotes an equal correspondence of the quantities.

Question 40 B

Question Type: Recall
Strategies: SaL, PoE; P12 S1

Question 41 C

Question Type: Evaluation Question (Main Idea)
Strategy: SI; P11, P12
This question requires your comprehension of Paragraph 11's main idea. Knowing the meaning of the word "paradox" would also help you determine the answer accurately.

"Paradox" means self-contradictory or contrary to common opinion. This is already indicated in Paragraph 11 Sentence 1: "One would expect that the construction of such complex shapes would require complex rules, but in reality, the algorithms (equations) that generate fractals are typically extraordinarily simple." Option C rephrases this idea.

Option **A**, although verbatim from Paragraph 11 as well, cannot be the correct answer. The statement that the algorithms of fractals involve loops is simply a confirmation – not a paradox – that the repeating equations ('loops"), albeit simple, can produce such visually-rich results. This is further confirmed in Paragraph 12 Sentence 5.

B, **D**, and **E** do not also state a paradox. Rather, these either describe or support the mechanics behind fractals.

Question 42 B

Question Type: Recall
Strategy: SaL; P8 S1

Question 43 A

Question Type: True False Statements (Two Statements)
Strategies: SaL; P2 S4, P7 S1

Question 44 A

Question Type: Application Question
Strategies: SI, attention to details; P4
In Sentence 1 of paragraph 4, musical notation in the Western system, "the frequency ratio 1:2 is generally identified as an octave." This means that the note an octave below 400Hz is 200Hz while the note above it is 800 Hz. The answer is A.

Question 45 D

Question Type: Recall
Strategies: SaL, SI, P10, S3

Question 46 D

Question Type: Evaluation Question (Main Idea)
Strategies: PoE, OA, SI; P1, P5, P14, P15
A quick way to deal with this question is to eliminate the most obvious wrong answers first. A is quite absolute in stating that math can be found in ALL music. Paragraph 14 notes, "Many algorithms that have no immediate musical relevance are used by composers as creative inspiration for their music." This means that mathematics is not really present in all music, but they merely serve as springboard for some – but not all – musicians.

C, on the other hand, is too specific. The passage does not solely discuss about the golden ratio or the Fibonacci numbers. **E** sounds somewhat possible. Still, nothing in the passage confirms the duplication of music and math in terms of content, at the very least. This leaves our possible choices between **B** and **D**.

The passage has indeed demonstrated that musical compositions and structures can be analyzed through the (B) use of mathematical patterns. However, this concept can also be included in the more encompassing statement found in option **D** – that is, "an intricate yet measurable relationship between music and math" has been observed and is being utilized by some composers through the use of math principles and algorithms. The best answer is **D**.

Question 47 A

Type of Question: Recall
Strategy: SaL; P13 S2

Question 48 C

Question Type: True False Statements (Statement and Reason)
Strategies: Sal and SI; P4
The first statement "The name of a note an octave above A is also A" is verbatim of Sentence 5 in Paragraph 4. However, the reason for this has to do with octave equivalency, which considers two notes an octave apart (for example, an octave above A) basically the same except in pitch. Hence, notes an octave apart are given the same note name (in the given example, also named A).

The reason given in the question, that the duplication in a note's name has to do with its combination with another note, is therefore, wrong.

Question 49 D

Question Type: Evaluation Question (Main Idea)
Strategies: PoE, OA, attention to details; P17

Similar to Question 46, the correct answer can be easily determined through a process of elimination. In addition, you have to note that the question specifically asks for the most possible closing statement for the last paragraph of the passage. This means that you also have to consider both the general idea of the passage AND the last few statements that will best connect to the given options.

The phrasing of Option **A** makes this choice wrong because it emphasizes math as the main subject of the passage. The passage, as well as the last paragraph, revolves around the relationship between math and music.

B is a true-sounding statement, but this is not mentioned anywhere in the passage or the last few paragraphs.

In Option **C**, the first half of the statement sounds applicable to the main idea of the passage. However, the second idea about mathematicians and musicians liking the other's discipline is not clearly suggested in the passage or the last paragraph.

This leaves **D** as the only best choice. Indeed, the last paragraph refers to certain mathematical applications or algorithms being employed to create beautiful music. This statement also applies to the idea of the passage in general.

Question 50 B

Type of Question: Recall
Strategy: SaL; P1 last sentence

Question 1 B

See: PHY 4.4; CHM 8.8, 8.9
During an elastic collision, there is conservation of momentum and kinetic energy. Kinetic energy is not conserved in inelastic collisions. The Second Law of Thermodynamics suggests that the total entropy (randomness or disorder) increases in any real system.

Question 2 C

See: PHY 4.1, 4.1.1
Translational equilibrium implies zero acceleration which means that it is not moving (at rest) or moving with constant velocity.

Question 3 E

See: PHY 2.5, 2.6
The ball is falling down, in the negative direction, with increasing velocity which is acceleration. Thus both the velocity and acceleration vectors are pointing downwards.

Question 4 D

See: PHY 9.1.4, 9.1.5
The potential energy (Ep) of a charged object can be calculated from the following equation:

$$Ep = kQq/r$$

where Q = the charge setting up the field, q = the charge brought into a distance r from Q and k = coulomb's constant. In this example, the potential energy of the charge at point a will be equal to the potential energy of the charge at point b since the radius and the charges are the same in both cases. As a rule, no work is done when a charge is moved along an equipotential surface or line since the force component along the line is zero.

Question 5 A

See: PHY 7.1.3

Interference is the summation of the displacements of different waves in a medium. The highest number in the range of amplitudes possible (= 8) will represent the maximum constructive interference of the 2 waves where the crests of the waves are exactly overlapping. The lowest number (= 4) of the range corresponds to the maximum destructive interference, where the crest of one wave overlaps the valley of the other wave. Answer choice A is correct since the maximum constructive interference will be (6 units 2 units) 8 units while the maximum destructive interference is (6 units - 2 units) 4 units.

Question 6 D

See: PHY 2.1, 2.2

Weight of the block = 10 kg x 10 m/s^2 = 100 N

Force due to gravity pulling the block down the plane = sin(30) x 100 N = 50 N

Net force accelerating the block = ma = 10 x 2 = 20 N

Thus: external force applied to block parallel to the plane = 20 + 50 = 70 N.

Question 7 D

See: PHY 9.1.1

For some reason, these types of questions are popular with the OAT. Just keep in mind that opposite charges attract and like charges repel. Before the rod is introduced, charges on the spheres are happily neutral with positive and negative charges paired up all over the sphere. When the negative rod is introduced between the spheres, the spheres suddenly become polarized (= a separation of charges into different regions). Thus the negative charges on the spheres are repelled so they run towards Regions I and IV while the positive charges are attracted to the rod and so run towards Regions II and III. Thus, whatever the charge on the rod happens to be, Regions II and III will share the same charge.

Question 8 C

See: PHY 2.4

F = GM_1M_2/r^2 (PHY 2.4), where G is the gravitational constant, M_1 the mass of the planet, M_2 the mass of the man and r the distance from the center of mass of the planet and the man. Therefore, F is proportional to M_1/r^2. If M_1 is doubled, F will double. If r is doubled, F will be quartered. Thus, if M_1 and r are both doubled, F is halved.

Question 9 C

See: PHY 7.1.2

The duration of one cycle of oscillation of the mass measured in seconds is referred to as the period (T). Note that the period is the inverse of the frequency (f), measured in Hz (= sec^{-1}). The amplitude is the maximum displacement of the mass in one direction from the equilibrium point, in this case, 0.20 m.

Question 10 B

See: PHY 5.1, 5.7

Any number of watts refers to Power. Power can be defined as the rate of work or W/t. Thus W/t x t = W which is work or energy in the units of joules. You should know that "mega" is an SI suffix meaning 10^6 so that 1 megawatt is 10^6 watts.

Question 11 E

See: PHY 2.4, 2.6

In the absence of air resistance, gravity is the only force acting on a projectile. Since gravity affects the projectile in the vertical direction, the horizontal speed of the projectile is unaffected and will remain unchanged from its initial value.

Question 12 D

See: PHY 7.1.2, 7.1.4

Resonance involves a system vibrating at its natural or intrinsic frequency, and under these conditions, the system vibrates at maximum amplitude. Energy and power are both proportional to the square of the amplitude, so they will also be at their maximum values. Speed in not relevant.

Question 13 B

See: PHY 1.6, 2.6, 4.3, 4.4

There are two parts to this problem. We begin by calculating the impact velocity of the 0.2 kg ball using the equation for speed V at any time t (i.e. PHY 1.6, 2.6): $V = V_o$ + at, where V_o is the original speed. Since the ball starts at rest we get:

$V = 0 \text{ m s}^{-1} + (5 \text{ m s}^{-2})(5 \text{ s}) = 25 \text{ m s}^{-1}$

Using the principle of Conservation of Momentum and momentum = mass x velocity, we get:

Total momentum before collision = total momentum after collision

$(0.2 \text{ kg})(25 \text{ m s}^{-1}) + (0.5 \text{ kg})(0 \text{ m s}^{-1})$

$= (0.2 \text{ kg})(0 \text{ m s}^{-1}) + (0.5 \text{ kg})(x \text{ m s}^{-1})$

Isolate x: x = 10.0 m s^{-1}

Of course, for the OAT, your calculations must be quick and efficient. You won't have to calculate for every question because there are quite a number of theoretical questions, but your calculations must be sharp so practice makes perfect!

Question 14 E

See: PHY 11.5

Using the magnification (M) equation:

$M = - i/o$

where i = image distance, o = object distance (positive i, o values = real; negative i, o values = virtual). Recall that: (a) if $M > 1$, the image is enlarged; (b) if $M < 1$, the image is diminished; (c) positive M = erect; (d) negative M = inverted. In this example, the question states that the image is real so according to the conventions above, i and o will be positive values and $M = - i/o = - (+)$ = negative (inverted image). In the diagram, the focal length, measured as the distance from Fo to the objective, is more than 3 times less than the distance between the object and the objective. Therefore, $i < o$, and $M = -i/o < 1$ (diminished image). The real image is inverted and diminished. The presence of the eyepiece is not relevant.

Question 15 C

See: PHY 7.1.3, 11.1, 11.3, 11.4

When light rays encounter obstacles in their path, such as the slits in the Young slit experiment, they bend around them to some extent and fill the region behind the obstacle, a phenomenon called diffraction (this is a result of the wavy nature of light). Refraction is the bending of light rays due to a change in velocity when waves go from one medium to another. Reflection occurs when light rays bounce back into a medium from a surface with another medium (e.g. a mirror reflects light). Selection has something to do with biology!

Question 16 E

See: PHY 1.3, 1.4, 1.4.1

Graphs with questions relating to displacement, velocity or acceleration on the OAT are common. When you look at the velocity vs. time graph, you would notice that there are 3 regions: (1) the graph has a positive slope indicating that velocity is increasing at a steady rate (= constant acceleration); (2) the graph is flat indication constant velocity (= 0 or no acceleration); and finally (3) where the velocity is increasing at a faster pace than (2), in other words, the slope is steeper meaning the acceleration is greater. Only answer choice E shows each of these: constant positive acceleration followed by 0 acceleration followed by a higher constant acceleration than previous.

Question 17 C

See: PHY 1.3

Speed of sound in water = $(343 \times 4)\ m\ s^{-1}$

Time taken to return = 20 s

Therefore, time taken to reach = 1/2 x time taken to return = 10 s

Depth of region = $(343 \times 4)\ m\ s^{-1} \times 10\ s = 13\ 720\ m$

Question 18 B

See: PHY 7.2.1

At equilibrium the force of the weight (W = mg) will be equal to the spring force ($F_s = -kx$), thus:

$kx = mg$, $k = mg/x = (1\ kg \times 10\ m\ s^{-2})/(0.5\ m) = 20\ kg\ s^{-2}$

Work done (spring) = $1/2\ kx^2 = 1/2\ (20)(0.5)2 = 1/2\ (20)(1/4)$

$= (20)/(8) = 5/2 = 2.5$ J.

{Note F = mg, g is estimated as $10\ m\ s^{-2}$}

Question 19 B

See: PHY 3.2, 3.2.1, 3.4

Since the 200 N block is not in motion, the value of the frictional force is equal and opposite in direction to the applied force, that is, 10 N.

Question 20 B

See: PHY 9.1.2

From the equation $F = kq_1q_2/r^2$, if the distance r is doubled then $(2r)^2 = 4r^2$, which means $4 \times r^2$ in the denominator. Thus the original force is quartered (= decreased by a factor of 4).

Question 21 E

See: PHY 3.3

The velocity vector at any instant in uniform circular motion is tangential to the path of motion; however, the acceleration vector is directed radially inward (i.e. towards the center of the circle).

Question 22 A

See: PHY 4.1, 4.1.1

A simple torque force problem: let the fulcrum (= the center of gravity of the bar) be the pivot point (draw a vector diagram i.e PHY 4.1.1):

$\sum L = CCW - CW = (100\ kg \times g \times 0.5\ m) - (75\ kg \times g \times x) = 0$

Thus $(100\ kg \times g \times 0.5\ m) = (75\ kg \times g \times x)$

g cancels, manipulate to get: $x = 50/75 = 2/3\ m = 0.67\ m$

(CW is to the right of the fulcrum).

Question 23 B

See: PHY 6.1.1

The collector is heating the water. Liquids expand on heating and thus occupy a greater volume. Since density = mass/volume, the density of the liquid decreases when it is heated. Thus the heated water leaving the collector in draining pipes is less dense than the water being supplied to the collector. Of course, 1 L of the less dense water would yield a lower weight.

Question 24 B

See: PHY 3.3

The acceleration of an object which is moving in a circle (centripetal acceleration) acts toward the center of the circle when the object is at constant speed (that is, along answer choice C.). However, since the speed of the plane is decreasing, it experiences a deceleration (= negative acceleration) which acts along the tangent to the circle opposite to the direction of its velocity (that is, along answer choice A.). The resultant acceleration vector can be obtained by finding the vector sum of A. and C., and this gives vector B. {Had the speed been increasing, we would add C. plus a vector to be drawn in the direction of the velocity at point 'P' (i.e. opposite to A. which is E.); the sum vector would be in the general direction of D. See PHY Chap. 1 for vectors}

Question 25 C

See: PHY 6.1.2

On the Surface: one easy way to imagine the situation is that the liquid in the reaction vessel is acting as though there is an explosion (i.e. gases evolve). Therefore, the higher pressure coming from the reaction vessel will "push" on the water in the left arm of the manometer and increase the level of the water in the right arm, as shown by answer choice C.

Going Deeper: The pressure in the container can be calculated relative to atmospheric pressure by comparing the height (Δh) in the two arms of the manometer according to the following (PHY 6.1.2):

$\Delta P = \rho g \Delta h$

Question 26 B

See: PHY 1.5, 2.6.1

Using the following equation and keeping in mind that the stone was dropped which is another way of saying that it started with a velocity of zero.

$d = v_{initial}t + (1/2)at^2$

$= (1/2)gt^2$

$= 5 \times 100$

$= 500$ m

Question 27 D

See: PHY 10.1, 10.2, 10.3

If you needed to run fast, would you choose a hallway with a lot of resistance or one with very little resistance? Well, it is similar with current. Current would prefer the path of least resistance. Of course, current emanates from the positive terminal, goes up the left side of this particular circuit and encounters some resistors (bulbs) connected in parallel: R3 on top and R1 and R2 in series. Well, preferably current would take the path of R3 because it is easier (less resistance). Since R3 has more current, it is brighter.

Remember Ohm's Law: V = IR. Since R is the same for all 3 resistors but the current is highest with R3, that means that V is also highest for R3. Thus answer choice D is correct.

Oh, just as an aside . . . !

The symbol for a battery (one cell):

A battery with more than one cell:

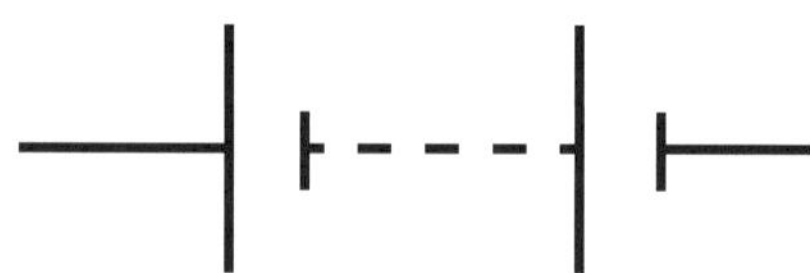

Please note, for any type of battery, the larger terminal is positive and the smaller terminal is negative.

For a DC battery:

AC batteries are not specifically tested on the OAT.

Question 28 C

See: PHY 12.1

Since a neutron has no charge, it would not be impeded in its motion by the positively charged nucleus, unlike the similarly charged proton. *{Note: answer choices A. and B. are false; answer choice D. is true for both a neutron and a proton and is thus an inappropriate answer; all things being equal, because a proton weighs somewhat less than a neutron and thus has less inertia, it should move faster making answer choice E. false.}*

Question 29 E

See: PHY 11.5

Using diopters = 1/(focal length in meters) Number of diopters = $1/(0.50 \times 10^{-2}$ m$) = [10^2/0.5] = 10^2/(1/2) = 2 \times 10^2 = 200$.

If you did not remember that equation from your Physics review, you will certainly remember it when you get into Optometry!

Question 30 B

See: PHY 4.1, 4.2, 4.5

Rotational motion is on the topic list for the OAT. This question is as difficult as you'll get!

1) The quantity mr^2 is proportional to the moment of inertia of a point mass about the center of rotation. Whether you consider from the point of view of *B* or *A*, either way, the mass m doubled and so the term *"mr^2"* doubled while the radius r, of course, did no change. In summary, with respect to either *B* or *A*, the moment of inertia has doubled.

2) Angular momentum is the rotational momentum that is conserved in the same way that linear momentum is conserved. So the angular momentum of *B* before the "collision" is equal to the angular momentum of *B* + *A* after the collision. Constant!

3) For a rigid body, the angular momentum *(L)* is the product of the moment of inertia and the angular velocity: $L = I\omega$. So if L is constant and I has been doubled, then the average angular velocity (ω, Greek letter omega) must be halved.

Question 31 C

See: 5 PHY 3.2, 3.2.1

The force of friction $F = \mu N$ where μ is the coefficient of friction and N is the force normal.

The normal force on an object always acts perpendicular to the surface, in this case, the road. Friction depends on the normal force. Since only a component of the weight of the car acts perpendicular to the hill, the value of the normal force decreases.Since the coefficient of friction remains the same, the value of the maximum frictional force decreases. *{Once an object is on an incline: N < weight of the object as determined by the cosine of the angle of the incline; this is worked out in PHY 3.2.1}*

Question 32 A

See: PHY 6.1.1, 6.1.2

Recall that the specific gravity of a substance is the ratio of the density of that substance to that of water. Since the density of water = 1 g/cm³, the specific gravity of a substance is equal to its density in g/cm³. For this example, where ρball = 0.5 g/cm³, and 3/4 of the object is submerged:

$\rho_{ball}/\rho l = 3/4 \rightarrow \rho l = \rho_{ball}(4/3) = 0.5 \times 4/3 = 1/2 \times 4/3 = 2/3 = 0.67$ g/cm³.

Question 33 B

See: PHY 7.1.2

Using velocity = frequency x wavelength:

7.5×10^3 m s^{-1} = x x 1.5 m

Thus x = (7.5×10^3 m s^{-1})/(1.5 m) = 5.0×10^3 s^{-1} = 5.0×10^3 Hz

Of course that means that most of the information given in this question was not needed - this forces you to focus on what is important.

Question 34 B

See: PHY 11.4

Both velocity and wavelength (= different colors) change (think of white light going through a prism making colors or the example of rainbows where white light is split into colors; also, recall velocity and wavelength are directly proportional, PHY 7.1.2). One should also know that the intensity (= the rate of energy propagation through space, PHY 8.3) of a light ray decreases when it passes through a medium other than air (its velocity decreases in the medium and this leads to an overall loss of energy). Identifying frequency is remaining constant is a common question type.

Question 35 C

See: PHY 8.5, 8.2

On the surface: When a siren drives by you, as it approaches, the frequency goes up, when it leaves, the frequency goes down. This means that you would expect the reflected wave to have a higher frequency than the original wave. The question is asking about the original wave so we expect it to be a relatively low frequency. For a given temperature and medium, the following is constant: velocity = frequency x wavelength. So if the frequency is relatively low, the wavelength is relatively high and, since it is happening in air and the temperature is not changing in those few seconds, the velocity is indeed constant.

Going deeper:

From the equation $f_o = f_s(V +/- v_o)/(V +/- v_s)$Since the distance between object and observer is decreasing, use v_o and $-v_s$, and given $v_o = 0$, we get:

$f_o = f_s(V)/(V - v_s) > fs$, thus fo > fs

{The preceding is true because the term $(V)/(V - v_s)$ is necessarily greater than 1 (plug in any real, which means positive, imaginary values), thus f_o must be greater than f_s} Therefore, the observed frequency is greater which means that the wavelength is lower from the observers point of view (from velocity = frequency x wavelength). Thus the wavelength from the source (= the original wavelength) is higher. As long as the environment (i.e. temperature) is relatively constant, the velocity of sound is constant (PHY 7.1.2, 8.2, 8.5).

Question 36 A

See: PHY 10.3.1

Kirchoff's Law I: the sum of current at a junction is equal to zero. The junction is like an intersection where all the roads join so it is the point pretty much in the center of the diagram. Let all current arriving at the junction be positive while all current leaving the junction is negative:

Q + T - S - U + R = 0

7 A + 8 A - 4 A - 11 A + R = 0

15 A - 15 A + R = 0 A, thus R = 0.

Incidentally, current is measured in amperes or amps which can be symbolized with just the letter A.

Question 37 D

See: PHY 9.2.3

Whether you are viewing this problem on a piece of paper or on a computer screen, if you follow these steps, you will understand how to assign the direction of magnetic fields forever! And yes, this is a common enough OAT type of question.

The easy way to remember the "right hand rule" is that if you grab the wire with your right hand, as your fingers curl, the tips of your fingers describe the direction of the magnetic field.

STEPS: (1) your thumb must ALWAYS point in the direction of the movement of positive charge (= current). To do this, stick out your thumb as though you will be hitchhiking, now uncurl your fingers and face the image. The only way that your thumb, which is still sticking out at 90 degrees from your hand, can point in the direction of the current is if your palm is facing the ceiling (i.e. if you are looking at a screen); (2) Grab the wire! So VERY slowly, imagine that you are curling your fingers around the wire: notice that above the wire, your fingers are moving towards you but below the wire, your fingers move away from you. So there it is! The magnetic field moves in a circular motion around the wire, towards you above the wire, and away from you below the wire.

Now you will look forward to magnetism questions on the exam!

There are 3 vectors that are all perpendicular to each other (like the x, y, z axes): the direction of the current, the direction of the electric field and the direction of the magnetic field (PHY 9.2.3).

Question 38 E

See: PHY 1.1, 5.2

A vector quantity has a direction and a quantity like force, electric field, acceleration and velocity. A scalar quantity has a number but no direction like speed, mass, charge, temperature or energy.

Question 39 B

See: PHY 2.2

You will usually get at least 1 question on the OAT referring directly to units. Everyone should remember that Newton's 2nd Law is F = ma and that mass is kg and acceleration a is m/s^2. So that means that the unit for force F must be $kg \cdot m/s^2$.

Question 40 A

See: PHY 12.3

An alpha particle is defined as a (doubly positively charged) helium nucleus.

Question 1 A

See: QR 3.2, 3.2.1, 8.2, 8.2.1

This is a rate problem with two initial values and two rates of growth. These can be combined into two expressions, one of Stephen's height and one of John's height. Let t be a variable for time in months:

Stephen: 4 ft + (.5 in/2 mo) t

John: 3 ft 10 in + (1 in/3 mo) t

Keeping track of units of measurement is very important in this kind of problem! Let's simplify these expressions by converting feet to inches. Remember, 12 inches to a foot. This gives:

Stephen: 48 in + t (1/4) in/mo

John: 46 in + t (1/3) in/mo

To find the time when their heights will be the same, simply set these expressions equal to each other and solve for t:

$$48 \text{ in} + t\,(1/4) \text{ in/mo} = 46 \text{ in} + t\,(1/3) \text{ in/mo}$$

$$2 \text{ in} = (t/12) \text{ in/mo}$$

$$t = 24 \text{ mo}$$

Finally, to find the height they will both be after 24 months, plug 24 back into the original expressions:

Stephen: 4 ft + (.5 in/2 mo) 24 = 4ft + 6in

John: 3ft 10 in + (1in/3 mo) 24 = 4ft + 6 in

Note: Evaluating both expressions is a quick way to check your work. If they aren't equal, something is wrong with your solution.

Question 2 E

See: QR 4.6, 4.6.1

First add 7 to both sides to set the quadratic equation equal to zero:

$$x^2 - 7x + 12 = 0 .$$

Next, check if you can factor the quadratic equation easily. In this case, you can:

$$(x-3)(x-4) = 0$$

$$(x-3) = 0 \text{ or } (x-4) = 0$$

$$x = 3 \text{ or } x = 4$$

Question 3 C

See: QR 7.2, 7.2.2

Remember, the "mean" is the average value of the set of numbers. Add the numbers together and divide by how many there are:

$$(7 + 7 + 8 + 10 + 13) / 5 = 9.$$

Question 4 A

See: QR 5.2, 5.2.2

Read the question carefully! It says this is an equilateral triangle, which means all of the sides are the same length and all of the angles are 60°.

Question 5 D

See: QR 7.1

First we need to find the probability that a single roll will turn up an even number. There are three possible even numbers (2, 4, and 6) out of six total possible outcomes. So the probability of rolling an even number once is:

$$p = 3/6 = 1/2.$$

Now to find the odds of rolling three even numbers in a row, multiply:

$$(p)(p)(p) = (1/2)(1/2)(1/2) = 1/8.$$

Question 6 C

See: QR 4.1, 4.1.4

We can treat $f(x) = 2f(x)$ as an algebraic equation with $f(x)$ as the variable. All we need to do is solve for $f(x)$. Subtracting $f(x)$ from both sides gives:

$$0 = f(x)$$

The function is equal to zero, no matter what x we put in. So $f(1) = 0$ is the solution.

Question 7 D

See: QR 2.4.3, 8.3

We are looking for the amount of berries produced over the course of two years. All we need to do is find the number produced in the first year and add it to the number produced in the second year. Let x be the number produced in year 1 and y be the number produced in year 2. Then:

$$x = .30\,(400) = 120$$

$$y = .85\,(400) = 340$$

$$\text{Total} = x + y = 120 + 340 = 460.$$

Question 8 D

See: QR 2.6

We are given the identity 2 km = 1.2 mi. We want to find an identity for 3.5 mi. If we divide both sides by 1.2, the right hand side will be 1 mi and we can then multiply by 3.5 to obtain:

$$(3.5/1.2)\ 2\text{ km} = 3.5\text{ mi}$$

The expression on the left is the solution we are looking for. Since the problem asks for an approximation, there are many ways we can approach it. Here is a simple one. Start with $(3.5/1.2)\ 2 = 7/1.2$. Now convert 1.2 to the fraction 6/5.

$$7/1.2 = 7/(6/5) = (7 \times 5)/6 = 35/6$$

All we need to do now is approximate 35/6. Notice:

$$35/6 = (36/6) - (1/6) = 6 - 1/6$$

But 1/6 is just a bit less than 1/5 = .2, so we can approximate the expression by:

$$6 - .2 = 5.8.$$

Question 9 D

See: QR 6.1, 6.1.4, 6.2, 6.2.1

Remember the definition of cotangent as cosine/sine. Also notice that $7\pi/6$ is in the lower left quadrant of the unit circle, where both cosine and sine are negative. These negatives will cancel and cotangent will be positive, the same as it is in the upper right quadrant. So:

$$\cot(7\pi/6) = \cot(\pi/6)$$

$$= \cos(\pi/6)/\sin(\pi/6)$$

$$= (\sqrt{3}/2)/(1/2)$$

$$= \sqrt{3}$$

Question 10 B

See: QR 5.1, 5.1.1, 5.2, 5.2.2, 6.1, 6.1.1

The key in this problem is to think of the line from the origin to the point (5 , 1) as the hypotenuse of a right triangle with legs of length 5 (along the x-axis) and 1. Then we can use the identity $\sin\theta$ = opposite/hypotenuse. The opposite leg has length 1. We can use the Pythagorean Theorem to find the length of the hypotenuse:

$$5^2 + 1^2 = c^2$$

$$c^2 = 26$$

$$c = \sqrt{26}$$

Therefore $\sin\theta = 1/\sqrt{26}$.

Question 11 C

See: QR 2.6, 3.2, 3.2.1

We are given the identity 1 cup = 360 g. We want to know how many cups are in 20 kg, so the first thing to do is convert grams to kilograms. Remember, 1 kg = 1000 g, so:

$$1 \text{ cup} = (360/1000) \text{ kg} = 0.36 \text{ kg}$$

Now set up the ratios, cross multiply, and solve for the unknown variable:

$$0.36\text{kg}/1\text{cup} = 20\text{kg}/x \text{ cups}$$

$$0.36x = 20$$

$$x = 20/0.36 = 2000/36 = 500/9$$

We can avoid finding the exact solution to this if we just notice that 500/9 is a little more than 500/10 = 50. The only solution close to 50 is 55.6.

Question 12 E

See: QR 2.5, 2.5.2

Since the solution options are all multiples of 1.5, we only need to figure out the order of magnitude. First consider the powers of 10:

$$(10^3 \times 10^8)/10^7 = 10^{11}/10^7 = 10^4$$

Now consider the multipliers. They approximately equal $(7 \times 4)/2 = 14$. So we have:

$$14 \times 10^4 = 1.4 \times 10^5$$

Therefore the correct answer is 1.5×10^5.

Question 13 C

See: QR 5.2, 5.2.2, 6.3, 6.3.3

The diagonal of a rectangle forms the hypotenuse of a right triangle. The legs are the sides of the triangle, in this case of length 3 and 5. To find the length of the diagonal, use the Pythagorean Theorem:

$$c^2 = 3^2 + 5^2 = 9 + 25 = 34$$

$$c = \sqrt{34}.$$

Question 14 E

See: QR 3.1, 3.1.1

We can convert the hours and the days to minutes separately, and add all of the resulting minutes together to get the total:

$$\text{Total} = 26 \text{ min} + 14 \text{ hr}(60 \text{ min}/1 \text{ hr}) + 3 \text{ days}(24 \text{ hr}/1 \text{ day})(60 \text{ min}/1 \text{ hr})$$

$$= 26 \text{ min} + 14(60 \text{ min}) + 3(24)(60 \text{ min})$$

$$= 26 \text{ min} + 840 \text{ min} + 4320 \text{ min}$$

$$= 5186.$$

Question 15 B

See: QR 5.2, 5.2.3, 6.3, 6.3.3

The key in this problem is that the diagonal of a square inscribed in a circle is the diameter of the circle.

$$\text{Diameter} = 2 \times \text{radius} = 2 \times 3 = 6$$

The sides of any rectangle and its diagonal are related by the Pythagorean Theorem. Since all sides of a square are the same length a, we can use b = a, c = 6:

$$6^2 = a^2 + a^2$$

$$36 = 2a^2$$

$$18 = a^2$$

$$a = \sqrt{18} = 3\sqrt{2}.$$

Question 16 E

See: QR 2.4, 2.4.2

This problem translates to an equation with fractions on either side:

$$3x/6y = 5xy/Z$$

Z is the value we are looking for. We can reduce the fraction on the left, and then cross multiply:

$$x/2y = 5xy/Z$$

$$Zx = 10xy^2$$

$$Z = 10y^2.$$

Question 17 B

See: QR 4.1, 4.1.1, 4.3, 4.3.1

First we want to get rid of the parentheses by distributing the 2:

$$(3x + 2)2 - x = 6$$

$$6x + 4 - x = 6$$

Next, combine like terms:

$$5x + 4 = 6$$

Next isolate the x term on one side:

$$5x = 2$$

Finally we want a single x on the left, so divide both sides by 5:

$$x = 2/5.$$

Question 18 E

See: QR 6.1, 6.1.2

Use the trigonometric identity $\cos\theta$ = Adjacent / Hypotenuse. This gives:

$$\cos 30^\circ = S/4$$

$$\sqrt{3}/2 = S/4$$

$$S = 2\sqrt{3}.$$

Question 19 B

See: QR 6.1, 6.1.4, 6.2, 6.2.1

Since cosecant = 1/cosine, we know that:

$$1/(\cos x) = 2/\sqrt{3}$$

$$\cos x = \sqrt{3}/2$$

Whenever $\cos x$ is $\sqrt{3}/2$, $\sin x$ is either ½ or –½ depending on which quadrant of the unit circle x falls into. Since we are given that $\sqrt{3}/2 < x < 2\pi$ we know x is in the lower right quadrant. Therefore $x = 11\pi/6$ and $\sin x = -½$.

Question 20 E

See: QR 4.2, 4.2.2

Before we worry about the different options given, let's isolate the x terms on one side and the constants on the other:

$$(2/x) + 3 > 5 - (1/x) = (3/x) > 2 = (1/x) > (2/3)$$

Now be careful. It is tempting to multiply through by x to try and clear the denominator, but we don't know whether x is negative or positive. If it is negative, the direction of the inequality will change. We cannot tell whether (c) or (d) is the correct inequality. Therefore we can only say that (a) must be true.

Question 21 A

See: QR 5.3, 5.3.3

The surface area of a cylinder is:

$$A = (\text{circumference of its base}) \times (\text{height}) + 2(\text{area of base})$$

$$A = (2\pi r)(h) + 2(\pi r^2)$$

The radius of the base r = diameter x ½ = 3.

$$A = (6\pi \text{ cm})(10 \text{ cm}) + 18\pi \text{ cm}^2 = 78\pi \text{ cm}^2$$

To approximate this value, let $\pi = 3.1$

$$A = 78 \times 3.1 \text{ cm}^2 \approx 242$$

So the best approximation given is 245.

Question 22 B

See: QR 2.6

This is a ratio problem. You can think of it as asking, 65 miles is to 1 hour as 25 miles is to x hours. Mathematically, set it up like this:

$$65\text{mi}/1\text{hr} = 25\text{mi}/x$$

All we have to do now is cross multiply and solve for x.

$$65x = 25$$

$$x = 25/65 = 5/13.$$

Question 23 B

See: QR 2.2, 2.2.3

Since this is an approximation problem, we can save time by rounding the given values to the nearest integer before doing any operations. \$39.99 becomes \$40 and \$15.75 becomes \$16. Then the total spent is approximately:

3(\$40) + 4(\$16) + 12(\$3)

= \$120 + \$64 + \$36

= \$220 .

Question 24 B

See: QR 2.4, 4.2

Convert 75% to a fraction, then multiply the two fractions together:

75% = 3/4

So 75% of 7/2 is:

$$(3/4)(7/2) = 21/8.$$

Question 25 C

See: QR 2.5, 2.5.2

This question is asking the value of y in the equation:

$$(5.97 \times 10^{24})\,y = 1.90 \times 10^{27}$$

Since this is an approximation problem, it will make things easier if we round $5.97 \approx 6$ and $1.90 \approx 2$. Then:

$$y \approx (2 \times 10^{27})/(6 \times 10^{24})$$

$$= (1/3) \times (10^3) \approx .33 \times 10^3$$

$$= 3.3 \times 10^2$$

Our approximation is slightly different than the solution given due to different rounding, but clearly the correct answer is 3.2×10^2.

Question 26 E

See: QR 2.6

This is a ratio problem. We can write it in equation form like this:

$$2.2\text{lb}/1\text{kg} = x \text{ lb}/4.5\text{kg}$$

Now cross multiply and solve for x:

$$x = (2.2)(4.5) = 9.9\ .$$

Question 27 C

See: QR 4.5, 4.5.2, 5.1, 5.1.1

We can use the properties of right triangles to solve this problem. Simply think of the line segment connecting the two points as the hypotenuse of a right triangle. Drawing a picture can help you visualize this. The lengths of two legs of the triangle are the horizontal and vertical distance between the points given:

$$x = 10 - (-2) = 12 \text{ and } y = 6 - 1 = 5$$

Now we can use the Pythagorean theorem to find the hypotenuse:

$$c^2 = 12^2 + 5^2 = 144 + 25 = 169$$

$$c = 13\ .$$

Note: this is a 5-12-13 triangle. If you memorize this relationship, you can save time by skipping the last calculation.

Question 28 A

See: QR 7.1, 7.1.2

First add the number of blue and yellow marbles to find the total, 20 marbles in the container. The probability of the first ball drawn being yellow is:

$$(\#\text{ yellow})/(\text{total }\#\text{ of marbles}) = 8/20 = 2/5$$

Since the problem specifies that there is no replacement the probability of the second ball being yellow is:

$$(\text{new }\#\text{ yellow})/(\text{new total }\#) = 7/19$$

The odds of both events happening is equal to the product of their individual probabilities:

$$P = (2/5)(7/19) = 14/95\ .$$

Question 29 E

See: QR 4.5, 4.5.4

To define a line we only need 2 points in a plane, so the problem gives more information than is necessary. We can pick 2 of the 3 points to use. To make calculations easier, choose any point with 0's or 1's first, then opt for points with integers closest to 0. In this case let's use (1 , 0) and (–1 , 3) to find an equation for the line in slope-intercept form:

$$y = (\text{slope})x + (y\text{–intercept})$$

Remember, slope = rise/run:

$$\text{slope} = (0-3)/[1-(-1)] = -(3/2)$$

$$y = -(3/2)x + b$$

To find b, plug a point into this equation (the point (1 , 0) will be easiest to use):

$$0 = -(3/2)1 + b$$

$$3/2 = b$$

So the final equation is:

$$y = -(3/2)x + (3/2)$$

But this doesn't appear as a solution option, so we need to try putting (c) (d) and (e) in slope-intercept form. It makes since to start with (e) since there are 2's and 3's as coefficients in it. When we rearrange, we see that (e) is in fact correct.

Question 30 C

See: QR 2.4, 2.4.2

First convert the integers to fractions with denominator 5, then combine:

$$[2 - (6/5)] / [1 + (2/5)]$$

$$= [10/5 - (6/5)] / [5/5 + (2/5)]$$

$$= (4/5) / (7/5)$$

$$= 4/7\ .$$

Question 31 E

See: QR 2.6

Since there are 7 men to every 4 women, 7 out of every 11 students are men. So 7/11 of the students are men. Multiplying this by the total number of students, we get:

$$(7/11)(143) = (7)(13) = 91\ .$$

Question 32 B

See: QR 2.4, 2.4.1

Options (c) (d) and (e) are easy to rule out since they are all greater than 1/2, whereas (b) is less than 1/2. The tricky one is (a). Here is a shortcut: using the fact that $\sqrt{3} < \sqrt{4} = 2$, we know that $1/\sqrt{3} > 1/2$. So the only solution less than 1/2 is 11/23.

Question 33 A

See: QR 2.4, 2.41, 2.4.2

First get rid of all decimals because the fractions are easier to work with. Multiply the left side by (100/100) and both sides by 10:

$$(60/270)(81/x) = 54$$

Now cancel common factors and solve:

$$(2/9)(81/x) = 54$$

$$(2)(9/x) = 54$$

$$1/x = 3$$

$$x = 1/3\,.$$

Question 34 D

See: QR 8.2, 8.2.3

This is essentially a compound interest problem. We have a present value of 4 meters, and a growth rate of 1.4 per year. So after three years:

$$\text{Future Height} = 4(1.40)3 = 10.976 \approx 11$$

But the problem is asking for the change in height, not the height itself. Therefore the solution is:

$$\text{Future Height} - \text{Present Height} = 11 - 4 = 7\,.$$

Question 35 B

See: QR 4.3, 4.3.1, 4.3.3

Notice that there are a lot of binomials hanging around this equation. First look for ways to cancel whole binomials, since that would simplify the equation quickly. Before we do that, though, we need to factor $(x^2 - x - 6)$. We need a two numbers whose sum is –1 and whose product is –6. –3 and 2 work. So:

$$(x^2 - x - 6) = (x - 3)(x + 2)$$

Multiplying the equation through by this factorization we get:

$$2(x - 3)/3 + 3(x + 2) = (5x - 1)$$

Distribute the coefficients and combine like terms, then solve for x:

$$(2x - 6)/3 + 3x + 6 = 5x - 1$$

$$(2x - 6)/3 = 2x - 7$$

$$2x - 6 = 6x - 21$$

$$15 = 4x$$

$$x = 15/4\,.$$

Question 36 C

See: QR 2.2, 2.2.1

Round 9.7 up to 10 and round 17.4 down to 17. Since we rounded one value up and the other down, at least a portion of the error will cancel itself out, but to be sure we are obtaining a close enough approximation (and assuming you have enough time) you can always multiply the original numbers for an exact solution.

$$10 \times 17 = 170.$$

Question 37 E

See: QR 3.1, 3.1.1, 8.2, 8.2.2

The total trip was 18 min + 12 min = 30 min long. Over these 30 minutes, the average speed was 28 mph. First find the total distance travelled, then divide by 2 to get the one-way distance from the house to the store:

$$(28 \text{ mph})(30 \text{ min}) = (28 \text{ mph})(1/2 \text{ hr}) = 14 \text{ miles}$$

$$14 \text{ miles} \div 2 = 7 \text{ miles}$$

Now we can solve for the value we are looking for. We know the distance (7 miles) and the amount of time it took to cover that distance (12 min):

$$x = (7 \text{ miles})/(12 \text{ min})$$

$$= (7 \text{ miles})/(1/5 \text{ hr})$$

$$= (7)(5) \text{ mph}$$

$$= 35 \text{ mph}\,.$$

Question 38 D

See: QR 7.1, 7.1.2

There are three events in this problem: the first green ball drawn, the second green ball drawn, and finally a red ball drawn. The probability of all three of them happening is equal to their individual probabilities multiplied together. Remember, the second and third events are dependent on the previous ones because the problem specifies that the balls are not replaced:

$$P(\text{1st ball is green}) = 3/9$$

$$P(\text{2nd ball is green, given the 1st was green}) = 2/8$$

$$P(\text{3rd ball is red, given the 1st and 2nd were green}) = 6/7$$

$$P(\text{all three}) = (3/9)(2/8)(6/7) = 1/14\,.$$

Question 39 A

See: QR 2.4.3, 8.3, 8.3.3

To find the percentage of juice in the mixture we need to find the weighted average of the ingredients:

$$[(0)2\text{cups} + (0.9)1\text{cup} + (0.6)3\text{cups}]/6 \text{ cups}$$

$$= 2.7/6$$

$$= 0.45 = 45\% .$$

Question 40 D

See: QR 7.2, 7.2.2

A good strategy for this problem is to convert all the fractions so they have the same least common denominator. In this case, 12:

4/12 got a 10

1/12 got a 9

3/12 got an 8

The rest $= (12 - 8)/12 = 4/12$ got a 7

Now we can think of the class as having 12 students total in it. Then the score breakdown is:

$$\{10, 10, 10, 10, 9, 8, 8, 8, 7, 7, 7, 7\}$$

To find the median, count 6 from either side and draw a line:

$$\{10, 10, 10, 10, 9, 8 \mid 8, 8, 7, 7, 7, 7\}$$

The median is the average of the two numbers on either side of the line, in this case 8 and 8. So the median is 8.

The Gold Standard OAT

Answer Document 1

Test GS-1

CANDIDATE'S NAME ______________________ STUDENT ID ______________________

Mark one and only one answer to each question. Be sure to use a soft lead pencil and completely fill in the space for your intended answer. If you erase, do so completely. Make no stray marks.

Survey of the Natural Sciences

1 Ⓐ Ⓑ Ⓒ Ⓓ Ⓔ	35 Ⓐ Ⓑ Ⓒ Ⓓ Ⓔ	69 Ⓐ Ⓑ Ⓒ Ⓓ Ⓔ
2 Ⓐ Ⓑ Ⓒ Ⓓ Ⓔ	36 Ⓐ Ⓑ Ⓒ Ⓓ Ⓔ	70 Ⓐ Ⓑ Ⓒ Ⓓ Ⓔ
3 Ⓐ Ⓑ Ⓒ Ⓓ Ⓔ	37 Ⓐ Ⓑ Ⓒ Ⓓ Ⓔ	71 Ⓐ Ⓑ Ⓒ Ⓓ Ⓔ
4 Ⓐ Ⓑ Ⓒ Ⓓ Ⓔ	38 Ⓐ Ⓑ Ⓒ Ⓓ Ⓔ	72 Ⓐ Ⓑ Ⓒ Ⓓ Ⓔ
5 Ⓐ Ⓑ Ⓒ Ⓓ Ⓔ	39 Ⓐ Ⓑ Ⓒ Ⓓ Ⓔ	73 Ⓐ Ⓑ Ⓒ Ⓓ Ⓔ
6 Ⓐ Ⓑ Ⓒ Ⓓ Ⓔ	40 Ⓐ Ⓑ Ⓒ Ⓓ Ⓔ	74 Ⓐ Ⓑ Ⓒ Ⓓ Ⓔ
7 Ⓐ Ⓑ Ⓒ Ⓓ Ⓔ	41 Ⓐ Ⓑ Ⓒ Ⓓ Ⓔ	75 Ⓐ Ⓑ Ⓒ Ⓓ Ⓔ
8 Ⓐ Ⓑ Ⓒ Ⓓ Ⓔ	42 Ⓐ Ⓑ Ⓒ Ⓓ Ⓔ	76 Ⓐ Ⓑ Ⓒ Ⓓ Ⓔ
9 Ⓐ Ⓑ Ⓒ Ⓓ Ⓔ	43 Ⓐ Ⓑ Ⓒ Ⓓ Ⓔ	77 Ⓐ Ⓑ Ⓒ Ⓓ Ⓔ
10 Ⓐ Ⓑ Ⓒ Ⓓ Ⓔ	44 Ⓐ Ⓑ Ⓒ Ⓓ Ⓔ	78 Ⓐ Ⓑ Ⓒ Ⓓ Ⓔ
11 Ⓐ Ⓑ Ⓒ Ⓓ Ⓔ	45 Ⓐ Ⓑ Ⓒ Ⓓ Ⓔ	79 Ⓐ Ⓑ Ⓒ Ⓓ Ⓔ
12 Ⓐ Ⓑ Ⓒ Ⓓ Ⓔ	46 Ⓐ Ⓑ Ⓒ Ⓓ Ⓔ	80 Ⓐ Ⓑ Ⓒ Ⓓ Ⓔ
13 Ⓐ Ⓑ Ⓒ Ⓓ Ⓔ	47 Ⓐ Ⓑ Ⓒ Ⓓ Ⓔ	81 Ⓐ Ⓑ Ⓒ Ⓓ Ⓔ
14 Ⓐ Ⓑ Ⓒ Ⓓ Ⓔ	48 Ⓐ Ⓑ Ⓒ Ⓓ Ⓔ	82 Ⓐ Ⓑ Ⓒ Ⓓ Ⓔ
15 Ⓐ Ⓑ Ⓒ Ⓓ Ⓔ	49 Ⓐ Ⓑ Ⓒ Ⓓ Ⓔ	83 Ⓐ Ⓑ Ⓒ Ⓓ Ⓔ
16 Ⓐ Ⓑ Ⓒ Ⓓ Ⓔ	50 Ⓐ Ⓑ Ⓒ Ⓓ Ⓔ	84 Ⓐ Ⓑ Ⓒ Ⓓ Ⓔ
17 Ⓐ Ⓑ Ⓒ Ⓓ Ⓔ	51 Ⓐ Ⓑ Ⓒ Ⓓ Ⓔ	85 Ⓐ Ⓑ Ⓒ Ⓓ Ⓔ
18 Ⓐ Ⓑ Ⓒ Ⓓ Ⓔ	52 Ⓐ Ⓑ Ⓒ Ⓓ Ⓔ	86 Ⓐ Ⓑ Ⓒ Ⓓ Ⓔ
19 Ⓐ Ⓑ Ⓒ Ⓓ Ⓔ	53 Ⓐ Ⓑ Ⓒ Ⓓ Ⓔ	87 Ⓐ Ⓑ Ⓒ Ⓓ Ⓔ
20 Ⓐ Ⓑ Ⓒ Ⓓ Ⓔ	54 Ⓐ Ⓑ Ⓒ Ⓓ Ⓔ	88 Ⓐ Ⓑ Ⓒ Ⓓ Ⓔ
21 Ⓐ Ⓑ Ⓒ Ⓓ Ⓔ	55 Ⓐ Ⓑ Ⓒ Ⓓ Ⓔ	89 Ⓐ Ⓑ Ⓒ Ⓓ Ⓔ
22 Ⓐ Ⓑ Ⓒ Ⓓ Ⓔ	56 Ⓐ Ⓑ Ⓒ Ⓓ Ⓔ	90 Ⓐ Ⓑ Ⓒ Ⓓ Ⓔ
23 Ⓐ Ⓑ Ⓒ Ⓓ Ⓔ	57 Ⓐ Ⓑ Ⓒ Ⓓ Ⓔ	91 Ⓐ Ⓑ Ⓒ Ⓓ Ⓔ
24 Ⓐ Ⓑ Ⓒ Ⓓ Ⓔ	58 Ⓐ Ⓑ Ⓒ Ⓓ Ⓔ	92 Ⓐ Ⓑ Ⓒ Ⓓ Ⓔ
25 Ⓐ Ⓑ Ⓒ Ⓓ Ⓔ	59 Ⓐ Ⓑ Ⓒ Ⓓ Ⓔ	93 Ⓐ Ⓑ Ⓒ Ⓓ Ⓔ
26 Ⓐ Ⓑ Ⓒ Ⓓ Ⓔ	60 Ⓐ Ⓑ Ⓒ Ⓓ Ⓔ	94 Ⓐ Ⓑ Ⓒ Ⓓ Ⓔ
27 Ⓐ Ⓑ Ⓒ Ⓓ Ⓔ	61 Ⓐ Ⓑ Ⓒ Ⓓ Ⓔ	95 Ⓐ Ⓑ Ⓒ Ⓓ Ⓔ
28 Ⓐ Ⓑ Ⓒ Ⓓ Ⓔ	62 Ⓐ Ⓑ Ⓒ Ⓓ Ⓔ	96 Ⓐ Ⓑ Ⓒ Ⓓ Ⓔ
29 Ⓐ Ⓑ Ⓒ Ⓓ Ⓔ	63 Ⓐ Ⓑ Ⓒ Ⓓ Ⓔ	97 Ⓐ Ⓑ Ⓒ Ⓓ Ⓔ
30 Ⓐ Ⓑ Ⓒ Ⓓ Ⓔ	64 Ⓐ Ⓑ Ⓒ Ⓓ Ⓔ	98 Ⓐ Ⓑ Ⓒ Ⓓ Ⓔ
31 Ⓐ Ⓑ Ⓒ Ⓓ Ⓔ	65 Ⓐ Ⓑ Ⓒ Ⓓ Ⓔ	99 Ⓐ Ⓑ Ⓒ Ⓓ Ⓔ
32 Ⓐ Ⓑ Ⓒ Ⓓ Ⓔ	66 Ⓐ Ⓑ Ⓒ Ⓓ Ⓔ	100 Ⓐ Ⓑ Ⓒ Ⓓ Ⓔ
33 Ⓐ Ⓑ Ⓒ Ⓓ Ⓔ	67 Ⓐ Ⓑ Ⓒ Ⓓ Ⓔ	
34 Ⓐ Ⓑ Ⓒ Ⓓ Ⓔ	68 Ⓐ Ⓑ Ⓒ Ⓓ Ⓔ	

The Gold Standard OAT

Answer Document 2

Test GS-1

CANDIDATE'S NAME ______________________ STUDENT ID ______________

Mark one and only one answer to each question. Be sure to use a soft lead pencil and completely fill in the space for your intended answer. If you erase, do so completely. Make no stray marks.

Reading Comprehension Test

1	Ⓐ Ⓑ Ⓒ Ⓓ Ⓔ	26	Ⓐ Ⓑ Ⓒ Ⓓ Ⓔ
2	Ⓐ Ⓑ Ⓒ Ⓓ Ⓔ	27	Ⓐ Ⓑ Ⓒ Ⓓ Ⓔ
3	Ⓐ Ⓑ Ⓒ Ⓓ Ⓔ	28	Ⓐ Ⓑ Ⓒ Ⓓ Ⓔ
4	Ⓐ Ⓑ Ⓒ Ⓓ Ⓔ	29	Ⓐ Ⓑ Ⓒ Ⓓ Ⓔ
5	Ⓐ Ⓑ Ⓒ Ⓓ Ⓔ	30	Ⓐ Ⓑ Ⓒ Ⓓ Ⓔ
6	Ⓐ Ⓑ Ⓒ Ⓓ Ⓔ	31	Ⓐ Ⓑ Ⓒ Ⓓ Ⓔ
7	Ⓐ Ⓑ Ⓒ Ⓓ Ⓔ	32	Ⓐ Ⓑ Ⓒ Ⓓ Ⓔ
8	Ⓐ Ⓑ Ⓒ Ⓓ Ⓔ	33	Ⓐ Ⓑ Ⓒ Ⓓ Ⓔ
9	Ⓐ Ⓑ Ⓒ Ⓓ Ⓔ	34	Ⓐ Ⓑ Ⓒ Ⓓ Ⓔ
10	Ⓐ Ⓑ Ⓒ Ⓓ Ⓔ	35	Ⓐ Ⓑ Ⓒ Ⓓ Ⓔ
11	Ⓐ Ⓑ Ⓒ Ⓓ Ⓔ	36	Ⓐ Ⓑ Ⓒ Ⓓ Ⓔ
12	Ⓐ Ⓑ Ⓒ Ⓓ Ⓔ	37	Ⓐ Ⓑ Ⓒ Ⓓ Ⓔ
13	Ⓐ Ⓑ Ⓒ Ⓓ Ⓔ	38	Ⓐ Ⓑ Ⓒ Ⓓ Ⓔ
14	Ⓐ Ⓑ Ⓒ Ⓓ Ⓔ	39	Ⓐ Ⓑ Ⓒ Ⓓ Ⓔ
15	Ⓐ Ⓑ Ⓒ Ⓓ Ⓔ	40	Ⓐ Ⓑ Ⓒ Ⓓ Ⓔ
16	Ⓐ Ⓑ Ⓒ Ⓓ Ⓔ	41	Ⓐ Ⓑ Ⓒ Ⓓ Ⓔ
17	Ⓐ Ⓑ Ⓒ Ⓓ Ⓔ	42	Ⓐ Ⓑ Ⓒ Ⓓ Ⓔ
18	Ⓐ Ⓑ Ⓒ Ⓓ Ⓔ	43	Ⓐ Ⓑ Ⓒ Ⓓ Ⓔ
19	Ⓐ Ⓑ Ⓒ Ⓓ Ⓔ	44	Ⓐ Ⓑ Ⓒ Ⓓ Ⓔ
20	Ⓐ Ⓑ Ⓒ Ⓓ Ⓔ	45	Ⓐ Ⓑ Ⓒ Ⓓ Ⓔ
21	Ⓐ Ⓑ Ⓒ Ⓓ Ⓔ	46	Ⓐ Ⓑ Ⓒ Ⓓ Ⓔ
22	Ⓐ Ⓑ Ⓒ Ⓓ Ⓔ	47	Ⓐ Ⓑ Ⓒ Ⓓ Ⓔ
23	Ⓐ Ⓑ Ⓒ Ⓓ Ⓔ	48	Ⓐ Ⓑ Ⓒ Ⓓ Ⓔ
24	Ⓐ Ⓑ Ⓒ Ⓓ Ⓔ	49	Ⓐ Ⓑ Ⓒ Ⓓ Ⓔ
25	Ⓐ Ⓑ Ⓒ Ⓓ Ⓔ	50	Ⓐ Ⓑ Ⓒ Ⓓ Ⓔ

The Gold Standard OAT

Answer Document 3

Test GS-1

CANDIDATE'S NAME ______________________ STUDENT ID ______________

Mark one and only one answer to each question. Be sure to use a soft lead pencil and completely fill in the space for your intended answer. If you erase, do so completely. Make no stray marks.

Physics Test

1	Ⓐ Ⓑ Ⓒ Ⓓ Ⓔ	21	Ⓐ Ⓑ Ⓒ Ⓓ Ⓔ
2	Ⓐ Ⓑ Ⓒ Ⓓ Ⓔ	22	Ⓐ Ⓑ Ⓒ Ⓓ Ⓔ
3	Ⓐ Ⓑ Ⓒ Ⓓ Ⓔ	23	Ⓐ Ⓑ Ⓒ Ⓓ Ⓔ
4	Ⓐ Ⓑ Ⓒ Ⓓ Ⓔ	24	Ⓐ Ⓑ Ⓒ Ⓓ Ⓔ
5	Ⓐ Ⓑ Ⓒ Ⓓ Ⓔ	25	Ⓐ Ⓑ Ⓒ Ⓓ Ⓔ
6	Ⓐ Ⓑ Ⓒ Ⓓ Ⓔ	26	Ⓐ Ⓑ Ⓒ Ⓓ Ⓔ
7	Ⓐ Ⓑ Ⓒ Ⓓ Ⓔ	27	Ⓐ Ⓑ Ⓒ Ⓓ Ⓔ
8	Ⓐ Ⓑ Ⓒ Ⓓ Ⓔ	28	Ⓐ Ⓑ Ⓒ Ⓓ Ⓔ
9	Ⓐ Ⓑ Ⓒ Ⓓ Ⓔ	29	Ⓐ Ⓑ Ⓒ Ⓓ Ⓔ
10	Ⓐ Ⓑ Ⓒ Ⓓ Ⓔ	30	Ⓐ Ⓑ Ⓒ Ⓓ Ⓔ
11	Ⓐ Ⓑ Ⓒ Ⓓ Ⓔ	31	Ⓐ Ⓑ Ⓒ Ⓓ Ⓔ
12	Ⓐ Ⓑ Ⓒ Ⓓ Ⓔ	32	Ⓐ Ⓑ Ⓒ Ⓓ Ⓔ
13	Ⓐ Ⓑ Ⓒ Ⓓ Ⓔ	33	Ⓐ Ⓑ Ⓒ Ⓓ Ⓔ
14	Ⓐ Ⓑ Ⓒ Ⓓ Ⓔ	34	Ⓐ Ⓑ Ⓒ Ⓓ Ⓔ
15	Ⓐ Ⓑ Ⓒ Ⓓ Ⓔ	35	Ⓐ Ⓑ Ⓒ Ⓓ Ⓔ
16	Ⓐ Ⓑ Ⓒ Ⓓ Ⓔ	36	Ⓐ Ⓑ Ⓒ Ⓓ Ⓔ
17	Ⓐ Ⓑ Ⓒ Ⓓ Ⓔ	37	Ⓐ Ⓑ Ⓒ Ⓓ Ⓔ
18	Ⓐ Ⓑ Ⓒ Ⓓ Ⓔ	38	Ⓐ Ⓑ Ⓒ Ⓓ Ⓔ
19	Ⓐ Ⓑ Ⓒ Ⓓ Ⓔ	39	Ⓐ Ⓑ Ⓒ Ⓓ Ⓔ
20	Ⓐ Ⓑ Ⓒ Ⓓ Ⓔ	40	Ⓐ Ⓑ Ⓒ Ⓓ Ⓔ

The Gold Standard OAT

Answer Document 4

Test GS-1

CANDIDATE'S NAME ______________________ STUDENT ID ______________

Mark one and only one answer to each question. Be sure to use a soft lead pencil and completely fill in the space for your intended answer. If you erase, do so completely. Make no stray marks.

Quantitative Reasoning Test

1	Ⓐ Ⓑ Ⓒ Ⓓ Ⓔ	21	Ⓐ Ⓑ Ⓒ Ⓓ Ⓔ
2	Ⓐ Ⓑ Ⓒ Ⓓ Ⓔ	22	Ⓐ Ⓑ Ⓒ Ⓓ Ⓔ
3	Ⓐ Ⓑ Ⓒ Ⓓ Ⓔ	23	Ⓐ Ⓑ Ⓒ Ⓓ Ⓔ
4	Ⓐ Ⓑ Ⓒ Ⓓ Ⓔ	24	Ⓐ Ⓑ Ⓒ Ⓓ Ⓔ
5	Ⓐ Ⓑ Ⓒ Ⓓ Ⓔ	25	Ⓐ Ⓑ Ⓒ Ⓓ Ⓔ
6	Ⓐ Ⓑ Ⓒ Ⓓ Ⓔ	26	Ⓐ Ⓑ Ⓒ Ⓓ Ⓔ
7	Ⓐ Ⓑ Ⓒ Ⓓ Ⓔ	27	Ⓐ Ⓑ Ⓒ Ⓓ Ⓔ
8	Ⓐ Ⓑ Ⓒ Ⓓ Ⓔ	28	Ⓐ Ⓑ Ⓒ Ⓓ Ⓔ
9	Ⓐ Ⓑ Ⓒ Ⓓ Ⓔ	29	Ⓐ Ⓑ Ⓒ Ⓓ Ⓔ
10	Ⓐ Ⓑ Ⓒ Ⓓ Ⓔ	30	Ⓐ Ⓑ Ⓒ Ⓓ Ⓔ
11	Ⓐ Ⓑ Ⓒ Ⓓ Ⓔ	31	Ⓐ Ⓑ Ⓒ Ⓓ Ⓔ
12	Ⓐ Ⓑ Ⓒ Ⓓ Ⓔ	32	Ⓐ Ⓑ Ⓒ Ⓓ Ⓔ
13	Ⓐ Ⓑ Ⓒ Ⓓ Ⓔ	33	Ⓐ Ⓑ Ⓒ Ⓓ Ⓔ
14	Ⓐ Ⓑ Ⓒ Ⓓ Ⓔ	34	Ⓐ Ⓑ Ⓒ Ⓓ Ⓔ
15	Ⓐ Ⓑ Ⓒ Ⓓ Ⓔ	35	Ⓐ Ⓑ Ⓒ Ⓓ Ⓔ
16	Ⓐ Ⓑ Ⓒ Ⓓ Ⓔ	36	Ⓐ Ⓑ Ⓒ Ⓓ Ⓔ
17	Ⓐ Ⓑ Ⓒ Ⓓ Ⓔ	37	Ⓐ Ⓑ Ⓒ Ⓓ Ⓔ
18	Ⓐ Ⓑ Ⓒ Ⓓ Ⓔ	38	Ⓐ Ⓑ Ⓒ Ⓓ Ⓔ
19	Ⓐ Ⓑ Ⓒ Ⓓ Ⓔ	39	Ⓐ Ⓑ Ⓒ Ⓓ Ⓔ
20	Ⓐ Ⓑ Ⓒ Ⓓ Ⓔ	40	Ⓐ Ⓑ Ⓒ Ⓓ Ⓔ